Finding Our Way
A Mother's Journey With Her Son

Finding Our Way

A Mother's Journey With Her Son

by Paula Horowitz

Menasha Ridge Press
Birmingham, Alabama

Copyright ©1994, by Paula Horowitz

Printed in the United States
by Menasha Ridge Press
3169 Cahaba Heights Road
Birmingham, AL 35243
First edition, first printing

Library of Congress Cataloging-in-Publication Data
Horowitz, Paula, 1934-
    Finding our way: a mother's journey with her son/by Paula Horowitz
        p. cm.
    1. Backpacking. 2. Horowitz, Paula, 1934-   —Journeys. 3. Mothers and
sons—United Stated—Case studies.
I. Title.
GV199.6.H67   1994
796.5'1—dc20   94-30204
                                                                                      CIP
ISBN 0-89732-162-6 (hardcover)
ISBN 0-89732-171-5 (pbk.)

Table of Contents

Flying Lessons

The dimming of the lights triggers my witless state of panic—shallow breaths, damp palms, that sort of thing. I've been afflicted this way since Jason's first recital at age eight. In those days I used to stand close by in the wings, perhaps more for my comfort than for his.

Tonight I watch from way back in the hall as he walks into the bright light to take his bow. A hush falls over the audience as heads lift in expectation. The conductor raises his baton, and the melancholy opening phrase of Chausson's *Poème* fills the house.

The music suits my bitter-sweet mood—sweet my joy in Jason's accomplishments, bitter the widening distance between us, a prerequisite for boys to grow into men. Why? I don't know.

Joe stands by the side door, to the left of the stage. He slipped in at the last moment; we were late, and couldn't find a parking place. I wonder how he feels at this precise moment. Proud? Worried for his son? Or is he thinking back to the beginning of his own career? But Joe's sentiments are off the record.

When the orchestra ebbs to silence, Jason lifts his violin toward the solemn B flat introducing the finely framed melody. Music will be his life's work; he's at the beginning.

Jason is our third child, born nine years after his brother, Brett, twelve after Gaia. He has benefitted nicely from this position, often to the detriment of the older children on whom sudden maturity was inflicted. There was more time for him, a bit more money.

From his earliest years we took him camping. It was the

only kind of vacation we could afford with three children. We always went to the coast of Maine, put up a large tent, and grubbed around in tide pools or swam in the ice cold water. Until, eventually, the two older kids and I tired of the circumscribed camping space. By then Joe took the family to Europe, either on sabbaticals or for other professional engagements, and Gaia, Brett, and I ventured on longer and longer forays into the mountains of Switzerland and France.

During the summer of '77, when Jason was only six, he was initiated rather cruelly into this footloose behavior when Brett and I took him on a long hike across the tundra of Iceland. We learned the hard way that a mountain silhouetted on a horizon of barren grassland is farther than you think. Jason kicked and screamed at his big brother for carrying his tired body on his shoulders the last few miles, because he didn't want to be thought a sissy. An ever wakeful sun and lack of a watch had us returning from no man's land at midnight, running to catch the last bus back to Reykjavik.

With the help of a map we figured out that we had hiked over twenty miles—a good day for anybody and remarkable for a six-year-old. I felt enormous admiration for Jason's valor, and set out at once to exploit it. He would be my new hiking buddy. Gaia was away at college and Brett's ventures had grown beyond my capabilities.

The summer after Iceland I took Jason to Maine to climb Mount Katahdin. He was so short that I had to haul him up cliffs. On the infamous Knife Edge I hung on to him for fear the strong wind would blow him over the edge. The round trip to the summit took us ten hours. Jason was furious when I made him help me carry firewood on the way down—enough was enough. I made a sickly fire and served swimming eggs for dinner.

When we returned home Jason told Joe: "Daddy, when we climbed the mountain we had nothing but raw eggs to eat all day!" but there was more pride than complaint in his voice.

For the next thirteen years we were called back to the hills with the steadiness of migratory birds. We learned to make fires in the rain, use an ice axe, a compass. And we got to know each other—there was time for that in the woods. Ultimately the definition of our walks lay in our being together.

After the concert, while waiting for Joe to get the car, Jason is still charged. I tell him how impressed I was with his performance.

"Thanks," he says, preoccupied.

"Did you forget your roses?" I ask. He was presented with two bouquets after he played, stooping awkwardly to receive them in his hands full of violin and bow.

"No Mom, I gave them to a friend." He sounds irritable, defensive. I'd been the beneficiary of his flowers in the past, and now I hope they have gone to a pretty girl. I am curious about the girl.

"That's good," I say to his closed up face. At that moment several of his fellow musicians from the conservatory gather around. The young men slap Jason's shoulders and the girls hug him. They bundle into a rowdy mass. He looks happier among his own, more relaxed.

When Joe drives up, Jason withdraws from the group. As usual, we are to have coffee and dessert together. I say to him, "Listen darling, maybe we'd better skip dessert. It's late, and Dad has to teach tomorrow."

"You sure?" he says gratefully.

We stand in the city rain trying to bear each other. He stirs a small puddle with the toe of his shoe. I try to accommodate the stab of my superfluity.

"Well, thanks for coming," he says, at nineteen still vaguely torn between conflicting loyalties.

God, how I will miss him.

On the drive home to Amherst, I say to Joe, "I don't know why I always feel so bad when we leave Jason behind in Boston. I should be happy, he was a success."

He doesn't answer right away; he searches for my hand. "I'm sad too," he says then, an admission only possible in the darkness of the car.

"Do you know why?"

"Probably for the same reason as you," he says—a remark suggestive of our combined confusion. "I'm hungry. You want to

3

stop for a snack?"

It's after two when we get to bed. I try reading, but my mind keeps wandering—parting with Jason is as important as his being with us has been. A wet maple branch sweeps mournfully against the side of the house. Next to me Joe sleeps. I turn off my reading lamp and look up through the skylight into nothingness.

After a while my eyes begin to adjust to the dark, and the longer I watch, the more stars reveal themselves.

The Rising Sun

When leafing through my old journal of Vermont's Long Trail, I find a desiccated bug, a streak of dried blood, a black feather, a trillium petal. There are pages with names and addresses of people we met and meant to write, and short musical compositions by Jason. One is scored for voice, harp, and oboe. My side of word-game contests confirms the many rainy hours spent in the tent. I rotate the book to read the notes in the margins: Good water at Peru Peak. Ten miles to Sucker Brook. Country store one mile west on Vt. 103. Ice cream!! The last underscored with double lines.

It was a simple enough thing, our walking together. The time was August, 1983, a summer of uncomplicated sweetness. Including a side trip to the White Mountains of New Hampshire, we walked more than three-hundred-fifty miles, from the Canadian border to Massachusetts. Jason was twelve; I called him Grasshopper on account of the spindly legs beneath his backpack. I loved hiking with him. Like the forested hills, his quiet and dreamy nature revealed a sudden splendor that might have been overlooked in a busier child. It was his very isolation that touched me—and his wind-tossed curls that shone like horse chestnuts from bathing in lakes and streams.

People have asked me if spending a month in the woods with a child and a Doberman didn't get boring. No. Our life under the stars was full of adventure. With every mountain climbed I felt more at home. It seemed as though I were convalescing from an undiagnosed illness.

When we returned home, it was hard to explain this aspect of our walk. We talked about people we met, proudly demonstrated hardened muscles, bragged a little about twenty-two mile days we put in. But the reflective moments had come when we sat side by side on a hill top drinking from our canteens, or drowsily sat and watched dying embers.

Around eight p.m. on July 31, Joe dropped us off at the unpaved North Troy Jay Road in northern Vermont. We hauled our packs from the back seat and opened the tail-gate for our dog, Thor, who was whimpering with anticipation after the long ride from our home in Amherst, Massachusetts. Jason said he wasn't feeling well, but I figured he was just apprehensive.

Concerned, Joe put his hand on Jason's forehead. "He looks flushed," he said.

"He'll be all right." I tightened the belly band of Thor's saddle bags while Jason clamped the eager animal between his knees. The road ahead looked desolate; it would soon be dark. I sighed inadvertently.

"You should stay at a motel tonight and start off tomorrow," Joe said.

"And then walk back here from North Troy? No, we'd better get going," I said, fiddling with my hip belt to take some of the weight of my pack off my shoulders. I had repacked several times in an effort to get the weight below fifty-five pounds, which was half my own.

"I'm glad you have Thor with you." Joe embraced our bulky shapes. "Are you sure you want to do this?"

We said yes, of course we were.

"Well, I'll see you in two weeks then, if all goes well." Joe looked at us dubiously. "Look after each other."

"Don't worry, we'll be fine."

"Please be careful!" he called after us.

We heard the gravelly crunch of the tires grow thin. I knew he had misgivings leaving us at the top of Vermont; as would-be conquerors of the wilderness we lacked credibility. The farther north we had driven, the more pensive he had become. It was always easier to be in the fray of things than to sit at home, wondering.

Thor had no second thoughts whatever since he was under the mistaken impression we would protect him.

For some time, we walked toward the setting sun. It would be two weeks before Joe would bring us clean laundry and news from home. We'd be only half-way then! A month was longer than we'd ever been out on a stretch.

"Isn't this great, Jay?" I said.

"Yeah....What time do you think....Hey, you come back here!" Thor suddenly crashed through the undergrowth.

"Must be some rodent," I said, following him into the bushes where he stood growling.

"I wonder what's bugging him," said Jason, but then we saw. It was a ghost. A grayish shape without precise contours seemed to be drifting in our direction.

"Let's turn around," Jason whispered. I peered through the foliage; the ghost swam in an upright position. Instinctively I backed up a few steps, then, in full retreat, we called Thor, who clearly wasn't planning to take on the phantom by himself— judging by his prompt obedience.

Before long we regained our wits. There were, after all, just silence, long shadows, and an amber sky.

"This is ridiculous," I said.

Jason shrugged, "Let's go on then. It's fine with me if you want to risk your life."

"C'mon now," I said, "nothing happened, did it?"

We stayed close together as we neared the ominous spot; I held Thor by his collar, but the frenzied dog charged ahead. From this distance the ghost seemed non-threatening; its movements were fluid, laid back.

Suddenly Thor grabbed the spook by the throat and shook him violently, forgetting that ghosts are already dead. Prancing, he tried not to stumble on the captive drooping from his jaws: a man's union suit.

"Our first night out and we're fleeing from long johns! We'd better not let that get out," I chuckled.

"Mom, where there's men's laundry, there must be a man. Let's go back to the road; it's too dark here. We could fall into a hole!"

7

I was about to whistle for Thor when we heard the cocking of a gun.

"Don't shoot!" Jason cried, running toward a small clearing, "Don't shoot my dog!"

A bald, bandy-legged little man in a red and black flannel shirt climbed out of the underbrush, his pate gilded by the sun. But for the gun, he looked a benign, gnome-like figure.

I held up the wad of dreary rags. "We were looking for you. I'm afraid our dog ripped up your, eh, laundry. We owe you some money. I'm really sorry...."

The barrels of the shotgun pointed some place near my toes. The man stared at me uncomprehendingly. I repeated the apology and the offer of restitution.

"That's my son," I said, somewhat irrelevantly. I smiled at the man. I was afraid of his dull eyes. I didn't know what to do.

"C'mon, Mom," Jason whispered.

"Right. Well, goodnight then," I made a silly little wave, clamping the long johns under my arm. I felt the mute man's eyes on my back.

We found Thor lying on the path with his chin on his front feet. He seemed disheartened; he had to be prodded to get up.

It had taken weeks to train him to carry his bags, laden with dog chow, his tent, night clothes, and rain coat. And a pair of pliers in case he stuck his nose into a porcupine's business. But the hardest thing for him to learn had been his position in the line up: the middle. He ached to be first. But not tonight.

My pack dug into my hip bones. I kept thinking about our encounter and about the movie, *Deliverance*. On this, our first night out, I had been as ineffective as a child. Jason never mentioned that. It was something new I learned about him.

He did ask me if I thought the stranger would follow us. "He must be mad at us," he said. I thought that, indeed, the little man probably was mad as hell, and shouldn't carry a gun, but I said not to worry—he wasn't interested in us.

We had expected an open lean-to, but Journey's End Camp had four walls. Thor refused to eat; he picked out a bunk, sighed, and went to sleep. We leaned our packs against the door. I lit a candle and made hot chocolate on our camp stove while we whis-

8

pered like fugitives. Jason spread out the map. Tomorrow we would walk nine-and-a-half miles to the Laura Woodward Shelter; we wished we could go there tonight, farther away from the man with the gun.

At the break of day I put on my down vest and sneaked out, barefoot, with Thor on my heels. He immediately busied himself, but I stood still and watched the sun touch the wet ferns. I crossed the brook, then, noiselessly on the pine needles, followed an animal trail. Suddenly, when rounding a corner, I came upon two foxes, their heads lovingly intertwined, their black-tipped ears quivering. A ray of sunlight fired their royal coats, but they knew of no vanity, absorbed as they were in each other. I watched them until Thor returned from his own revelations and with a shriek sent the pair scampering for cover—two white-plumed tails sweeping in different directions.

Slowly I walked back to camp where I found Jason sitting in the cabin doorway, offering peanuts to a nervous chipmunk. The chipmunk skittered closer, retreated, came closer still, twitching with greed and fear. In the end, standing on his hindlegs, the chipmunk leaned the upper part of his body in Jason's hand and filled his pouches.

Predictably, Thor brought anarchy to this scene as well when he blundered back and once more had his self-esteem injured, this time by a few ounces of rodent that managed to become invisible right in front of his nose. To save face, he grabbed a stray woolen sock and paraded so joyfully for us that even Jason, who was disgusted with him, began to laugh.

We would have to become more efficient with our packing routine if we wanted to be home in four weeks. Jason swept out the cabin while I tried to divide Thor's load evenly among his saddle bags. The sun was high overhead when we finally got under way.

Half an hour later we reached the U.S.-Canada line post and the north end of the Long Trail. This was the true beginning of our walk, duly marked for future reference by Thor. Twigs snapped under our boots as we walked beneath summer oak and maple. Everything was exactly as I had imagined it—sunshine, bird songs, solitude, and two dear companions. Even the physical effort of lugging our household along added to my satisfaction, though as the hours passed we did considerable grunting and groaning.

On top of Burnt Mountain we had a long rest. We had been eating squashed Mars bars to stave off hunger; now the sardines were like caviar. Not until after the coffee did I fully take in the view: mountains to the south and the north, a valley below, the wind-shaped clouds above. No telephone wires or T.V. antennas to scratch black lines through this panorama.

Jason lay on his stomach; Thor had snuggled close enough to rest his head on the only soft place of Jason's body. I estimated another four hours to the shelter. We had no need of a watch—perhaps it was four o'clock, maybe earlier, I thought drowsily....

When I woke up, the sun had shifted to the west. Looking about me I felt as though I had awakened on the Isles of the Blest. Only one night out and already my boxed-in bed at home seemed an oddity—what could be easier than a mattress of moss, a blanket of sun?

Thor, alert to my stirring, started licking Jason's neck forcefully. "I was dreaming about Frodo," Jason said, stretching, and began to tell a long, complicated tale. His head was singing with Tolkien's legend.

I said, "Hobbits would be at home here, huh? You can imagine Frodo and Bilbo having tea right there on that boulder."

"No Mom, hobbits like the woods, and anyway, they hate us. People have wrecked Middle-Earth."

"How?"

"With bombs, of course, and factories and highways...."

"Hold on! Nobody bombs Hobbits. As for factories, where do you think your backpack was made? And you need highways to get from here to there, right?"

"You didn't have to go anywhere when it was still beautiful everywhere."

"It's still beautiful here." He started to lace up his boots. "Jay? Don't you think it's lovely here?"

He shrugged. "Everybody in the whole world is going to die. The kids in school say that we're going to have a nuclear war."

The enormity of the pronouncement took my breath away. Is that what he thought about? I said, "That isn't true. Nobody wants to blow up the world. The kids are wrong." But his knowledge was sophisticated.

"There could be a nuclear accident, or sabotage or something. I think it sucks."

When I walked over to where I had parked my boots, I found that a rabbit had neatly deposited a heap of scat on one of my socks. I angrily shook it clean. Five minutes earlier I would have been delighted that small animals had shared the ledge where we were sleeping.

Jason took up the subject of his dream again while we hiked. I listened absentmindedly. He was really talking to himself now and an occasional "Incredible!" or "Really?" was all he needed from me.

I had been much younger when I lived with bombs. Bombs from the Allies that landed on Dutch hospitals and homes by mistake, aborted V-2s aimed at London that whined through the night. Life was laced with fear and every day worthy of celebration. And celebrate we did. Over a piece of chocolate traded for a watch on the black market; a few lumps of coal stolen from a German truck when a soldier's back was turned. My older sister got her first period during the war and we celebrated her survival into womanhood. Our lives were full of hope. Even though we ate flower bulbs to stay alive I had never doubted the arrival of a new dawn. But my children, with their full bellies and their freedom, had lost hope for our survival as a species.

We had been climbing steeply westward and now followed a ridge over saddles from peak to peak. Our packs were too heavy; we would have to send some things home with Joe. Jason was lagging behind and getting grouchy. I waited for him.

"We're nearly there," I said.

"You don't know where we are," he answered testily.

"Common sense. We're tired, so we'll make camp as soon as we find water."

"There's the rub."

"We each have about half a bottle....I guess that won't do for Thor."

"We shouldn't have brought him along," he said.

Miffed, I strutted on. Thor scrambled ahead in his usual

fashion with his nose to the ground. I didn't have the energy to keep him behind me and gambled he wouldn't run off. The next time I looked around, Jason was sitting down with his head in his hands.

"Are you okay?" I shouted. I knew I could count on him to keep going no matter how tired he was. There was neither water nor a flat place to pitch a tent in sight. I put down my pack.

"That's okay, honey, we'll just sleep right here tonight." When he caught up, he gave me a dark look and marched ahead of me until we reached the lean-to.

"Good job," I said, noticing how exhausted he looked. I tried hugging him, but he shook me off and set out to get water at the spring.

Thor showed no interest in his rations. Instead he urinated around the periphery of what he decided was our rightful territory. He then backed up on his markings, sniffing with furrowed brow to make sure he hadn't overlooked anything. He had never done this before. I assumed his genes were beginning to remember their original wildness. I admired his proficiencies and knew neither man nor beast could cross his line of scent without his permission. With a satisfied air he wolfed down his food, turned a few circles on the lean-to platform and settled down for a good night's sleep. We put his sweater on him and clipped his chain to the rafters.

Even minor duties in the woods were time-consuming. We worked by flashlight; it was probably past ten when the dishes were washed and our boots tied up and hung away from mice and chipmunks. We had set up the tent on the lean-to floor. To be warmer and away from bugs, we said; but there was more to it— we had not yet accepted the wild. Ostrich-fashion, we made believe the flimsy nylon would shield us from—whatever.

"I'm not tired anymore," Jason said. Indeed, neither was I. Once the load was off our backs, we could fly. We had been scurrying around; now it was time to be aware of the sighing trees, the tiny gurgle of the spring—grace notes of the mountains.

We dangled our legs off the deck and listened. The moon was in its last quarter, the sky deep. We'd had our attention directed downward, and nearly overlooked the meteorites shooting through the sky, flaring up and fading into the void. Awed by superhuman concepts of space and time, we watched burning boulders fly until our imagination grew dizzy and our necks cramped.

I thought, we may destroy as much of the natural world as we can get our hands on, but there's nothing we can do to this. It will go on in spite of acid rain, Three Mile Island, the Bomb. The sun will rise again.

"Really important things don't change," I said softly.
Jason didn't see the relevance of that remark. He fell asleep almost at once.

At least he knew I loved him.

Binding Steeple to Distant Steeple

Even in mid-summer the northern end of the Long Trail was sparsely traveled. Five days out and we hadn't seen a soul. The trail was overgrown. Wasps had nested without fear of boots, stinging nettle grew waist-high. Sharp crests and rugged slopes without switchbacks tired us out quickly, and in flatter areas downed spruce repeatedly blocked our passage.

We were bug-bitten, scratched up, muddy, and we were hungry. The provisions we carried proved to be insufficient to replenish the calories we burned. As we didn't eat meat, an hour after a supper of dried soup, rice, or instant mashed potatoes, we longed for breakfast. Fresh food and hot showers were memories we kept vivid by fantasizing in the darkness of the tent. And the next day again, we sweated up mountains and picked our way through bogs, stopping only to drink Gatorade. Flies made resting or eating impossible. Our exasperation came out in long silences and impatience with Thor and each other.

We could quit, of course. Roads cut through the Green Mountain ridge at intervals, and if you walked east or west you'd get to a village eventually. I knew Jason wouldn't give up so easily and neither would I, but I thought about it a lot that first week.

Finally, late one afternoon, we met a human being, more in spirit than in flesh, of which he had little. He was amazingly clean. Thor checked his credentials inch by inch while we formally shook hands.

"Socrates," said the stranger.

"Iphigenia," I wanted to say, but gave my real name.

"Headin' south?"

"Yes. Where did you start from?" The flies had a hey-day, running with their sticky toes over our faces and legs. Swatting had become second nature to me, but Socrates didn't seem to mind them. He only narrowed his eyes.

"North Adams."

"Ah yes. Well, you're the first person we've seen in days."

"That's good! If you don't mind, I'd like to give you some advice. Last night I camped near Mansfield. Let me tell you...."

"Wait a minute. Mount Mansfield? That's almost forty miles from here, isn't it?"

"Thirty-five. I got up early. Anyway...."

"When did you leave North Adams then?" That was the southern terminus of the Long Trail where we hoped to arrive in three weeks.

"Eight days ago. Look. Get off at Vt. 109. Mansfield is crawling with tourists. Day hikers, you know. You can pick up the L.T. later. Stay in the farm country, it's beautiful and it's quiet."

Eight days! He had averaged more than twenty-five miles per day on a rugged trail and with a backpack! We'd done about eight, with difficulty. I said, "You're in a hurry!"

"How can you walk thirty-five miles in one day?" Jason asked.

"Day hikers," Socrates said wryly. We chuckled. Anybody would run to get away from *them.*

"I guess we'll stay off the trail for a while then; by tomorrow we have to find a grocery store anyway," I said.

Socrates counseled us to ask the farmers for permission to camp on their land. He had another bit of wisdom before he loped off.

"You folks carry too much. My pack never weighs more than twenty pounds."

"What a skinny guy!" Jason said, "Lucky we met him, huh Mom? I bet all the shelters around Mansfield are full."

"Probably."

"Are we getting off tomorrow?"

"I'd be just as happy to walk out tonight if you're not too tired. I'm sick of flies."

The comforts of civilization seemed overwhelmingly

16

desirable. I hadn't thought much about clean sheets and bathrooms with running water, and suddenly I wanted to hear music. I wanted to read in bed with a pillow under my head.

"Could we still find a place to sleep, Mom?"

"Oh, sure. It won't be that late when we get out of the woods."

There was no moon that night; we hiked along a logging road that led to an open field where timid sparks of fireflies winked through the tall grass. Side by side we sat quietly taking in the mysterious night-blooming meadow.

When we reached Davis Neighborhood, Jason said, "I'm going to have an egg salad sandwich when we get there," without a hint of where "there" might be.

"What? You've never had egg salad in your life! And I want a shower first."

"Where are we going to get a shower?" he asked suspiciously. Not until then did I remember that his ethics forbade sleeping in motels or any other place one had to buy. I had agreed not to lessen the achievement of the hike with amenities.

"This is different. I didn't expect to leave the woods," I said. "We have no choice, really, we can't walk around like tramps!"

He said I always changed the rules. As far as he was concerned motels were out. We should have stayed on the trail if I were going to ruin the whole plan. I said you had to be flexible; he called it cheating.

"So you won't mind asking some stranger if we can camp on his property," I said.

"You have to do that," he said earnestly.

When all was said and done, there were neither motels nor farms; we set up the tent next to an overflowing trash can in a parking area.

Later, a car drove up with a couple of teenagers. Jason had fallen asleep, but I thought we were probably not allowed to camp there and I was on edge. Another car arrived with more kids and soon a beer party was underway. The radios boomed fortissimo. Jason rolled himself into a ball and descended to the bottom of his bag, moaning.

Thor leaned against the tent, trying to be close. I opened the zipper a few inches, so I could reach out and stroke his head to calm him. The combined smells of dog and garbage had replaced fresh mountain air. I've turned into a hobo, I thought disgustedly.

After the cars had screeched away, I lay watching the intermittent green-yellow flash of a tiny firefly on the nylon ceiling.

Camp was broken early and fast. We marched along the blacktop for about an hour until we found a homey looking restaurant. Thor, whose shiny black coat had turned gray with road dust, was tied to a post. Seated on bar stools, we ordered three two-egg omelets, keeping a covetous eye on the preparations. The cook, whose apron resembled an artist's palette, suggested we try his wild blueberries. He proved their juiciness by rubbing them between thumb and forefinger, then adding deep purple smears to the art work on his stomach. He made great pancakes. We brought Thor his food on a paper plate that he pushed along the sidewalk until he figured out he should put a paw on it.

After the meal our energy returned. There were no mountains to climb, no 'blow-downs' in our way. Convenience stores provided snacks—suddenly life was easy. We petted cows and horses, bought apples, and kept on walking south through Vermont's farm country. The road was fringed with day lilies and tall stalks of chicory. Orderly white fences climbed up the hills and down again, like rows of first communion children, binding steeple to distant steeple.

The people, the clouds, the very day moved slowly, as if in contemplation. I thought I could walk on, girding the globe, and not tire except that my body was forever clamoring either for more or for less of one thing or another. We had grown accustomed to the weight of our packs and were able to go many miles without resting.

I did develop painful cramps in my calves, perhaps from walking on a hard surface. After each rest it was so severe that I hobbled and grimaced with pain, to the delight of Jason who mimicked my gait. We both had bruised collar bones; occasionally I would slip off one of the pack's shoulder straps to give a bruise a break, only to cringe more when I swung the pack straight again. A more serious problem was the sun. By the time we found a drug store and bought hats and lotion, we were red.

Thor had a problem with the hot pavement. He scanned the road for shady spots, making his moves methodically and with reluctance. A woman who was watching this chess board behavior from her porch brought him a bowl of water, and just to rub it in, he made as though he wanted to stay with her.

We walked through the villages for four days, one day more or less like the next—rain and sun, pain and joy. Our sleeping arrangements were colorful. The second night we asked some women we met if they knew of a place we could camp.

"Sure, there's a nice campground just up the road on a lake. They got hot showers, too, and there's a little store. Me'n Bunny go swimming there."

Relieved, I thanked her too warmly for the information; she looked me up and down and shrugged, "Sure...." I didn't blame her for not realizing what emotion the word "shower" generated. Jason, who is likely to think of the next logical question while I still exult in the answer to the first, asked, "How far is it?"

"Oh, seven or eight miles, no more, huh Bunny?"

Bunny agreed it was not.

We snickered after they were out of earshot. To think they considered a seven mile hike to go to bed "just up the road!"

"We'll get there by breakfast. Easy," Jason said. I don't know if he thought the Lord or I would provide, but he never showed anxiety about walking in the dark on a strange road with no place to sleep. For me, it wasn't like that any more, though I had also left such worries to my parents when I was small.

When I was five we were evacuated from the North Sea coast because the Germans feared a British invasion. We were packed in a train that rode on until evening. When it stopped it was raining. People spread out and started walking. When I became too tired I rode on my father's neck with my face in his wet hair. We went from farm to farm, and while my worried parents pleaded with the farmers for lodgings, I discovered the odor of rank black soil, and I was excited by this new world.

"Are you tired?" I asked Jason.

"Dead."

"We'll ask at the rectory." I should've thought of that earlier. We had just kept going because there wasn't much else to do, nor had there been an obvious place to camp.

The house next to the church turned out to belong not to the minister, but to a Mrs. Morgan who opened the door with a smile big as a harvest moon. She was a heavy woman with short gray hair and a competent manner.

"Put the luggage in the garage and don't go away. I'll be with you as soon as I can."

After twenty minutes or so she reappeared, giving away that smile again.

"So!" she said, "that's done. Now I can invite you in."

I protested, repeating that we just needed permission to camp in a field or a barn. Perhaps she could advise us whom we could ask? Mrs. Morgan, however, had arranged things in her mind to her satisfaction. We were to have soup with her. She called Jason "young man" and Thor "poor thing." The poor thing was fed in the garage and given her own dog Pet's blanket. Pet himself seemed to be out on the town.

While we sat in her tidy dining room in our not too tidy outfits, she told us her husband was dying of stomach cancer. She'd had to get him ready for bed, which was why she'd kept us waiting.

It was late in the evening, and after a day of nursing duties she was cooking us soup. "I made it earlier today," she said, "as if I expected you. Do you like brownies, young man? Of course you do. My own son—wait I'll show you."

Out came a portrait of a man with his bride on his arm. By now I had become intrigued with her and was all too pleased to hear the family history. A daughter as well. Grandchildren. Mrs. Morgan had been a grade school teacher, her husband a construction worker, "a good man." She had a collection of fossils that made her forget about the soup. We sat at the table examining the skeletal shells of leaves and insects and bones.

"It looks like a valuable collection to me. Is it?" I asked.

"Oh, it is rich! Rich! But not in terms of money. It just gives me such pleasure to know these imprints are left behind....I see the young man understands."

I considered it indelicate then to ask where she had gotten so many fossils. Jason was fingering them respectfully. "How old do you think this snail is?"

The two of them bent over the stones again, her gray head brushing his silky one. In the next room a life was ending; yet this was our moment under the lamplight.

"What's the name of this town?" I asked, and with that pedestrian question we returned to the soup, hearty lentil, and, to our relief, without meat. Over brownies we studied Mrs. Morgan's map. We had walked twenty-six miles that day! She told us her son was a backpacker, which explained her empathy to some degree.

"Godspeed, and don't forget to write how it all turned out," Mrs. Morgan hugged Jason goodbye.

Although, according to him, we weren't allowed to cover any part of the distance by means other than our feet, he didn't object to a ride from Mrs.Morgan's friend to the camp ground. It was nine miles away.

We never did write. But that smile is etched in my mind as permanently as an imprint of a dragonfly wing in stone.

-4-

Just Be Glad

I don't know how many miles we covered the following day, but by evening my muscles felt satisfied. Jason was bronze and lean. His eyes seemed to have lightened a shade. I even imagined he had grown.

Toward evening we found ourselves in a similar fix as the night before: Tired, hungry, no campground. The town where we stopped was vintage New England—clapboard houses, a covered bridge, a welcoming church atop a green hill. There was also a motel, but we asked for shelter at the church. At the time I felt no embarrassment at this rather awkward arrangement.

The pastor's wife offered us the use of a recreation room as long as we tied our dog in the church yard. We shortened his chain so he wouldn't pee on the grave stones. The apartment had four couches, a bathroom, and a small kitchen. The linoleum tiles were polished and cool underfoot; symmetrical stacks of folding chairs leaned against the wall.

All this luxury drove us to the laundromat so that we might be worthy. Afterwards, we were as hungry as we'd ever been. We bought Alpo, hot baked beans, Italian sandwiches piled with vegetables and cheese, and a quart of milk, then rushed back to the church for supper. The cardboard tubs of beans were steaming on the coffee table, and the sandwiches, luscious with oil and garlic, lay at the ready in their wax paper wrappings when the pastor came in to greet us.

"Great!" he said, "great!" This seemed to be in reference to our names. And what were we doing here, exactly?

"Great! That's just great."

"Yes. We're enjoying it. We just bought some supper." I poured the milk.

"Looks great," he said.

We praised the room, the church, and the laundromat that had come in so handy. Jason was leaning heavily against me in a cloud of garlic and beans. The ebullient pastor began to discuss our great home town.

"Why don't you start," I said to Jason, alerting our host to our keen interest in the food. At last he retreated with the announcement that services would be at ten. I had wanted to leave earlier, but found it safer to be agreeable, so he would let us eat.

The most memorable thing about the morning service was that the elderly parishioners called us "the young people" when they surrounded us on the lawn afterwards. I tried to stand up straighter.

We were well past the heavily traveled section of the Long Trail, but until we could locate an approach to it, we had to keep to the roads. The local people didn't know what the Long Trail was, let alone where, even though one of the oldest long-distance hiking trails in the country had been in the vicinity since 1931.

On Sunday evening we found ourselves moving approximately south-west, again in search of a place to camp. It was reasonable to assume that our luck would run out, but the laconic New Englanders accepted us with good humor.

A farmer gave us permission to pitch the tent by a stand of poplars near a shallow stream that ran behind his huge red barn. When he dropped by at dusk for a social visit, Thor bared his teeth and yapped at the man's jeans. I thought he probably had grounds for this unusual behavior, but scolded him self-righteously. Fortunately he had just grazed the farmer's leg, but it was a case of biting the hand that fed us—too embarrassing for any words that immediately came to mind. We were told to get the goddamn dog out of there, and did.

I would have overruled Jason and stayed at a motel that night if there had been one. Some miles later we called at a dark-stained and sagging parsonage. The minister opened the door just wide enough to present himself. Assisted by a bad case of ring around the clerical collar, he resembled a stove pipe—rigidly dark and dusty.

"This happens to be a very bad time," he said, twisting his thin lips into an upside-down smile. "I have to get ready for the evening service."

I could see that having a couple of vagabonds at your doorstep at dinner time on a Sunday night could be construed as being "a bad time." I stammered an apology, the blood rising to my face. It was quite startling to watch him break into a smile—all the yellow droopy folds were ironed out as if by magic. With cheerful goodwill he invited us into the vestibule and phoned one of the church elders.

This very shy fellow drove us to his house, one in a row of ranches with fenced-in lawns.

"There she is, and you're welcome to 'er," he said, barely audibly, indicating an aluminum camper. Water was available at the garden hose. There were two beds in the trailer with piles of covers. Our gentle host smoothed out the blankets apologetically. Thor was allowed to stay with us; he received an affectionate patting.

"If you need anything just holler....I'll be back after church. Eh, better not bother my sister. She's in there." He pointed to a shack in his back yard.

"No, indeed not. You're very kind, and we don't need another thing."

"People are incredible," Jason said, "imagine trusting total strangers with all your stuff."

"We're not likely to lug off too much in our backpacks," I said.

"Mom, why can't you be nice?"

"I'm not nice?"

"You act like it's nothing"

"I know it isn't nothing. Actually, all these favors embarrass me."

"Just be glad about it, that's all."

While washing most of myself under the hose, I happened to glance at the rickety cottage and saw an almost bald woman peering through the window with no pretense of hiding her curiosity. I felt goofy kneeling there among my bubbles; it seemed too intimate an operation to perform in front of a stranger.

"Guess what, Mom," said Jason, while I sat on the trailer's threshold squeezing the water from my hair.

"Hm?"

"There's no toilet."

"Of course there is," I said. On closer inspection we found a potty-like contraption, but we had no idea how it was used, since there was no water.

"It's no big deal for you," I told him, "just go out back. Only watch the wire." An electric fence ran between the back yard and the pasture.

"What if someone sees me?"

"Then they'll figure out that you're peeing, but I'm really in a fix. I guess I'll have to wait until dark."

I could ask the shy man for the use of his bathroom when he came home, but I hated to. The more I thought about it the more urgent the problem became. Thor, who lifted his leg nonchalantly on the rose bushes, was unconcerned with the complexities of civilization, but Jason refused to take advantage of the back yard accommodations if I couldn't. On many occasions during our wanderings I observed his principled behavior and respected it too much to interfere, though usually his adversities only added to my own. It was through our all too human vulnerabilities that we got to know new things about each other.

We had dozed off over our books when suddenly we were startled by a strange sound.

"Did you hear that?" whispered Jason. A noise like scraping knives sounded close by.

"Sh....there it is again. What in God's name....Did you lock the door?" I asked.

"There's no lock."

I climbed on his bed to look out of the only window and saw nothing but a yellow glow in the direction of the shack.

"Someone seems to be sharpening an axe," I said. It occurred to me that I didn't even know the name of the village.

"No Mom, I think it's a big knife, or a machete...."

When I came down off the bed and stepped on Thor, I

screamed. The noise outside stopped. We hung onto each other until the pounding of our hearts calmed down. Then we made for the rose bushes. Suddenly, the eerie noise started again, but now it sounded as if metal plates were clapped together. Though I was scared silly, I was not, at that moment, in a position to run.

"Hurry up, Mom," Jason urged, but I was ready to die for an empty bladder.

"Don't you dare move," I told him, as he was shielding me from possible road traffic.

I had been in a similar situation during a trip to Egypt. The country had recently been opened to tourists; we rode a bus from Israel through the Sinai desert for ten stifling hours—non-stop for fear of marauders. When, at last, the bus came to a halt at the Suez Canal, the passengers were greatly relieved. At least they thought they were going to be. Everybody tried to act casually while circling the one building in search of a door that could lead to a bathroom. There wasn't one. The bus passengers provided great amusement to the Arab merchants sitting on the wharf, also waiting for the ferry. Having drunk a large amount of fresh orange juice before leaving the Gaza Strip, I was near tears with misery when a fellow passenger pointed further up the Nile. "Right over there!" he said, laughing at our up-tight expressions.

Sure enough, by following one's nose it was easy to locate a hole in the ground surrounded on three sides by a canvas screen where it counted, i.e. between the ankles and the waist, and facing the canal. I defeatedly took my turn, trying to hold my breath against the stench. Smack in the middle of the proceedings, an enormous German ship steamed alongside; cameras with lenses like torpedos were whipped out to record my posterior for posterity.

After our stop at the rose bush we set out to investigate the source of the commotion. Like a couple of shady characters we crept around to the cottage where the clanging appeared to originate. Under the yellow light of the porch, the bald-headed woman sat half-naked on an overturned bucket. Her breasts swung as she heaved a large tin platter repeatedly against the rain pipe with raw energy. Perhaps it was a gesture of frustration or an archaic urge for rhythm, but the unearthly lament made me shudder.

The tormented woman beat her drums through the night.

Her brother drove us to a diner for breakfast, his face set in remorseful rumples. He stayed with Thor while we ate, then took us to the trail head. We expressed thanks inadequately.

It wasn't long before Jason and Thor disappeared ahead of me, eager for the freedom of the hills. "Let's not leave the trail again for anything," Jason called over his shoulder.

It was good to be solitary. I touched the lobed sassafras and watched the light sift through the branches. My tread was noiseless; I was beginning to fit in.

In a world of walls and parking lots, I stretched time only when I irritably waited for a plane, in a doctor's office, or for the rice to boil. Even then I could be seen with some reading material in my hands, so as not to "waste time." Electricity removed the inconvenience of sundown, and Mondays piled on Sundays as if to get it over with.

Here the open day lasted until the light was gone; we bedded down when the flowers closed their petals and the animals put a furry paw over their nose. Life was immediate. We watched the sky for changes in the weather, awakened exuberant as frogs in a pond. Yet I knew I would eventually get restless and would have to continue my ill-defined search outside the forest. I hoped I wouldn't stop looking.

Later, dropping my pack and pulling out a pan, I asked Jason, "Do you think?"

"Think what?"

"Just that. Do you do it when you walk."

"I don't think so." He giggled.

"C'mon. Be serious."

"If you really want to know, mostly I feel things."

"Yeah, me too. I thought I would be meditative, you know? But I'm more or less in a stupor. I seem to just let things happen."

"Well, you're thinking about that at least."

"Yes. But I'm mostly occupied with mundane things. Like being thirsty, or having a sore neck."

"Can I have Swiss Miss? I'll get the stove going."

"What do you mean, you 'feel' things?"

"What? Oh, I don't know....I'm just not scared here. In school I feel different from everybody else; it makes me nervous. It's like, you know, in orchestra when people play out of tune? I hate that. Everything's in tune here, everything...."

"That's a beautiful analogy. When we live with other people I think it's normal to feel out of tune sometimes. I bet all your friends feel 'different.' That's because everybody is."

"Oh gimme a break!" he said contemptuously. "That's not what I mean. I don't even know what I mean."

Maybe. At any rate he wasn't going to explain. Oh Jason, I thought, watching him set his jaw, I'm going to kick you out into the world so unprepared. You'll be lonely no matter how many miles we walk together.

"I've got an idea, Jay; let's bushwhack to that mountain— no, that one," I said, putting my arms around him and rotating his head like a weather-vane.

He took a compass reading in line with the mountain's summit—a boulder, or some other feature; we walked to it and took another reading. While the trail resembled a Japanese garden only briefly concealing what lay around the turns, this uncharted course demanded our full attention.

Thor, with his barometer sensitivity, wasted much energy trying to coax us back to the trail, pointing out that we were going nowhere.

The summit was farther than I had expected. We would have to backtrack before sunset or we'd get lost. I knew Jason had no misgivings about my lack of reliability when it came to orienteering. It kept surprising me that he didn't worry about safety or shelter. I wanted to be more trusting, but when I didn't know what lay ahead I started fretting, and so I could never be truly free.

We sat down on a ledge in the middle of the sky, looking down on Vermont's gentle landscape. There was no sign of highways cutting the hills; the Long Trail itself was invisible. I laid my shirt out to dry and we took off our hot boots. Thor looked on studiously while we gathered blueberries from the low bushes in the crevasses, then did a little grazing of his own, but more efficiently. He simply put a whole branch in his mouth and raked off the ripe berries between his teeth.

"He doesn't know he's a dog," Jason laughed.

Tea drinking on a windy mountain top was the ultimate luxury. With our fresh supplies we even had cookies. I was absurdly flattered when a monarch butterfly couched on my knee and Jason told me it thought I was a flower.

"Skunk cabbage, maybe," I said.

"Just be glad," he reminded me, and I was.

"Do you want to do a sun salutation?" he asked. I thought this was the right place, and so we turned toward the sun and placed our palms together and closed our eyes. We went through the yogic motions—bending, stretching, and returning to the still starting position with folded hands, adapting to each other's rhythm of stillness and movement.

Afterwards we chanted "Aummm" facing eastward. I had never done this on a mountaintop before. The sound flooded the valley, beyond Mrs. Morgan and her good man, Bunny, the bitten farmer, the minister; beyond the mad woman and her gentle brother, and on to the end of time.

-5-

Measuring Miles by Inches

Thor scraped the baked surface off the trail and wriggled his belly into the cool peat. The afternoon stillness—filled with the busy living of rodents and insects—hung among the trees.

I leaned against a boulder, bending my knees a little to let it support my backpack. It was in the nineties and humid; we'd done a good fifteen miles uphill and down. My shirt was drenched. Rounding my back to drag the pack onto my shoulders again, I said, "Okay, let's go, pooch," nudging Thor's rump with my boot. He frowned at a tree frog blundering near his nose, but didn't move.

I went on my way. Somewhere a white-throated sparrow trilled its astounding variations. Swept along with its exhilaration, I called back and imagined the small, invisible bird answering. Why were humans pleased to be acknowledged by animals? How this green world filled me with joy all the long, hard day!

Thor didn't come when I whistled. I dropped the pack and jogged back; he wiggled his stumpy tail penitently, putting on his best tragic air. I unfastened the belly bands of his bags and lifted the weight off him.

Just then Jason, whom I had estimated to be some twenty minutes ahead of me, came trotting back, panting, "Didn't you hear me call? What's going on! I found your pack and I thought...."

"Is there any water up ahead? Thor won't move. His nose feels like an old tire." Sweat stung my eyes; I wiped them with a corner of my shirt. "We may have to build a stretcher, Jay, to get him to the lake. We could hide our packs in the bushes."

"Mom, he weighs ninety pounds! Let's give him the rest of

the Gatorade. Be right back." He'd also left his backpack behind. I stroked Thor's head; he moaned softly. He needed water, and soon.

Red, and still breathing hard, Jason handed over the bottle. The parched animal greedily slurped the greenish liquid I poured between his teeth until he tasted the lime, which had a restorative effect on him. Grimacing, he dodged his benefactors, evidence that he could move pretty well. We applauded his character and carried his saddlebags between us on a stick. Hanging his head, Thor played his role of victim to the hilt—I had no doubt that he was a casualty of our neglect until he started to chase a chipmunk. I thought he'd gambled away the last of his strength, but he had smelled the sun-dappled water before we saw it. Soon he was cruising through the lake like a dilapidated motor boat, drinking his fill.

Farther down the shore we noticed a bright-orange, one-man tent, the only prop on an otherwise pastoral stage. The pebbled beach was pristine, though undoubtedly it served campers daily. "Through hikers," that is people who hike long distances, rarely litter. Gum wrappers and beer cans are found near trail heads accessible by car.

We picked a spot where the grass was still matted from a previous tenant. Jason was in the water before I could start my organizing. Why not, we had hours of daylight left. I had to rummage through plastic bags tied with rubber bands to locate my bathing suit. We had just arrived and already the place looked like a flea market.

While Jason swam out I dallied at the water's edge, savoring the soft coolness washing over my tired feet. This sweet tranquility was disturbed by Thor sounding his alarm. Fortunately he was tied up, because the man who approached was naked. He called, "Hi! Mind if I join you?"

Ordinarily I would have been terrified of a man without his accommodations, but his boldness challenged my preconceived notions about dress codes.

"Not if I can keep my suit on," I said. He chuckled.

"Is that your son? Fine swimmer."

I was glad when he sat down, though I worried about the sharp stones. He was in his thirties, a Robert Redford type, with fine eyes and a blond beard. He'd been hiking for six months, off and on, starting in Georgia. I didn't ask what he did during "off" times; for some reason these brief camp encounters didn't deal with people's lives outside "The Hike." I was sticky and smelly, anxious to get into the water.

My daily hair washing had earned me the name Shampoo Lady. Because of his immersion in Tolkien, Jason was nick-named Halfling. People acquired their new names at campsites, where they observed each other's peculiarities. I could think of some cute names for the stranger, but he claimed he was Dale.

Dale and I swam, then he carried water for me to rinse the soap from my hair, so as not to pollute the lake.

Later, the black flies were joined by mosquitos and deer flies; all of us did a lot of dancing. Dale offered to pitch our tent.

"Thanks," I said, "I'll snap the poles together. Do you think we need to put on the rainfly?"

"Look at that," said Dale.

"Right." The wispy mare's tails meant rainfly weather was on the way. I tossed him the tent bags. "Jay, where are the poles?"

"Dunno."

"Well, help me look."

"There isn't too far to look here." He poked things around with his foot while I made an uneasy assessment of the day's ventures. The poles had been tied to the outside of my pack and must have slipped out when I threw it down to check on Thor. I could have missed them in their tan cover, especially if they had rolled away from the pack. "That must be it," I sighed.

"What must be it?" Dale stood hugging the tent bags. I told him how I'd been preoccupied with carrying Thor's stuff. I hated to look incompetent.

"How far back is it?" Dale asked.

I was putting on my shorts over my wet suit. "I don't know exactly. Two miles, maybe."

"Right or left side?"

"Right. Would you mind keeping an eye on the dog?"

"I'll go. You should get your supper; you can use my tent if the bugs get to be too much. Tan bag, and you're sure about the right side of the trail?"

33

"Yes, from here. No! Are you crazy? You'll never find them, and besides...." He was gone already. "Dale, please come back here!"

"Besides what, Mom?" Jason was unruffled.

"Besides he's stark naked. Besides it's our problem. Besides he'll never find them. He should mind his own business. Damn!"

"He'll find them."

"You should always be suspicious of people without clothes, you hear me? You act as if it's normal! I'm surprised you didn't offer to go with him!"

"He didn't want me to."

"That's not the point. Do I have to spell it out? He's a streaker for Pete's sake!" I was furious.

"You liked him yourself. He's doing us a favor." Jason started walking toward the orange tent. He looked sad, even from the back.

We ate our supper and washed the dishes. I was fighting a quiet battle with myself. It was ugly to be suspicious of Dale; he'd been kinder than kind. I didn't know how to protect Jason from harm without destroying his faith in people. I had to trust his instincts; at least his were still fresh.

When Dale brought back the poles, we set up the tent while he went to "get y'all a treat."

The lake changed from grey to gold before vanishing under thick haze. Dale's body too, would be dressed by the night.

I should've known. In the fuzzy distance it looked like a piece of chalk was stalking the beach—he was wearing a black long-sleeved jersey, a long white cotton wrap, and sandals.

We huddled in our tent, eating chocolate chips, and listening to Dale's stories.

He'd spent three days with a sick old man in a lean-to in Pennsylvania. "It was April," he told us, "I can still see him....lying on the floor in his army surplus bag, a green cap pulled over his forehead, his eyebrows curled over the edges."

I listened to the lilting lake; a small animal scurried nearby. Dale was staring into the candle flame.

"He'd been walking for over thirty years. Death wasn't a

big deal to him, but it was private. I just stayed around to give him sips of water." Long silence.

"He died as gently as animals in the woods." Dale tugged at his beard, nodding his head absentmindedly, as if approving of such easy living and dying.

"Did he look like Gandalf?" asked Jason.

Dale left his reminiscense then. He chuckled. "Let's see. He was short, with a powerful chest and a beautiful white beard."

Jason sat up straight. "And his eyes?"

"Funny thing about his eyes. They were pitch black. Not what you'd expect somehow in a dying man. And who is this fellow, Gandell? Someone you know?"

"Gandalf! You know, the Wizard in *Lord of the Rings*?"

"Oh. I haven't read that."

Jason gave a synopsis of the legend and decreed that our tent was the Last Homely House east of the sea, except it was west. It was a place for story telling, eating, and singing. "For sleeping also," I added, "so get your toothbrush."

"But Dale saw Gandalf," Jason said excitedly, "could I just tell him about the feast in Elrond's house with Frodo?"

I was pretty sure Dale knew the tale and had given Jason a chance to tell a story.

Before parting, we lingered by the shore. Dale put his arms around us as we watched puffs of cloud float on the water, a scene right out of Mirkwood. For a few eternal moments, life was exquisite. Dale kissed my hair before he walked off into the haze.

Jason whispered, "Gandalf fooled him, Mom. He's a wizard. He didn't die."

"Oh," I said, touching the spot on my ribs where Dale's hand had been.

The next morning the orange tent was gone. It wasn't raining but would be soon. A wet tent would be heavy; we hurriedly broke camp. With luck, we could breakfast between showers. My mood was as grey as the air we plowed through. Jason was humming a few paces behind me, fragments from the *Queen of the Night*. He wore his hobbit outfit: a yellow sweatshirt and green shorts.

"What've you got to be so cheery about?" I wanted some-one to brood with. "We'll be drenched if this keeps up all day."

There was no point in donning rain gear; sweat would get us quite as wet. Only around camp did we make an effort to stay dry. Thor, in the lead, called a halt to the sorry parade now and then for a spontaneous shake. I kept colliding with him and saying unkind things.

Around ten the rain was mostly compact fog. We found refuge on a ledge under a shallow cave. I could see neither sky nor mountains, only billows of silver mist. Thor immediately took the best place and started shivering. I put his pack out of the way near the edge of the overhang, where my boot accidentally shoved it overboard.

"Mom!" Jason cried. I didn't even hear the pack hit the ground. Peering over the rim of the ledge, all I could see was the top of scrub; no telling how far down, down was. Jason had al-ready changed into a dry shirt; the soggy yellow one lay in a heap.

"Just a sec, I'll get it." He put on a sweater and his poncho and vanished into the soup. To compensate for the mishap I hastily started a fire with birch bark in a corner of the burrow, and hung Jason's shirt to dry. Thor's fierce sneezing bounced back in a muted echo. Baffled, he tilted his head. He looked so comical, I laughed, "What was that, Thor!" It was all the encouragement he needed to get to his feet and bark excitedly at the mountains barking back at him. I tended the fire, changed, then fished up a box of stale crackers and a tin of sardines. The coals were ready for cooking and still Jason hadn't returned.

"Shut up, you moron," I told Thor. I shouted "Jason!" and heard "....ason, ...ason," faintly among dog salutations. But then Jason materialized abruptly and tossed the pack on the shelf.

"Hey, I was getting worried about you! Thanks for getting it. You're all scratched up!" I pulled him up.

"A fire, great! The pack was dangling off a branch—good thing it's red."

"You're freezing! Here, I made hot chocolate." It tasted unbelievably good. Trail cuisine, though inedible in civilized surroundings, tastes, my father used to say, like an angel pissing on your tongue.

"If you give me your Swiss Army knife I'll open the sardines."

"I'll do it."

When he turned to wipe the knife clean on a wet leaf, crafty Thor moved in and gobbled up our precious food. At exactly the same time, we caught him licking out the can. Jason, who had been such a sport, threw down the knife, kicked the tin, called Thor damned and rotten, and said he had lost his appetite and was, furthermore, sick to death of hiking, of muck, of the stinking, wet beast.

"And he's spoiled and unruly." Maybe there was more, but I laughed until my stomach ached. The scene was the epitome of absurdity: the fuming boy, the crouching dog still savoring his plunder—all this drama among the weeping trees. In the end, Jason laughed with me from nervous reflex, but he stayed pretty angry.

Toward the middle of the afternoon, we stopped again to make tea on our gas stove. Walking around in circles, we drank while fishing soggy corpses out of our tea. It was hard not to be able to rest. We'd been walking through low land, our boots grabbing the mud. I always tried to keep my feet dry, even if it meant detouring, but Jason just sloshed through. In spite of my efforts, I was as muddy as he.

"We'll stop at the first lean-to, Jay." He unfolded the limp map and marched over it with index finger and thumb, measuring inches that would be miles.

"It's a good four miles, but no steep climbs," he said.

"We'll get there early enough so there'll be room. Let's hope we won't have to set up the tent."

"It looks like it's rained a hundred days."

Somber hills. Where yesterday we had walked the sun's path, decay reigned. Fungi were born overnight, the birds were mute. Puddles collected in the footprints we left behind, and in our necks, our pockets, our hearts. The desolate afternoon slowly wore away.

I slipped off a stone while crossing a river, and with every step bubbles squeaked out of the lace holes in my boots. A pale, pink whisper of sun broke through briefly. Birches threw anorexic shadows, filtering transparent lines through the green.

Then, "I see it!" Jason said. I jogged to catch up with him. Sure enough, the corrugated roof of a lean-to crouched among a stand of evergreens.

"None too soon, let me tell you. Do you hear anything yet?"

"Not yet."

Well, we were still too far. I hoped the lean-to would be empty. If we had to share the place, Thor wouldn't be tolerated on the platform, especially in his present ragged state. That meant setting up his tent and him knocking it over on purpose. He preferred being scolded to being segregated. Contemplating such inconveniences, I almost wished we could keep on walking until the weather changed. Few things were more gloomy than arriving soaked at a cold, damp shelter, and being called upon to tend to bodily needs. I felt mud seeping through my brain as well as my toes.

There was only one fellow at the camp. "Hi!" Jason greeted him. The stranger didn't respond.

"What a creep," Jason whispered.

"Maybe he's deaf." We dumped our packs on the platform. Still no reaction, even when Thor jumped up. At least that was something. The young man sat as if petrified, staring somewhere in front of his dangling legs. His hair looked like a forsythia bush in the grip of winter.

Jason and I went through our routine: getting water, spreading out a plastic sheet, and putting our sleeping pads and bags on it. Feeding Thor. The man got up and started gathering twigs for a fire. Jason looked bluish around his mouth and his hands were stiff with cold. We lit the little camp stove to make bouillon from cubes. In the meantime the silent man expertly got a fire going.

"Let's help," Jason shivered.

"Give me your boots," our housemate spoke for the first time and in a most amiable way. He put Jason's boots up on sticks he'd pounded into the ground, close to the fire. His movements were methodical—not slow, exactly, but singularly focused. He looked somewhat mad, with all that wild hair and those short legs.

"My name's Johnny," he sang in a seductive tenor, "I always take care of my boots." I was startled by the mis-match of voice and appearance. He took a black gummy tube out of his pocket. "We'll put this on 'em when they're dry," he said gravely, and fussily slid the tube back in his pocket.

"Very kind of you," I said, turning my head to hide my amusement. Wet boots were messy, but the fellow acted as if he were about to save the world.

Gathering firewood was a slow process. We had to cross a full river, jumping from slippery boulder to boulder, straying ever farther from camp to find dry wood. The lower, dead branches of pine burned well, but briefly. I could barely navigate the river empty handed; with my arms full of sticks it became a stunt. Johnny never spoke. His elfish figure could be seen balancing on high ground in the middle of the stream, camouflaged under a load of firewood. He gave himself unstintingly to the creation of a massive woodpile.

We worked solemnly, as though part of a chain gang. The path leading from the river to the camp had turned into a rich, muddy sponge. I decided to surprise Johnny and build a rock walkway. Egged on by the halo that I imagined over my wet head, I rolled and tumbled and heaved rock upon rock to construct a river crossing. Bruised but swelling with good will, I surveyed the much improved approach when Johnny returned with a dead tree on his shoulder. While I stood smiling modestly he marched over my beautiful bridge without so much as a nod.

I continued my forays into the woods, taking some pleasure in my raw hands and stringy hair. I felt disdain in Johnny's silence; he employed a sneaky weapon, by which I found my insecurities. Faced with malice, my reaction would have been one of energetic defiance.

Evening came early; our attention centered on a blazing fire. Jason's boots were steaming on their stakes; Johnny was roasting nuts. Thor, for his part, lay low in a corner, politely staying off our sleeping bags. I hoped no one would remember he was a wet dog and shouldn't take up room in the small shelter. The trees were dripping; a narrow stream had formed in front of the lean-to, where water poured off the roof.

My glance followed a stray leaf funnelling by until it was smashed under Johnny's boot. He bent down to give me a handful of nuts. That was the first time I really saw his face, guileless as a spring morning, with eyes concealing nothing. In his baggy pants and drab plastic poncho, Johnny with his bare heart seemed more exposed than Dale had been. I watched him while he rubbed goo into Jason's boots, again totally committed to the task at hand. Jason sat cross-legged on the floor, scribbling notes on the back of a mashed potatoes pouch while moving the fingers of his left hand on an imaginary fingerboard.

Later, sitting side by side, we ate in chaste meditation in synergy with the forest. We were drawn into Johnny's peace; the usual backpacking jokes were superfluous that night.

Eventually, we did have to scamper about with tooth-brushes and disappearances in various directions for private under-takings. Jason lost the soap downstream. We smelled like pepper-mint sticks after washing with toothpaste. Jason said, "The best thing about backpacking is the people you meet. I really like Johnny."

I put my arm around him; together with our grotesque shadows we walked back to camp, our path weakly lit by the flashlight.

Johnny was already in his sleeping bag, his bushy mane propped up on neatly folded clothes. We tied our boots together and hung them from the rafters. Thor lay with his legs stretched out, thereby taking up one quarter of the floor space. Jason gener-ously bedded down next to him; I was between the two boys.

The work was done. My muscles were warm from labor, my mind free of concerns about tomorrow. I closed my eyes and took a delicious gulp of rainbow-flavored air in the very midst of which Thor jumped up, ears pricked, muscles hard. His nervous nose never lied, and soon a dripping person under a large backpack appeared. Her name was Miriam. She eyed the possible vacancies on the platform.

Johnny's greeting: "If you wouldn't mind setting up your tent, we wouldn't have to put the dog out."

It was by far the most ridiculous thing he could have said. I got into my boots, curling my toes against contact with their squelchy insides. "No, of course the dog'll sleep outside!"

"I'll put up my tent, leave the dog be," Miriam said. If that wasn't surprising enough she added, "Goodnight, Johnny." Sheepishly I climbed into my bag once more, thinking, whatever I say or do will be wrong.

Johnny lit a candle, anchoring it meticulously in dripping wax. I watched him secretly through my eyelashes.

"That was a good idea, building a bridge," he said. I guiltily squeezed my eyes shut. "It made wood-carrying more fun," he added. Did I imagine a smile in his voice?

"Thanks," I said. You-should-have-thanked-me-you-holy-so-and-so, my brain added without permission. Johnny took a small Bible from under his pillow and started to read with that voice of his.

"The earth is the Lord's and the fullness thereof." Jason had his eyes closed, but I sensed he was listening.

"Who shall ascend into the hill of the Lord?" I imagined violet sun on ice in winter, a broken barn door. The bottom of a baby's foot.

"....who hath not lifted his soul unto vanity."

Chocolates wrapped in silver, cobwebs in morning grass.

"Cease from anger, and forsake wrath: fret not thyself...."

Lilac soap, Mozart's Requiem, new sneakers. The thundering Maine coast.

"Should I stop now?" Johnny asked, laying a hand across the open Bible.

"More," Jason said.

Wave upon wave boomed against the rocks, spraying ocean water on my sun-filled eyelids as I lay in the sculpted sand, listening.

6

The Storm

We were ahead of schedule, having put in long twenty-mile days because of the rain. Enough rain to wet the sea. We learned to live with it and kept sloshing on to stay warm. Thor had become a heap of trouble. On days that we camped in the open he lay in his tent with his black head sticking out. It was depressing to see the rain pouring down on his face, and to go out in the middle of the night to repitch his tent when he yanked out the stakes. On lean-to decks, in spite of his warm sweater and the wind screen we rigged up, he wouldn't stop shivering. Thor could shiver on command. I was kept awake by the drum of his fraudulent chills. When I went to cover him up he conned me with his don't-worry-about-me-I'm-just-a-dog look.

"Sissy!" I scolded, and brought him into our tent where he lay with his long legs jabbing into my stomach and his wet fur assailing my nose. In the end I preferred spending the night outside, leaving man's best friend cuddled against Jason's back. We had reluctantly decided to send Thor home and called Joe from a country store. The meeting was to take place at a trailhead around noon.

At two o'clock Joe still wasn't there. We put on rain gear and huddled under a dripping canopy of leaves.

"Maybe the road is washed out," I said, despair creeping into my voice.

"He'll come, even if it is. He'll rent a truck or something."

I wasn't so sure. We couldn't wait much longer—we'd get hypothermia. Already we were shivering. What if we had misunderstood each other and Joe was waiting elsewhere? Something definitely had gone wrong; it wasn't like him to make us wait in the rain. He'd been chattier than usual on the phone, telling me about work, about the mail that had piled up. We looked forward to spending two days together. There was much to talk about!

"We'd better move around a bit," I said, "and if Daddy isn't here in another hour, we'll hitch to a town."

"Haven't seen one car."

My son looked like a soggy little tramp. I began to blame Joe for it all. I wanted dry socks so badly, I could hardly think of anything else.

Joe hadn't misunderstood directions and the road wasn't washed out. He had just "left a little on the late side."

I knew it wasn't a big deal. What were a couple of hours to people who'd been living in the woods for two weeks? Just the same, I was unnerved by the time Joe emerged from the car cheerful and groomed and fed. His civilized appearance made me feel ludicrous, like a child playing in the mud. He personified what I had been running away from. Knowing he'd taken the time to replenish our supplies and driven the distance made me angry at myself for being unreasonable. I wanted to grab my mixed-up emotions and my dry socks, and run.

"I think we'd better not leave the trail or we'll never find the courage to finish the hike," I said.

"That's what I was thinking," said Jason, to my surprise. Joe thought we should rest up and eat some good food.

"I knew it," said Jason. "Mom won't want to go back into the muck. I knew it!"

"Sure she will," Joe decided for me.

"Mom," and "she" began to feel ever more contrary. Wads of dirty clothes found their way from my pack into the car while I struggled to regain my equanimity.

"Well, at least you'll be home sooner than we thought," Joe remarked.

But I was not about to stray from my destructive course. "Actually, I've decided to go on to Mount Madison in the Whites."

Jason said nothing, though this was the first he'd heard of it. I didn't even mean it. I just knew I wasn't ready yet to return to walled-in living.

"Haven't you had enough? Do you want to wait until you both get sick?" Joe said gently. He had no idea that I was just being rotten.

"We won't get sick," I said.

"And how are you planning to get to the White Mountains, if one may ask?" Joe said, dropping the tailgate shut. I tried to ignore the water running off his slicker, drenching his nice, clean pants. Pale, green-veined stones gleamed in the mud of the logging road where we slouched against the car, its hood steaming.

"We'll switch to the Appalachian Trail and eventually we'll hitch to Pinkham Notch," I said.

"Do what you want." Joe had finally had enough.

Before he drove off he told Jason, "Take care of Mom." Jason gravely assented.

I wanted to undo the whole thing. I wanted to thank him and apologize, and shake him for letting me get away with my bull. But I couldn't.

At the Sherburne Pass junction, where the Long Trail and the Appalachian Trail cross, we began our big detour to New Hampshire's White Mountains. And that's how we came to sit out the storm with the Swat Team.

The first thing we always did when we arrived at camp was to read the log. We added our names, destination, and comments on trail conditions useful for people hiking in the opposite direction. Sometimes hikers wrote personal messages—things or people lost, requests to pass news along the trail by word of mouth. The pages abounded with derogatory statements about the steepness of the terrain. And once there was a communication by someone who had found Jesus.

According to the log, the Swat Team had started their two thousand mile trek in Georgia, where the A.T. begins at Skinner Mountain, and was headed for Mount Katahdin in Maine.

Supper in the crowded cabin was subdued. We no longer mentioned the rain that engulfed our spirits, but exchanged stories in measured tones while we stoked up our camp stoves and made hot drinks. All of us had chosen to tramp the woods like waterlogged rabbits; our fellowship was immediate.

I'd been asking people about the hike at the end of each day when we congregated in shelters, "Why are you doing this?" Never did anyone give a direct answer. People looked toward the mountains and said dreamily, "Oh, I dunno....How 'bout you guys," neither expecting nor receiving an articulate reply. Perhaps our answers wouldn't have differed much. The modern world had drowned out the wind in the trees, leaving us with nameless longing. Better take the dirt and the blisters, the tasteless food and the rain. Here in the forest, we were in touch with the very core of things.

The lean-to smelled of sweat and dirty boots. Of the nine people bunking together that night, I was the only woman. The last person to come in from the rain slept underneath one of the platforms along with a broom, a snow shovel, and mouse droppings. All I could see of him was his yellow hair. The rest of us were divided evenly between the two decks. In my corner I lay staring at the graffiti and the plastic bags crammed between the logs. Darkness would soon consolidate the array of limbs and gear lolling haphazardly on the decks.

Propping myself up to look over his shoulder, I asked Jason, "Don't you miss Thor?"

On the open page of the diary he'd drawn trellises stacked with notes round as rose buds. The pencil was still balanced in his sleeping hand. I pulled his bag up around his shoulders and watched grey rain fill the mountains until my eyes grew tired, and then I listened to the drops hammer on the roof.

The sleepers' dreams were hovering in the rafters. The rain had ceased and a dragon was making its nightly rounds, discharging long, reverberating rumbles. The hills lit up when fire rolled from its throat and reflected in the eyes of a horned owl. Thunder cracked overhead. I opened my eyes to white light. Jason lay with his head on the dirty planks. Another splintering jolt brought everybody to their feet.

We sat bumper-to-bumper on the edge of the lean-to, bare feet beach-white every time the light rocketed over the peaks. I huddled between two strangers, one of whom put his sweater around me. We felt the great storm bear down and resonate through our souls like Bach's D-major Fugue. Lightning bolts snaked through the ledges to where the dragon lived. Nine strong on our stage, our arms resting on each other's shoulders, we changed from dark mirages to brief bright clowns with naked faces and bushy heads. Ghostly too, the masked raccoon shuffling down from the picnic table, disturbed by the row of humans. During the cave-like dark between flashes I glimpsed things that are hidden in daylight. To think I might have spent this night in a motel....

When I woke up, the sky was swept clean and everybody was gone. Not a trace of seven men boarding, packing, or cooking. The resident raccoon sat on top of the picnic table.

"Hey Jay," I shook him, "did we have a thunderstorm last night?"

"Sure," he said soothingly, as if talking to a mad person.

"We did, right?"

He shook off the last of his sleep. "Where is everybody?"

Reassured I hadn't been dreaming, I teased, "Everybody who? What are you talking about?"

He wasn't flappable. "Nice of them to let us sleep, huh? I guess when you're hiking two thousand miles you learn to move quietly, like the animals. Except for Thor. He sounds like a tank when he gets up in the morning."

"That sweet soul," I said.

"That sweet soul would be wading in the soot pie there, and you'd be having a fit." The rain had mashed the charred wood and ashes of many old fires into a thick black goo in front of the lean-to.

"I would not," I said.

A few minutes later he made as if to walk through the muck on his way to the bushes, his red boot strings trailing.

"Hey, watch where you're going! Don't you have any sense?" I yelled.

He snickered with satisfaction.

We shook the water off low bushes to air the sleeping bags on them and unfolded the tent we'd packed up wet some days ago. While things were drying we scrubbed ourselves and our socks. Finally, we ate porridge made with powdered milk, apricots, and nuts.

On this shining morning, the tiny white-throated sparrows

warbled their high spirited call, but I found myself stiffly incompetent to express my joy.

One thing I haven't figured out about backpacking. You start out with a given amount of stuff. Every day you eat two meals and several snacks, and yet the load seems to swell. I usually had to pack Jason's things as well as my own. He got frustrated after several rearrangements of his gear and wasted energy on kicking and pounding. Even after squeezing the air out of the rolled up tent, pressing our plastic-bagged clothes into bricks, and removing any extra paper from food bags and squashing them, we still had to fight zippers and buckles.

That day, Jason had subjugated his possessions with much grunting when he discovered part of his load, a bag of stakes, still hanging on a twig. His face flushed in anger. He tore open his pack and everything tumbled out again.

"I'll help," I said quickly, but too late to forestall his fury.

"You never even asked me if I wanted to go to Madison!" he shouted, forcing his stuff into the bag on one side while it escaped on the other.

"Here, let me...."

He shook the pack empty and started to redo it. "I thought you said we were equal partners!"

"You're right, I should've discussed it with you, Jay, but I didn't know I wanted to go until I realized the trip was almost over. I was in a bad mood. I'm sorry; we don't have to go."

"I want to."

"We've done so much hiking; you must be getting tired of it. Sometimes I forget you're twelve because you never complain."

"Why should I?"

When we got going at last, the big blue backpack wobbled ahead of me above his scratched-up legs.

7

Doctor or Cook?

In Vermont, peaks over 2500 feet receive annually more than a hundred inches of precipitation, while the valleys get thirty-eight. A good part of the hundred inches must have fallen during the past week. The trails were severely eroded by vibram soles and had turned into streams of thick, sucking mud. Jason had grown accustomed to wallowing, but now that my boots were almost dry, I made an effort to keep them that way. I lost sight of him while I picked my way, the pans clinking inside my pack.

We had gotten a late start, what with all our housekeeping chores. I wanted to get off at U.S. 5 near Dartmouth College early the next day. Wondering what Jason would think of that, I yodeled a message for him to stop and wait. He never called back, which bugged me plenty. I supposed he thought one fishwife scaring the wildlife was enough. In the middle of a yodel someone called "hello," right behind me.

"You scared the daylights out of me," I said to a man in knickers. He was about thirty-five, had a pony tail, John Lennon glasses, pale skin, and wore, of all things, a tweed coat.

There was more traffic on the A.T. than on the Long Trail, but we rarely met more than one or two people during a day of hiking, and more often we saw nobody.

"I just said hello! I'm sorry!" the stranger smiled.

"That's okay. I was calling my son."

The man took off his pack and rested it on the toe of his boot. We exchanged "where're you headin" type questions. He said he'd become depressed and was thinking of quitting. The loneliness was getting to him. He'd been out only five days.

"Would you mind if I hiked with you for a couple of days?" he asked.

"We're actually planning to return to the Long Trail. This is a side trip for us. We're going to try to get a ride to Pinkham," I explained, tactfully turning the offer down.

I noticed the red claw of a plastic creepy-crawler lobster slip out of his pocket when Conrad (that was his name) stooped to hoist up his backpack. It didn't fit with his outfit of an impoverished Englishman, but it added a fine touch of color.

"Is that some kind of memento?" I asked, shaking claws with the lobster. Conrad seemed irritated with me. He pushed the lobster back in his pocket without answering. When we caught up with Jason, he spoke mostly to him.

Later in the afternoon, we sat straddling a fallen tree, drinking instant coffee. Rest stops were something we cherished, but now, instead of relaxing, I kept chattering. Conrad told us he'd done a fair amount of hiking, mostly in California, where it didn't rain. He said he was from "all over" and did "this and that" when I asked, so I knew I'd been too nosy.

"Maybe we'd better get to camp," he said, picking up his neatly folded jacket and putting it back on, not minding the wet heat. Jason looked at me nervously; he probably thought I would say the wrong thing again. I raised my eyebrows at him, but he was siding with Conrad.

"Lead the way, Jason," Conrad said cheerily, standing aside to let me pass.

So, we were going to camp together it appeared. For the first time, I hoped there would be other people at the cabin.

In dry weather we preferred camping away from shelters. I loved awakening in the tent and letting my eyes follow the channeled bark of maple or oak up toward the crown where tender light hinted of a new day. I would lie waiting for the ferns and grasses to straighten up, for the veeries and mourning warblers to begin their songs. Oh well, sleeping in a lean-to was less work, and tomorrow we would be on our way to Pinkham.

We arrived at Happy Hill Cabin about five o'clock. While I scribbled in the log, Jason and Conrad gathered wood, then Conrad disappeared for a long time. I wanted to gossip, but Jason simply said, "So what, I like him." He liked everybody for as long as possible.

"Too bad the Swat Team moves so fast," I said, "it was fun to sit up with them last night, wasn't it?"

"Yeah. It's different to be in the middle of the weather...." Just then, Conrad returned to Happy Hill. He looked very handsome in a white cotton suit. His hair was sleeked down; he had shaved. I was still wearing my canvas shorts and mud-trimmed socks.

"Did you watch the thunderstorm last night?" Jason asked Conrad, who proceeded to give a poetic rendition of his emotions. It had to do with the power of light and darkness. He trailed off into a Norse legend about rapacious Vikings, and drew pictures of battle axes, war hammers, shields, and daggers. Jason was captivated. His eyes followed the sketching pencil as it drew muscular, short-legged horses rearing beneath mace-swinging riders. In their male imagination they, too, were conquerors—foreign to me.

Buddies in arms, they lit the best fire we'd had. After it stopped flaring, Conrad surprised us with his cooking. He carried an assortment of spices, dried onions, and garlic, and made a good meal of our sorry rice and noodles. I vowed never to go backpacking again without spices. For dessert, he created a compote of fruit he'd dried himself.

Conrad and Jason kept up a lively discourse. I watched how their faces picked up the glow of the fire. What a nag I had been, prejudging this sweet, generous man.

It was a beautiful, warm night. We sat by the fire until Conrad declared bedtime. He doused the coals while Jason and I retreated for ablutions. Waxen moonlight sifted through the pines while we brushed our teeth. The sharp peppermint taste reminded me this wasn't a dream. Jason hooked his arm through mine as we walked back to camp and said, "I love being here." He was nearly as tall as I already.

Conrad sat tailor-fashion on the floor, grandiose in his white suit. He'd lit two candles, one placed near each knee—a picture too stark to be real. I tried to avoid stepping in his ring of light. At first I assumed he was fiddling with his toiletries, but that was not what they were. He had a velvet-lined leather case filled with surgical instruments. There were two scalpels, scissors, forceps, clamps, needles, and silk. Jason leaned over him, eager to see.

I spoke harshly to him, "Go to bed."

Conrad showed me how his scalpel could gash a blade of grass, its steel flashing. "A knife like this can slice a man in half," he said, his eyes twitching like a squirrel's tail.

"I bet."

"Come here," said Conrad.

"I'm already here." I didn't recognize my voice. Damn! We were camping with a lunatic! He'd brought spices to season us! The white suit—doctor or cook?

"I mean closer," he said. He handed me one of the scalpels. "Feel that!"

"Wow! Eh, why do you tote these things around?"

"What?"

I cleared my throat. "I said, what do you use them for?" I handed back the scalpel, the blade pointing toward me. "Be careful."

"You're all right," said Conrad. "You never know who you meet out here, you know?"

"That's a fact."

He returned the instruments to the case. "I don't like getting them wet. The night air, you know."

I pulled my sleeping bag closer to Jason's and lay stiffly on my back. Once, when I thought Conrad was asleep, I shone my flashlight on him, casually, as if it were an accident. He lay with his glasses on, his head propped up on an air pillow he shared with the lobster. I don't know why, but that unnerved me extremely.

Everything returned to normal in the morning. Conrad, gay and charming, was back in his knickers, cooking us breakfast. Jason was reserved; he understood that Conrad's possessions were not mere *objets d'art,* although we hadn't talked about it. I worried that Conrad would get weird again if we acted uneasy around him, so I tried to compensate for Jason's strained attitude with too much talking.

After we swept out the cabin and stuffed every last bit of trash in our packs, we filled our canteens and were on the trail before nine o'clock. We skirted Dothan Brook, then followed a dirt road through a young pine forest. Humming, Conrad kept up a fast pace while we were climbing a ridge. On the descent, two white-tailed deer bounded away; from the thicket they kept their mild eyes on us as we passed.

"I would walk ten miles to see that," Conrad said dreamily.

Jason scrutinized his face, trying to reconcile the two Conrads. "Yeah, I would too," he said.

About eleven the sky started to cloud over and the heat became oppressive. We had arrived in Norwich, where Jason and I planned on leaving the trail. Conrad treated us to ice cream at a drugstore before we said goodbye. He would stay in the woods a few more days, and thanked us for helping him through his depression. I felt lighter when the strange man shook hands and walked away.

8

Lilies of the Field

Jason, who had been especially pensive during our walk
with Conrad, now wanted explanations for last night's bizarre
display.

"Well," I said, "maybe he found them somewhere. I once
found a stethoscope."

"Do you think he kills people?"

"Of course not. He's just eccentric, that's all. These things
seem more creepy in the moonlight than they really are," I said,
sticking out my thumb to hitch a ride.

"Mom! That's not how you do it!" He was seriously embarrassed for a mother who didn't know how to be cool.

"Oh?"

Demonstrating the correct posture and thumb position, he
feigned an outrageous, street-wise mug. I did my best imitation,
and soon a Mercedes pulled up. We had thought more in terms of a
truck.

After the man loaded our gear in the trunk, the elderly
couple invited us to sit on their spotless, air-conditioned uphol-
stery. I felt smug that I had nabbed such a luxurious ride despite
my lack of talent. The sitting on something soft and clean had my
mind running away from the woods, but arrested by the woman's
"What a wonderful thing you two are doing."

When they heard how many miles we'd come, the couple
wanted to hear details of our days and nights in the Green Mountains. The woman, who was dressed in an expensive grey linen
dress, said that children learned by doing.

"I hope we're both learning," I said.

"These days people are too focused on achieving and acquiring; they have no time for their children," said the man.

"Well, the rest of the year we try to achieve and acquire too, I'm afraid," I said.

"No-no-no-no!" the man protested.

They took us all the way to Kinsman Notch, and when we parted, the woman reminded us that Jesus told the Jews not to waste time getting and spending, but to observe the lilies of the field. "You know," she said softly, holding my hand in both of hers, "I never had children."

Jason asked me about the lilies of the field.

"She meant we should go through life with open eyes and notice the beauty around us. And that we shouldn't be so occupied with tomorrow that we miss the present. I guess she was especially thinking of simple things."

"She meant all that?" he boxed my pack, teasing me with my pontificating. "You think that's the reason we go hiking?" he asked.

Our next ride was in the back of a pick-up whose solar bed grilled our bare legs. Then we walked for an hour until a semi-trailer rasped to a halt.

A man with reflecting sunglasses leaned out of the window. He was burned red except for a band of baby-white skin visible underneath his shirt collar, which made him look oddly defenseless.

"Ya'll wanna ride?" he asked, sliding the black mirrors to the tip of his nose. I shaded my eyes to look into his, way up there in the huge truck.

"We're trying to get to Conway."

"Hoppon!" The running board of the truck was nearly as high as my shoulders.

"You've got to be kidding. Do you have a ladder?"

That brought him away from the window and down on the other side of his truck. He picked up Jason, pack and all, and deposited him on the step. Jason dove in through the window after dumping his pack inside. From there, he was able to unlatch the door. The driver took my pack and I pulled myself up. Without ceremony he shoved a big hand under my bottom and heaved, "Hayaa!"

"Thanks," I panted.

There wasn't room for the three of us in the cab, so Jason was told to sit behind the seats. That's when we discovered we had a hostess as well. She lay folded in a nest of blankets.

When Jason hesitated, she welcomed him: "Set 'ere why don't ye."

All this time her husband had been laughing at us and shaking his head. He had a big belly, powerful arms, and hairy hands. His wife was a miniature with bird-like features. Jason was given half of her nest, where he looked predatory with his big hiking boots.

The semi labored into gear. I saw it hadn't been a small matter to bring the thing to a halt.

Bird-woman showed Jason pictures of her grandbabies and her bird dogs back in Tennessee, and Jason told her of our hike. The man was flabbergasted that anyone in the "U. S. of A." could be stupid enough to live for a month like a "doggon' possum."

"An' what does yer mammie feed ye in them woods, boy?" asked the man.

"Uh, sardines and things." The man smacked his thighs with a blow hard enough to finish both of us.

"Saardines? Ye hear that Mary-Sue? Hahaha. Saardines he says!" He wiped his eyes. "Oh sweet Jesus, they eat goddamn saardines."

Mary Sue chuckled, "Leav'em be Pappie."

"Ye like saardines, boy?" He found Jason in his mirror. "Do ye?"

"Yes, they're okay. We mostly eat rice and mashed pota-toes," Jason tried to salvage our credibility.

"Rice 'n mash....pfff...." Now both of them cracked up.

"Ye tell yer mammie to get ye some better grub, boy, if ye wanna get some size on ye."

"Don't worry," I grinned, "I'll take care of it." The bird-lady told me about the benefits of biscuits and grits with gravy. They had brought their boys up good, five of 'em not counting the one who'd died an itty bitty bugger God luv 'im 'n real cunnin' he was too.

They went out of their way and delivered us on the doorstep of Pinkham Notch Camp. The unloading left me with a squashed bosom.

"Ya'll have something good to eat now, ye hear?" The driver gave me a familiar pat on the tail and roughed up Jason's hair, as though we were two silly kids he'd dropped off at summer camp back in the hills of Tennessee.

"Those people are the salt of the earth, Jay."

"I hope they liked us—do you think they did?"

"I'm sure; I think they like everybody."

For a long time afterwards I had a smile in my heart.

At the lodge we received sheets, blankets, and a key to our bunk room. We ate a splendid home-cooked meal by candlelight with fifty or so other hikers, at long tables. After taking a slow shower, we slept.

In the morning we did more lazy eating and bathing. We'd made reservations at Madison Hut from Vermont and looked forward to a day of climbing. At the end of the day, shelter and food would be waiting for us instead of the usual camp chores.

It was one of those mid-summer days that move slowly. I felt as if we were wading through billows of heat that grew larger and more resisting as we pushed upward. The trail rambled over boulder fields where we hauled ourselves up on tree roots or bulges in the stone. I regretted not leaving earlier before the steaming heat was trapped in the woods. Once we reached the tree line there would be a breeze, and the going would be easier. It took us over an hour to do one mile of steady climbing.

By midafternoon the stillness widened and the sky took on the feel and hue of resin. Scrubby pine replaced the hardwood forest. We stopped to pick blueberries, saving a handful and throwing back our heads to pour the tangy fruit into our mouths.

"Here," Jason said, holding out dusty-blue gems in purpled hands.

I received his small gifts—the last Tic-Tac, the best spot on the floor, or the doing of an unpleasant task—and treasured them long and deeply.

The first nibble of wind freed the hair that sweat had glued to our faces. A young man came striding down the mountain, gesticulating "go back." He looked like Jason's pet tarantula "Paganini" standing on hind legs: all hairy motion. Closer, he was a bearded man in a hurry.

"Better go down fast," he said, "You won't manage the gusts up there. Once you're beyond that ridge," he pointed to where we'd first noticed him, "Oh boy, watch out! I'd say sixty with eighty-to-a-hundred gusts!"

"How's that possible? It's just a bit windy now and then. Feels great, actually. It was blood-hot below."

"The kid'll blow away, and you're not very big either. I could barely stand up myself." The man did look tattered.

"We made reservations at Madison; I couldn't stand going all the way down again."

"Suit yourself," he said, striding away.

"How much farther is it?" I called.

"Forty minutes in good weather. But I'd go down to the woods for the night anyway. There's no place to pitch a tent, so you'll get wet, but you'll live to tell about it!"

"All right! Thank you!" I shouted to the top of his descending head.

"A hundred-mile wind, sure! And just a breeze here," I said. "What do you think, should we go back down and stand under a tree tonight?"

"No way! I'm too tired and I'm hungry. The sky looks pretty dark over the summit though, Mom."

"Put on your windbreaker—it's getting chilly here." I looked forward to a bit of excitement with the cockiness of an apprentice. "Okay storm, here we come!"

The wind grew in strength the higher we climbed but was far from threatening. Until we cleared the next ridge. Here, a tempest tore at the treacherously brooding day, slamming us against the mountain's face. We should have returned to the protection of the forest then, but instead, we crawled to the side of the rib where the wind was less strong and clawed our way up through krummholz as fast as we could. I still did not believe this could be a hundred-miler.

Unfortunately, we needed the cairns on the rib to guide us, and minimum visibility forced us back there. With difficulty, we succeeded in tying ourselves together with a spare strap. Our windbreakers clapped like spinnakers; loose strings whipped our faces. It wasn't possible to stand upright; we hugged the slope, face down, waiting for an instant of respite before the next blast howled by. During these brief lulls I called "Go!" and we crept on knees and elbows like marines in boot camp, gaining a few feet before the gale had us clinging to the rock once more, buried beneath our backpacks.

While we were crouching against the slope, we had to scream to communicate—the words were wrenched from us by an omnipotent, invisible force.

"I'm sorry I got us into this," I yelled, and bargained silently for our safety.

"What?"

"Sorry!"

"Me too!"

"My fault!" I protested. His neck was bleeding, I supposed from a flogging buckle or string. Our hands were raw—we grasped at anything to stay grounded, not minding sharp edges or thorns. The cold anesthetized these minor wounds.

A full backpack bombed past, hurled by the wind like a wounded sparrow. Snowshoe hares were tossed by the storm like tumbleweed.

"We have to help them," Jason hollered, knowing we were powerless. "They'll be killed...."

It began to pour. Water barreled toward us in sheets, biting at our faces. Why in God's name had I not believed Tarantula Man? During a pause between gusts I let out a wail of frustration and fear.

"Don't worry, Mom, we'll make it," Jason said, holding on to a fistful of my sweeping hair. He added, "We have to."

"You're not afraid?"

"What?"

"Go!" I called.

We were on the mountain for hours. The sun set; the storm raged on. At last we saw the lights of Madison Hut blossom in the distance. The trail followed a level route here; we were over the summit, and the wind, its might diminished, leaned behind us. We could walk now, fly, in fact. The light was our beacon. We were almost home and would get a hiker's welcome, having braved such a storm, I thought, my confidence returning.

Two men and an older woman were sitting at picnic tables, reading, and didn't look up when we blew in. The cold and dismal hut apparently had no crew to check us in.

"Nice to see you too," I whispered to Jason.

"They look like mummies," he said.

We went to the bunk room and dropped our packs. Bunks were in stacks of three, with four or five folded, heavy wool blankets. Most were unoccupied, some had grey humps on them.

I lay down near the roof, Jason just below me. Rest didn't lessen my exhaustion, nor did the safety of the hut bring comfort. The blanket load pressed down on me and yet I shivered. I kept still as a corpse in order not to touch a cold spot.

Some welcome that was. They probably blamed me for going over the peaks in this weather. With a child. A bunch of professionals annoyed with neophyte trouble makers. We'd learned the hard way; I badly needed sympathy.

I whispered, "Hey, Jay! Psst!" but there was no answer. Obviously, he was making the best of it. I did myself in with projections and expectations, and when they were thwarted I lost my anchor. My face felt hot, but the rest of me shook with cold. At one point, I smelled coffee and fried fish and began to wonder if I were dead. In any case I was oh so tired....

The storm buffeted the creaking hut unabated and rain battered the murky windows. I sailed in and out of sleep.

Some time later I sat up and realized that my period had started a week too soon. When I climbed down, the bunks began to spin. I made it to the latrine in a daze and discovered that it was out of order. I went out into the wind and felt better after that.

In the meantime, Jason had woken up. He looked worn out. We hadn't eaten since breakfast and thought we might drum up a cup of tea. It was ten-fifteen, and the dining room had come to life. People were chatting and playing Scrabble. Tea and hot chocolate were available, and the crew, a young man and a girl with long dark hair, made us sandwiches without our asking.

"We thought we'd better let you guys sleep. You looked

pooped when you came in," the girl said. "Did you put Neosporin on your legs?"

"Hm?" We looked down. Our bare legs looked as though we'd had an argument with a mountain lion. The rain had washed the blood down into the cuffs of our socks.

"It's stopped bleeding," I said, before remembering she would know about mountain safety. "We'll put on Neosporin."

We'd been the last people to arrive, and the hut crew had watched our approach through binoculars, ready to help out if needed. Everybody was frazzled from the storm. Wind gusts had been clocked at one hundred miles an hour. And, yes indeed, there had been fresh fish for supper, and soup and salad, all prepared in the pantry on a gas burner.

"Where'd you get the fish?" I asked, glad my previous sulking wasn't written on my forehead.

The young man stretched and yawned luxuriously. His sweater was in need of underarm repair. "We go down every day for bread and veggies. Not the way you came up, but it's still a six hour round trip."

"And you carry food for twenty or more people? That's unbelievable," I said, "Every day!"

"Well, it has to be done, so...."

I smiled at Jason who didn't need applause either. He was enjoying the hot chocolate, and eating bread.

9

Strawberry Tuesday

We had four days hiking left and had just congratulated ourselves on attaining a certain adroitness when the fall came literally on the heels of pride—Jason stumbled on the downhill of Bromley Mountain.

We'd hit the trail early. By now our bodies were broken-in much like our boots, and we fairly waltzed over hill and dale. There were raspberries and sunshine, nuthatches busying up the trees, a pair of falcons overhead to get us high. I felt invincible. After walking over three hundred miles, we had become strong and sure of ourselves.

Then Jason fell face down, the weight of his pack smacking him against the ground. He chafed his hands and held them palms up for damage assessment.

"Darn," he said, "I must have tripped over a root or something." But it was not his hands that worried me. Blood sprouted sensuously from his knee. With a giddy stomach I rummaged through the first aid bag, while he discovered his real problem.

"Oh shoot," he said.

After sterilizing the tweezers to pick out the grit, I pressed a sterile pad on the wound. The cut was deep enough to expose a thin layer of fat. I tied my kerchief around his leg, but his cells kept on coming with amazing profusion.

Jason insisted he could walk. "That must be the one that cut me," he indicated a flint-edged boulder.

"You need stitches," I said.

"Can't you just sort of press it together, Mom?"

"No. You need a doctor. It'll get infected."

"What about our hike?"

"Well, we almost made it. Daddy'll have to come and get us. Our first problem is getting you off the mountain." He was losing a lot of blood and his face was beaded with perspiration. I had to get help, but I couldn't abandon him.

"Let's try to stop the bleeding; then after you rest a while we can walk out slowly," I told him.

The nearest town was Peru. We would have to climb back up the mountain and go down on the other side. It would take hours. I applied pressure to the mushy mess; he cringed. My hands were sticky with blood—I wiped my free hand on my shorts.

"It's slowing down, Jay. Are you okay?"

"Fine. Let's go."

"I'll hide your pack in the bushes."

"No Mom, I want it."

"I'll hide mine and carry yours." He wanted *his* pack on his back, and I said no, no extra stress on that knee. Just then a young man appeared who was on his way to Georgia.

It took a moment for him to figure out whose blood we were toying with—there was enough on me to suggest I was the patient. When he saw the knee he observed he didn't like the looks of it.

"Neither do we," Jason said, "we're vegetarians."

"Can you walk?" the man asked. He took off his bandana, tied it to a shrub to mark the location where he cached his backpack, and, shouldering Jason's, said, "Here we go."

It was the kind of gesture we'd come to expect on the trail—everybody taking responsibility for another's problems without discussion. We had readily shared our rations and fuel, and on one occasion, carried the pack of a man who had torn a muscle.

"By the way," said our new companion, "I'm Abe." He shook hands with Jason.

"I don't know what we would have done," I began, but Abe interrupted.

"The sooner we get him fixed up the better." Though Jason was still oozing, I knew he was reassured that somebody was making decisions.

I felt obliged to keep up with Abe, especially because Jason tried so hard. They ran back up the mountain with me puffing behind.

"When we get there," said Abe, "we'll see if they'll start up the chair lift."

"Ski lift," I puffed.

"Hm? No, I think it runs during the summer too, but not at this hour. If not, we'll carry him down on a stretcher."

There was a telephone on the summit and Abe managed to have the Big Bromley Chairlift activated.

"When I was your age I would have bawled," he told Jason before he left. That made me feel pretty good.

We were the only passengers. Below, Jason was ushered to a first aid station by two nurses who cleaned his wound. He lost consciousness while lying on the table. They called an ambulance, and by the time it arrived a few minutes later, Jason was sitting up, looking more befuddled than usual.

We were both dehydrated and given copious amounts of water and salts. The ambulance transported us to a medical center where a nurse led Jason away. I paced like an expectant father until I was called.

"This boy of yours," said the doctor, "insists he's going to finish the hike."

"No, of course not," I said.

"Well, it seems to me he has a point. You should finish what you set out to do. If it's important, and it is to him. So, I'm going to put in a stress suture. We've trussed him up pretty well. This kid's been watching to see if I did it right, huh Jason."

Good for him. I preferred looking at Cézannes's *Tulips in Vase* on the opposite wall.

When the repairs on Jason's knee were done, a taxi took us to Johnny Seesaw's, a rustic lodge where the host gave us pink drinks. We spent the evening playing chess in the heavy-beamed lounge, Jason's leg propped up on a chair.

At the end of two days of languishing by the pool, gourmet food, and leisurely walks with Rogue, the resident Black Labrador, to prevent Jason's knee from stiffening up too much, we were ready to leave. The innkeeper brought us to the trailhead in his truck after a brunch of Eggs Benedict and raspberries with cream.

Rogue, wearing a red bandana, kissed us goodbye.

I had been instructed to check the knee for red lines or pus. Armed with sterile bandages and antibiotics, we set out on the last leg of the Long Trail. Jason limped along.

Our progress was slow; flies were everywhere, especially on Jason's knee. We decided to hike over the summit and pitch the tent somewhere on the mountain's broad flank, hoping that higher up the flies would be blown away by the wind. This turned out to be a miscalculation.

In spite of the ubiquitous fly, we praised the view from Bromley Mountain. I engraved the present in my brain—Jason's profile against the sky, the pines, the rich-scented air, and the film of transparent haze in the valley—for recall when I would be too old to climb mountains.

By a slanted ledge was a spot of scrubby moss where we would put the tent; a gravel footpath meandered nearby. While I stomped around, clipping poles together, Jason stooped on his good knee—the slope was covered with wild strawberries. Soon he hobbled over, hands filled, a blush on each knee.

We hid from the bugs as soon as the tent was up. Though the spot had seemed fairly horizontal, it soon became clear we would be rolling east as soon as our muscles relaxed in sleep.

"Not only will we be piling up, but we'll have our feet pushing up our throats," I fussed. Jason could sleep in any position; I assigned him the bumpiest spot.

We had carried drinking water with us; for washing we used wet towelettes, an indispensable item on a mountain top. We brought out the stove, pan, mugs, Johnny Seesaw's sandwiches, teabags, and a citronella candle, and carried them to the highest part on our side of the mountain. After supper, we sat side by side, taking in the night.

"It's as if there's just us left in the world—it's so quiet here," Jason said pensively.

"Do you miss Yuki?" I asked.

He had been fighting tears when music camp came to an end a few weeks ago and Yuki returned to Japan. He wouldn't talk about it, but her picture stood on his nightstand in the dried-up garden of chained bluebells she had made for him. For her birthday we sent her an extravagant gift—an eighteen karat gold chain to reflect the immensity of his emotions.

I asked him if he was still so sad to have her gone. He looked away, his feelings safeguarded by shadows.

"A little."

"There'll be her letters when we get home."

He shrugged. "Right now I don't feel like going home."

"No. It's perfect here."

"It seems we've been gone much longer than a month. It'll be weird to live with problems again."

"What problems exactly?"

"You know, things that make you nervous."

"It's difficult out there, isn't it. Maybe you can choose not to let it bother you so much. Now that we've learned to keep a different pace."

I mused over what I'd just said. It had taken only four weeks to call the woods "here" and life in Amherst "out there." I knew I couldn't adjust completely to either place.

"Let's go to sleep," I said, weary suddenly. When we walked back to the tent, we noticed the lights of a village below.

As I lay anchored between our backpacks to keep from bumping into Jason, I let the strain from my muscles drain into the stone beneath me. How sane life was here. If I counted the hours I spent maintaining our lifestyle at home, acquiring, protecting, rearranging goods, fussing over them, what proportion of my life did I go around looking down, focusing my attention on objects? "They can steal the rug on the floor, that's okay with me," Porgy sang joyously. I would go home and do what was expected of me—what I expected of me....

"Mom? Are you awake?"

"No."

"Does God exist?"

Why didn't he ask me about flibbertigibbets or Valkyries. But of course he had nuclear weapons to think about. I wanted to say yes very badly. Yes, my dearest son, a compassionate God exists.

"I don't know," I said, "but I think so, Jason, I find it much more difficult to believe He doesn't. Especially out here."

While he slept I turned on the flashlight, aiming it away from his face. His hand lay on the tent floor, cupped, as if still holding the ruby berries. I watched his child's slumber wistfully. Then I, too, went to sleep.

Growling next to my ear awakened me. I knew at once it was a raccoon. There were, in fact, two raccoons. "Csh," I said, poised on all fours with only my head outside the tent. Bright moonlight turned the ledge chalk-white, forming a stark backdrop for the animals.

"Csh!" They were bold as brass, looking me in the eye. I clapped my hands. They growled. The animals were arguing over Jason's boot that sat between them. I picked up the other and hurled it at them with a mean cry. Impudent as they were, they only backed off a little. Still, I had yet another pair: mine. I put them on my hands, brandishing them like boxing gloves while I straightened up outside the tent. They zoomed up a tree.

"What are you doing?" asked Jason.

"Bringing our boots in."

"You woke me up."

All was peaceful again, his breathing, the rhythmic filing of crickets. I smiled in the dark at the raccoons' childlike behavior. Probably they had invented another game already. I felt heavy with sleep, but what a pity to miss the moonlit night....

Now what? I jumped up, trying to get out of my bag, but getting the zipper stuck. While drawing myself along inside my mummy bag like a mermaid out of water, I peered through the tent screen.

"Oh, Mom!" Jason accused me.

"Shh...."

"It's just a motorcycle."

"Up here? That's nuts." Then I remembered the village lights. There could be another way up Bromley. I didn't see a headlight, but the rumble grew louder. "What time is it?"

"We don't have a watch."

"Must be after midnight."

"Who cares, Mom, we don't own this place. It's probably some guy from that village, remember?" But he started groping through his belongings. I heard the click of his jackknife. I giggled—a middle-aged woman and a twelve-year-old boy on top of a mountain, armed with a three-inch knife.

I unzipped the front door just enough to peer outside.

Suddenly the strawberry patch was splashed with light. A motorcycle circled the tent.

"Keep still," I whispered.

On the blind side of the tent the motorcycle stopped. Exhaust stabbed my nose. Another spin around and the visitor seemed satisfied that the brown mushroom he had happened on was just a tent with who cares what inside, and roared away.

"Something about motorcycles," I said, "I guess they get bad publicity."

"I wasn't really scared until he stopped."

"Should we make tea? I'm so thirsty!" I was wide awake and jumpy.

"If you don't make me brush my teeth again," he said.

We went outside and sat around the blue hiss of the stove.

"I see Orion," said Jason, "and Gemini."

"When I was a child I thought the stars were holes in heaven," I told him.

"Neat."

Sipping tea, we listened to the forlorn hoot of a night owl. Jason said he was too tired to stay up, but didn't feel like going back into the tent. It had gotten clammy in there with the dew point so high and two bodies evaporating.

"We could sleep outside," I said. "Let's bring out the pads and the sleeping bags. You can watch Orion until you drift off."

We put on sweaters and snuggled into our bags.

"Night, Mom."

"Goodnight, Grasshopper."

I fluffed up the folded down vest I used for pillow, but couldn't get comfortable; my shoulders hurt and the sharp edge of a rock dug into my back.

"I hear something...." Jason popped up.

"I don't. You're just spooked."

He climbed over me, poking me in the stomach.

"Stop it," I said. He got his knife from the tent.

"There's a whole bunch of them," he said, and now I heard

it too.

The sound stretched like an evil smear. It was a scene from nightmares—three black-leathered men, huge and malevolent, rode through the strawberries. We sat mesmerized. I realized the first visitor had gone back to get his buddies; they could do awful things to us....

The engines slowed to idle, then ground to a stop. The lights went off. Boots scraped the gravel. The men dismounted in slow motion. They moved toward us, removing helmets. Two appeared to be in their forties. One man kicked his front tire, muttering to himself. He handed the others cans of beer.

Jason leaned against me; I held on to his sweater.

"Evening." The sudden sanity of speech seemed unnatural. One of the men knelt in front of us, dangling his helmet between his legs. He pulled the tab of a beer can. I was sitting up inside my sleeping bag, but my feet were stone-cold.

"You guys camping?"

I swallowed. I had a vision of our cat dropping dark entrails on the kitchen mat and I nearly gagged.

"Yes."

"Beautiful night," the sitting figure said.

I said, "Did you happen to see the other tents?"

"I didn't, did you Charlie?" Charlie had not.

"We sort of spread out. They're around somewhere, my husband and another couple. Not many flat places right here. For more than one tent, you know." I pulled my sleeping bag to my chin. Joe had told me to bring mace, but I had scoffed at the idea. I imagined myself squirting the men maliciously.

"Yeah, sure. Did you hurt yourself, kid?" Charlie spat out a piece of beef jerky he'd been chewing on.

"He just fell," I said, fixing the spot of the jerky spit in my mind so we wouldn't step in it.

"You guys seen any bears?" asked the sitting man.

"Bears?"

"There's a bear around. We've been tracking him. Like to get a shot at him. Christ, you can see clear as day tonight. But no shooting after dark of course."

"At least the bear is safe for now," I said.

"She sounds like your wife, Joe," Charlie grinned at the younger man.

I heard myself laugh. "My husband's name is Joe, that's probably why. C'mon, Jason," I loosened my grip on him. "Climb into your bag."

The sitting man replanted his helmet.

"We slowed the engines so we wouldn't wake you, but you were up anyway. I probably stirred you up earlier." He crushed the beer can and tossed it into the bushes.

"Yeah, we were up anyway. Well, happy hunting!"

The man swiped the dust off his rear with great black gloves. "Let us know if you see the bear; we'll be back in the morning. You're not afraid of bears, are you kid?"

The nightriders vroomed off, moonlight glancing off their helmets and the back of their boots.

God Almighty, I thought.

Arms around each other and drunk with relief, we walked to where the men had disappeared from view.

"Wasn't that scary?" I asked, bending down and resting my face on Jason's head as we stood barefoot in the damp grass.

10

Old Dog, New Tricks

"It isn't cheap, you know, and I don't know if I can do it," I said to Joe. We sat by the woodstove drinking red wine one late afternoon. It had been snowing all day and I had turned on the outside spotlight and kept the drapes open. The only other light came from the flames curling behind the glass stove door. This strategy of leaving the room in semi-darkness not only gave us a view of the snow-laden trees in the yard, but prevented Joe from picking up the *Times*.

"So? What do you think?"

"Think about what," he said, his trademark answer that never failed to drive me mad.

"Ice climbing. Expensive. Scary. Your opinion."

"How expensive can it be?"

Jason was in his room practicing his violin, and every once in a while he stopped. We thought he was trying to catch our conversation; he had ears like sonar. At every silence in the middle of an étude, we made up a fake conversation on a subject that wouldn't interest him; then the music would continue.

"What will you be teaching next term?" I asked, before we went back to the original topic. The bottom line was that Joe didn't care what we did as long as we didn't break our necks.

Needless to say it had been Jason's idea. He had become interested in mountaineering and sent for catalogues specializing in equipment. His reading these days consisted mainly of high-mountain adventure, and he had pictures and maps covering every available space in his room. I thought it was great until I was invited to participate.

"Ice climbing? What's that? Forget it," I said, "At my age?" He asked why I didn't just lie down and die then if I refused even to try something new.

"I'm afraid of heights," I said.

A few weeks later we signed up for a course at North Conway, in the White Mountains of New Hampshire.

As soon as we entered the Eastern Mountain Sports Climbing School, I felt all wrong. It was plain that Jason, at thirteen, was too young and I too old and the wrong sex. You had to be a male, in your twenties, sun-burned, muscular, and you had to wear different clothes. Woolen knickers and down parkas were definitely not *de rigueur.* I felt absurd when I asked one of the perfect men for the leader of the school, Joe Lentini.

"Hey Joe, your party's here," he called. We waited with trepidation among the coils of brightly colored climbing ropes, racks of axes, moon-walk boots, and crampons. I touched one of the twelve points of a crampon with my finger; it was apparent that they could gouge the hardest ice.

"Imagine falling with these skewers connected to you and getting tangled up like you do with cross country skis. Do you suppose they'll teach us how to fall?"

"I'll teach you not to fall. Hi, I'm Joe Lentini."

Tanned. Muscular. Young.

I said, "I think I'm too old for this. Maybe you could teach Jason." Joe laughed and tossed us jackets and pants and special rigid double boots to accommodate the crampons, while singing and tilting his head to judge our sizes.

"We have to put all this stuff on?" asked Jason.

"Trust me. We're gonna be on the ice for seven hours or so, in the wind. Here, try these." He handed us our helmets, then checked the fit.

It took a long time to put on five layers of clothing, the last one Gortex. And we weren't done yet. More socks, gaiters, two pairs of mittens, and finally the climbing harness.

"This stuff might be all right where there's no gravity," I said, "but how can you move this way?"

"You drive," Lentini said, shoving me out the door.

We loaded the car with ropes and climbing hardware. Our teacher carried a backpack filled with emergency equipment. He told us you would die quickly of hypothermia on the ice, especially after the sun set. All you had to do was twist an ankle, or screw up a knot. Or an anchor could loosen and swoosh! Away you'd fly.

"The technique works, but people make mistakes," he said. "You guys know your knots?"

"We learned them," I said.

"You know them or not?" Joe was getting impatient. Jason said yes, of course we did.

"We'll spend the day learning the basics on Cathedral Ledge. Tomorrow, if all goes well, we'll do Willey's Slide. That's intermediate."

Tomorrow we would be intermediate ice climbers? I thought it more likely I would be intermediate dead.

"I feel silly," I said to no one in particular, and Joe explained that most people who hadn't practiced the sport felt the same way. Tonight I would be one of "us," and though other people might call me crazy, I would know better. Yeah, right.

Cathedral Ledge offered big bulges of blue ice on a 180-foot slab. Things started off reasonably enough. All we had to do was stand still and listen to Joe teach. I tried to concentrate, but I was so nervous that I got flustered. Joe had seen that before.

"Calm down," he said, "you'll be fine. My best climber so far this year was a woman in her forties. Don't set limits for yourself."

We learned to screw in pitons, the meaning of "front pointing," climbing with *pied plat* (flat-footed), and using the French technique, the *aux canard* (like a duck). Then we roped up. Joe ran a rope to the top of the slab, anchored it, and came back down, tying himself in and arranging the rope to belay us when we started the climb.

"Aux canard," he shouted, and we dutifully practiced the duck step. "Straighten up!" When we finished the first stretch we waited for orders on how to proceed. It was getting steeper here. Joe moved within earshot again, the umbilical rope slack between us.

"Now Paula, jump!" he ordered.

"Jump where?"

"Guess."

"You mean down?" He was going to prove that the technique worked. I would jump, or rather let myself fall through the sky, and he would arrest.

I looked down. "I can't, Joe."

"You can't fall? That's odd, most people do it quite naturally."

I wasn't fond of being ridiculed. I looked at Jason who was dug in below me. "Okay," I said.

I didn't even have time for my life to pass before my eyes. As soon as my weight tugged the rope, Joe held me and I was able to replant myself on the ice. It had been rather fun actually.

We learned a lot that day. Joe said we were ready for the real thing.

"Wasn't that great, Mom? Pretty soon we'll be able to cross glaciers and go to all kinds of places in the winter. We could do Mont Blanc and...."

"First let's do tomorrow," I said.

I couldn't sleep all night. I was so apprehensive I hardly touched my breakfast. Jason ate a stack of pancakes and fried potatoes.

We met Joe at eight for the twenty-five mile drive to Willey's Slide. It was hard driving on the icy roads with my bulky clothes and big boots. I kept hitting the brake by accident. When we reached Crawford's Notch, the site of the Slide, I felt wretched.

Joe, surveying Willey's Slide with proprietary pride, arms akimbo, asked us if we could draw any conclusions about the place by looking at the forest growth.

"Birch," I said, "relatively new forest. Ah, there really must have been a slide?"

"Yep, a family of five named Willey and a couple of other people were wiped out here by a landslide in 1826. You've heard the expression 'it gives me the willies?'"

"Oh boy," I said.

We had to walk for half an hour through the woods to get to the foot of the ice fall. Joe, loaded down with his pack, slings, pitons and carabiners, clanged ahead, trampling the snow and making the going somewhat easier for us. We carried our own gear and fifty-five meter ropes. I didn't like wearing the helmet, but Joe forbade us to go without. Ice could break off, loosened by people climbing above us, and come careening down the mountain, he said.

At the foot of the 900-foot slide we got our first good look at the steep ice we were supposed to climb. I attributed the grim expression on Jason's face to a case of the willies.

"Don't worry," I said, "this guy knows what he's doing."

"I'm not worried," he said irritably.

"Neither am I. Just terrified."

"Not me!" He burst out laughing. From then on we hid our nervousness with lighthearted banter.

Joe repeated the safety rules and checked the knots, harnesses, and the gates (locks) of our carabiners. We did the first pitch, the distance between stances, without ropes; the angle was mild and our crampons anchored us easily in the frozen snow. Before Joe started the next one he gave us meticulous instructions. I was to come up first, Jason would follow and remove the pitons. (Joe had guessed correctly that Jason would give him a better chance to retrieve his pitons.) One person at a time would be climbing. Joe clambered up the second pitch, fixing ice screws for protection along the way. I tried to remember where he changed techniques so I could copy him.

"Awesome!" Jason said with admiration as we watched Joe march up the ice wall. When he reached his stance, a place chopped in the ice to stand on, he put in more screws, securing himself to the mountainside and me as well, since I was connected to his lead rope. I began to climb the moderate grade, which, I was acutely aware, took me farther away from level ground.

"Climbing," I shouted to Joe, indicating I was coming up on his rope. I took the following rope that was connected to Jason up with me and anchored it when I reached a piton, removing my own rope. I was very afraid of making a mistake and centered my concentration on the work to be done. Don't step on the rope with your crampons, you'll weaken it. Make sure Jason's rope is connected properly. Don't let your mittens whisk down the slide.

"Slack!" I shouted. Joe gave me a bit more rope. When I

arrived at the stance, I was elated. All had gone without mishap and I hadn't been hysterically scared.

"So," said Joe, "don't just stand there doing nothing. Always keep thinking. Be alert. Watch the rope for God's sake."

I sobered up. As we were still learning, Joe wouldn't trust me to belay Jason. I undid the following rope, handing it to him to bring up Jason. Then Joe continued the climb, setting up pitons for protection while we stood shivering on a narrow sill of ice.

"See ya," I said to Jason, starting the next pitch as soon as I heard Joe's signal, "Belay on."

"Good luck!" Jason clasped my shoulder.

The third pitch was the hardest at a sixty degree angle. About halfway up there was a blue vertical mound to conquer. I couldn't see Lentini and the obstacle appeared impossible.

"Joe! I'm stuck. What should I do here?"

"Think!"

I studied the ice obediently. It was vertical, glassy, interesting.

"Use double axe technique here! Piolet traction! Keep your heels down!"

Right, the hammer, the axe. Heels down.

"Come on up, Paula, you can do it." Joe had detected no movement on the rope. Going down was out of the question. I had wiped down from my mind. I couldn't keep clinging to the ice and knew darn well Joe wasn't going to help me. I slammed in the axe, then swung the hammer. It skidded off the ice, spewing pellets in my face. I tried again, aiming higher and off to the side as I had been taught. The strenuous effort made me swim in my tent of clothes. Once I started on the bulge, all my energy was directed toward survival. All that prevented me from falling to my death were the two short front points of my crampons and my tools jammed into the ice. If you didn't count the rope. I slipped once, but recovered before I tugged the rope.

When my head appeared in Joe's line of vision, he shouted, "You're doing great!" But a moment later he was scolding again. "I told you to lower your heels. Push off the ice! Straighten up! It's a matter of trusting your feet."

"I'm glad you're telling me that, you snotnose," I mumbled.

"No no, around the outcrop. Think!"

"Up rope!" I snarled. My calves were hurting. I muttered, "You sonofa.....," blaming my limitations on him.

It started to snow. When I reached Joe, I was exhausted and hungry. We hadn't brought a thing to eat, not even a candy bar. Oh, how I wished for a cup of coffee. I unzipped my jacket and lifted off my helmet to cool down and immediately my damp clothes turned frigid.

"Put that on," said Joe, indicating the helmet. When changing the belay, I fumbled a double fisherman's knot.

"You know what the trouble is with you? You're irrational. You're damn competent, but you're irrational!"

I smiled broadly. He said I was competent! You know what? I told myself, I am! I knew then that I would complete the course honorably. Here I was, stuck on this slick, tiny ledge hardly wide enough for my feet, hundreds of feet above the trees, grinning!

When Jason climbed, he had the same difficulties I had, except that he had the added problem of having to remove our hardware from the mountain. While we waited, Joe's attention was completely on the rope leading to Jason. I got colder and colder, and was impatient to get going again.

"He's doing well," Joe said, taking in rope steadily, patiently. "He's dependable. That's a good quality in a climber."

Jason's figure appeared small and forsaken among all the ice. I had been so busy with my fear that I hadn't considered how frightening it must be for him to be left behind, with no one in back of him. I had simply transferred all responsibility to Joe.

Jason was not in a good mood when he arrived. His hands were painfully cold and he felt weak from tension and exertion. After Joe had started on the next pitch, we huddled together as best we could, turning ourselves into snow sculptures.

"I'll be glad when we're done," I said.

"Not me. I love it," he said stubbornly.

"Belay on!" Joe called.

"I'll try and go a little faster, Jay," I said, brushing off snow.

"I'm fine, don't worry Mom." He was purple with cold.

The next few pitches were fun. I was feeling more sure of my feet and comfortable now with the slings and carabiners. When we arrived at the summit I wanted to do a wild dance.

"What a view huh?" said Joe. "Every time I climb this mountain....I never get tired of it." He stretched his arms to encompass the scenery and bellowed "I love it!" with a surprising show of passion. But immediately he focussed on the ropes lying in intricate loops at our feet, and began to separate them. "Now you'll be able to go places in the winter that are closed to other people. That's the point after all," he said.

He coiled the ropes, a task he didn't want to share. "I'm checking to make sure there are no weak spots." I was happy enough not to have to handle the cold rope.

"Actually, I was surprised to see you show up this morning," Joe said to me with a hint of irony, "but I'm glad you did. Once you made up your mind, you climbed."

"Well, it wasn't as bad as I thought it would be," I lied.

"The technique works!" Joe said triumphantly. "I love it!" Perhaps part of the "technique" was his pedagogy.

It was nearly dark in the woods on the way down the slope. The snow was deep and the rocks treacherously slick. Joe saddled us with the heavy, iced ropes.

"You didn't think I was going to carry them, did you?" he said. I fell many times and was so sore that I could hardly drive back to Conway.

Lentini had given us the name of a vegetarian restaurant where we finished the day. I felt completely wonderful and was just about as happy as I'd ever been. We were proud of each other and of ourselves, that we'd done the thing. That evening over pasta we laughed at everything.

It seemed reasonable to try out our newly learned skills while we were in the neighborhood. The weather was good; with luck we would make it to the summit of Mount Washington. Joe Lentini had told us there wouldn't be any technical difficulties, but the trip would take a good eight hours and would be tough. The mountain was infamous for its severe winter temperatures and the highest recorded wind speeds in the world.

Though the weather appeared stable, we were instructed by
people from the Appalachian Mountain Club at Pinkham Notch to
turn back at once if there was a change, which could occur at any
time. People had been killed by avalanches and from exposure. I
filled the thermos with boiling water and bought sandwiches and
eight candy bars.

The trail started in the enchanted forest behind the lodge.
Tree branches were coated with a fragile film of sun-lit ice, and
skis had left glistening tracks. We spoke excitedly about the pros-
pect of reaching the summit; if Jason harbored the same reservations I did, he didn't mention them. At the Tuckerman Ravine
Trail, some two miles later, we overtook two men and felt incred-
ibly cocky when they had to turn back for lack of equipment. They
admired the spanking new tools we'd purchased in Conway,
handling the axes as awkwardly as we had done three days ago.

My doubts about the hike grew in proportion to the difficulty of the terrain, but Jason was so enthusiastic that I didn't say
anything. On a particularly steep ice-covered stretch, I found
myself separated from him. He kept closer to a swatch of trees,
which gave him at least psychological support. Looking down, I
cringed. I didn't do anything I had learned from Joe Lentini. I did
not trust my feet; I leaned into the slope instead of depending on
my front points and standing up. Scaling the ice in the most inel-
egant way possible, panting and swearing, I finally reached the
Headwall. Quite unhinged, I joined Jason and two skiers, who
treated me with unearned respect. I immediately faked it and acted
as if I had used "the technique" confidently.

Savvy Jason had seen my bungled form; he gave me a look
that said, "you child," but had the grace to keep silent.

I had lost hope that the weather would rescue me from
having to continue. The sun was so bright that we had to don
goggles, and there wasn't a cloud. After chewing a tasteless, frozen
chocolate bar, we were faced with gigantic, iced-over boulders.
Though it was hard going, I was less scared than I had been on the
slope, partly because I wasn't so alone. We lost a lot of time on this
laborious section, picking our way carefully and resting often.

A thousand feet below the summit, the wind came tearing
over the mountain. We had less than a mile to go—too close now

to give up. The plateau between Huntington and Tuckerman Ravines was surely one of the bleakest places in the world. Everything was laminated with ice and appeared sterile. My crampons didn't grab the thin ice, so at every step I had to hack my feet in to keep from slipping. The grade here was gentle, and Jason, who had no fear of falling, moved on like a pro.

Close to the top, I overcame my anxiety in my haste to see Antarctica. For that is what it looks like on top of Mount Washington in the winter. The wind turns blood to jelly and the cold screams. It is a place where temperatures drop so low that the wind-chill is irrelevant. We dove inside our parkas so that only our eyes peeked out to take in the dead-cold landscape. The weather station was iced over and had become part of the rock. There was a cruel beauty here that didn't belong to the green earth. This place was like no place....all because of a dip in the jet stream.

We crouched under our space blanket behind the weather station where the wind was somewhat blocked, and quickly drank the hot water from the thermos. We didn't stay long in this blue-iced domain, but all these years later I can still feel Jason's shoulder pressed against my right arm, the scrape of frozen gravel under the heels of my boots. I can see the vapor of the water we drank fogging our goggles and feel the wind tugging the space blanket. These are the concrete details that recall an indescribable sensation on a sterile, winter mountaintop.

The trip down was almost too much for us. Jason got frostbite in his fingers.

"You and your mountain climbing. Better be careful you don't hurt your hands," the music teacher had warned. How we had laughed at his calling crampons "grapple irons."

I unzipped my parka so Jason could warm his hands under my arms. I was horrified at the hard, white skin. The moment that my hands were uncovered I felt my own flesh freeze. We couldn't stand still very long, but waited until his fingers began to tingle. Then he buried his hands under his sweater, making it difficult for him to keep his balance while we climbed down the mountain. It was dark when we got back and discovered I had lost the car keys.

Later, well, quite a bit later, we thought of these adversities as trifling, compared to what we had seen.

-11-

Cow Story

Toward the end of every school year we littered the dining room with backpacking equipment. Although it had been stored carefully, we always inspected the gear. The stove was taken apart, cleaned, and given a trial run, the tent pitched on the lawn to make sure the essentials were intact, the camp dishes given a fresh wash. We counted bandaids, breakfasts, suppers. Clothes pared down to a minimum were double bagged, ice axes sharpened. I enjoyed the organizing, the efficient appearance of the brightly colored paraphernalia. Backpacking had become a ritual, a benchmark of passing time, as reliable as other seasonal events.

I wished the entire family could go, but Jason, who had packed with me for seven years, didn't question the way things were done. During the summer, when his Dad was steeped in research, we went hiking, and on returning home we stayed up late with our stories. Joe was the best vicarious traveler possible—he was interested in every detail of the trip. His reactions were a mix of admiration and aversion. Much of the grubby side of backpacking didn't appeal to him, nor did the physical labor. I insisted that the rewards far surpassed any inconvenience, but words didn't adequately express the thrill of accomplishment at the end of a tough day, or the perfection of a wide open night. I wished he could be part of the experience so we could help each other remember how it was away from the glare of civilization. My faltering attempts failed to communicate the essence of backpacking—a possibility for understanding what counts and what ultimately doesn't.

That is not to say he didn't play a pivotal role in the success of our travels. Obviously, we wouldn't have gone anywhere against his objections, but more than that, he could be counted on to bail us out, to pardon mistakes, to encourage our endeavors. And he was always there, waiting for us at the end of the trip.

A consequence of the growing solidarity between Jason and me was that as a threesome, we had fallen out of step. When we did go somewhere together, Jason withdrew into himself and Joe got annoyed at my preoccupation with Jason's preoccupation.

Eventually an unspoken compromise was reached to combine backpacking trips with Joe's professional engagements whenever possible. That way we could spend the museum and concert hall parts of our travels together.

A fine opportunity for this presented itself when Joe had to go to Amsterdam for a math conference. The city was an exciting place to stay—and trains to the mountains ran on the hour.

Amsterdam, as everyone knows, is a city bent under the weight of history. I lived here as a child and saw people pulled from their homes and loaded onto German army trucks like so much scrap, the way I'd so often seen the rag man fling his tatters on his cart. First came the siren, then the screaming, the pulling, the kicking, the blood on dirty pavement. My father's hand covering my eyes. And always the fear that I would be the next child to be taken from my bed in the night. How was I to know I wasn't guilty of being Jewish?

I survived to walk again through the beautiful, old Leidschestraat with its preposterous display of luxury goods. To laugh when we blundered into the Red Light District on our way to the Rijksmuseum. To eat in elegant restaurants. As if I had forgotten that eighty-thousand Jews had been deported and killed. I could see the knowing in the old faces among the crowd still. The young are like tourists, I thought, like Joe and Jason, who know but can't know. And like me, who came for a good time.

When the week was up, Joe took us to the Centraal Station where we got on the train to Zürich. We waved from the window long after he'd become indistinguishable from others on the platform. I looked out over the flat polder land slipping away behind us, my head fairly bursting with a scrambled overload of past and present.

From Zürich we took a local train east in the direction of Scuol in the Engadine Mountains.

We arrived in Guarda in the evening. A bus climbed steeply from the railroad station to the village, about two hundred meters higher. Surrounded by snowcapped peaks, Guarda resembled a paperweight village—winding roads, a slim steeple, and a small hotel sequestered on a plateau tinted by the sun. Its few new houses were built in the style of the old ones, their elegant Romansh murals stressing the timelessness of the village.

We began searching for a bed and breakfast. A freckled dog led the way, protesting our backpacks with passion. There were flowers everywhere, behind lace curtains and hanging from clay pots in the courtyards. Farms were spread out over the lower slopes, but the main village was perambulated in minutes.

We dubbed the dog "Muttchen," for small mutt. He showed us the well in the center, which bubbled up sparkling water, a delicacy he didn't seem to care for. We told him, "Nein, we don't want a hotel, find us something cheaper," whereupon he led us to a farm.

The farmer's wife had a baby pressed against her full breast and two straw-haired toddlers clinging to her legs. *"Drei Buben!"* she shook her head in mock protest at the inconveniences three little boys caused, radiating pride.

"Ach," I said, "I have two of my own and a daughter as well. This is Jason. He's thirteen already!"

"Ach so! Yasohn!" she beamed. We were at once bound by our mutual fertility. *Drei Kinder* and not a moment to yourself, *so ist das Leben. Ja ja!*

She had four guests already—a full house. But we were welcome to the attic, which had to be cleaned first.

"Ich musz noch putzen," she insisted against our objections. We waited in the pasture while she readied the sleeping quarters. It seemed a good time to eat the buns we'd picked up, together with yogurt and apricots. The sun was sinking fast. Black conifers loomed beyond the rolling fields, their slender shapes standing out against the flushed zigzag of the alps. Muttchen lay down in expectation of an after dinner sweet and was pleased to see that the two cartons of strawberry yogurt were squashed; the

pink froth had trickled to the bottom of my pack. I laid my gummed up belongings on the grass while he held the leaky cartons between his paws, licking their contents with closed eyes.

The wood-frame beds were piled with snow-white, down coverlets. A strong draft from the floors below stirred up haydust and mixed with the odor of oiled harnesses hanging from the beams. If anything could have made our stay in Guarda more satisfying, this was it. We lay blissfully gazing at the rafters—eons from sense pollution.

The roosters started at dawn, soon joined by long melancholy moans of cows. Lightlines stretched through the windowpanes onto the timbers overhead; a baby's crying pealed through the rarefied air.

Already Jason's bed was empty. In the daylight the attic revealed itself as a place for the storage of metal-banded chests with great locks, a broken moped, twisted and curved farm contrivances, a dented feeding trough with rusted bottom. Our high beds were flanked by two chests and a velvet-covered barrel-back chair. One chest held a ceramic cow on each side of a ginger pot.

I hung out of the window as far as I could, snooping on village life. Women in shapeless cotton dresses and cardigans carried shopping bags or pushed strollers; two boys rolled a wagon wheel, hitting it with a stick and shouting with thin voices.

"Hurry up! Breakfast is almost over!" brought me back to a wet-haired boy.

"You showered," I said.

"I'll wait for you outside. You should see the mountains!" The day simply couldn't be put off. He climbed down the ladder, jumping the last rungs while I cautiously folded my bare feet around them.

One had to go outside and re-enter the house through a different door for breakfast. The room was reliably Swiss—checkered cloths, stone pitchers with foaming milk, round, dark loaves of bread. The floors were laid in black and white tiles; everything shone with purpose and order.

The farmer's wife volunteered that she had milked the cows, nursed the baby, fed the pigs and chickens, and seen to the needs of her other guests. She wiped her hands on her apron.

Would we like more tea? More cheese? Her husband would soon come in to take breakfast with the *Buben*. She smiled as though this commonplace event were a celebration.

When I asked if she'd heard the weather forecast, she shook her head. It would, of course, hardly change her routine of milking, cleaning, and mothering. She opened the brass-ringed curtains, lifted her head to the sky and pronounced the weather to be *schön*.

Our plan was to set up a camp high in the mountains, and, if the weather held, to climb one of the three-thousand-meter peaks: Piz Linard or Piz Buin. It would be our first experience with camping in snow, and we were keen to try our newly learned ice climbing skills.

For two days we hiked to the high pastures to acclimatize, descending to Guarda and the farm late in the afternoon. After dinner, we sat on the terrace at the hotel, looking at the mountains' changing aspect as the sun dipped lower. I already felt the melancholy of loss before our hike in the alps had even begun.

Good coffee and a seductive pastry display also begged our attention. The waitress smiled at me over Jason's head, as he stooped to scrutinize them under the glass dome. Cherry or Black Forest—that was the question.

Afterwards Muttchen walked us back to the farm, his tail straight as a compass needle.

On the day of our departure, the farmer's wife surprised us by delivering the weather forecast. "Snow at two thousand meters, visibility near zero." She wrinkled up her nose apologetically.

"Maybe they're wrong," said Jason.

"Not here, they have it together in this country. The weather wouldn't dare."

"Snow's better than rain at least." A wet fog enfolded the village, silvering the cobbled street. Even our freckled friend was hiding.

The road straggled up the lower slopes through forests of larch and Norway spruce swollen with a night of rain. It had been made barren by the climbing feet of cattle and men, but alongside, wildflowers prospered in the fat soil of the low pastures.

At two thousand meters—the treeline—the fine rain had

changed to snow, with an accumulation of four or five inches. We trudged along, heads down against the drift, the silence deepened by softly mounting flakes. I was happy to be walking in August snow. Now and then I caught a brief glimpse of the peaks, reminding me that this wasn't friendly territory, but a place indifferent to the specks climbing its back. Its rules would carry the day.

"Hey Mom, look!" Jason pointed to a postage stamp of blue in the grey sky desert. "Let's get out the chocolate."

"I don't know where it is," I stalled, putting off cold hands.

"Yes you do," he said cheerily.

While we hunched together, munching, a group of Guernsey cows wandered over, hunching together, munching. Snow clung to their lashes as it did to ours. Their fawn-colored flanks steamed, filling the air with warm life. Among the many patient, round eyes looking vaguely in our direction, I caught a set of cunning black ones staring at me. "Hi Boo, how are you?" I asked politely.

"You talk to cows?" Jason frowned.

"Why not? It's not what things are, but how you perceive them. For instance...."

"Okay, okay, I recognize your kinship with Boo," he grinned, inviting the snowball I aimed at his head.

He unfolded the map and began to translate meters into feet. "We're at nine thousand or so. We should take a bearing and head for that rib. According to this, it connects with the shoulder."

"The rib bone's connected to the—shoulder bone," I sang.

We cooled down quickly during the short rest. Snow settled on our necks and frosted our socks. From here, we estimated a three hour climb. The snow would be deep higher up and the altitude was already slowing us down.

"Bad luck with the weather, huh? Isn't it supposed to be good in the Engadine?" I asked, stuffing away the compass and candy wrappers.

"Look, it's clearing off!"

In the distance, the clouds began to break up. Maybe we wouldn't have to set up camp in a snow squall after all.

We climbed slowly, always gauging the route ahead and trying to avoid difficulties. For several hours we were almost oblivious of the alps, centering our attention on our feet, on the toil of the pitch. We scooped up snow to quench the thirst and every few steps upward, stopped to gulp thin air.

The sun came out when we finally reached the plateau where we would spend the night. We were beat. The packs weighed forty pounds each, not counting the axes and the rope. I couldn't have lugged mine much longer.

"Oh, Mom...." said Jason, awed by the new panorama that came into view. He rested his arm around my shoulders. The view was everywhere. Pristine snowbowls, crevassed glaciers with meters-thick blue ice, and vertical granite walls framed our campsite, while beyond, the peaks were silhouetted against a windswept sky.

Jason unzipped his parka, and, holding it by the hem, filled it with wind.

"You look like the Winged Victory," I said, inaudibly against the flapping nylon.

After scraping off a layer of snow, we found the campsite strewn with loose gravel; more sizable boulders had to be removed in order to accommodate the small mountain tent. Though we were between rocks and hard places, we were safe here from avalanches. With our axes we poked the boulders loose and rolled them out of the way. The spot was exposed; it would be bitter cold once the sun went down. The wind made it difficult to set up the tent.

"Damn it Jason, hold the corners down!"

"You do it then. I only have two hands."

"Use 'em, will you?" The fly flapped uncontrollably. I imagined us taking off over the snowy peaks, hanging on to the ballooning rainfly.

The tent had to be roped down, the ropes tied around boulders. Even then we had to discourage it from levitating by piling smaller stones inside, stones that vied for space with bodies and gear. Within the sun-lit dome we were out of the wind and warm enough to dispense with jackets.

I lit the stove while Jason held an aluminum sheet over it to protect the tent. It was dangerous, but we had no choice in this wind. Jason, who subscribed to *Summit*, entertained me with blazing tales related by mountaineers who had lit stoves in tents, defying manufacturers' "Do Not."

After a long wait, watching the pot that wouldn't boil, we made do with warmish freeze-dried cider. That finished off our water—we would have to melt snow from now on.

Impatient to explore the neighborhood, we booted up and went outside. Some ten minutes later, Jason located two small glacial lakes that would serve as our water supply. We surveyed the chaste snow, second-guessing crevasses and scanning the peaks for possible ascents on the first clear day.

"What do you think of that one?"

"No."

"How about that one?"

"No."

We couldn't agree. There were avalanche tracks every-where; we feared them, but didn't mention them. We'd heard their ominous roar and read the warning on the map: *"Lawinen Gefahr."* We probed with our axes as we moved on, wondering how deep the packed snow was. They sank only as far as recent accumula-tions, about a foot.

At the edge of an immense snowbowl, we paused. Its eastern basin was steeped in vermillion light; finely chiseled miniature avalanches hurried down like raindrops on glass. I had never seen anything so steeped in fragile splendor—it was like looking inside a limpid rose. Jason was affected as well; I was glad to huddle near a kindred soul, as if clinging to him would hold the moment.

Our anoraks slapped furiously as we climbed the rim of the bowl where we looked on miles of wild ice and granite, sheer faces and glaciers.

The temperature dropped suddenly and dramatically. We hurried back to camp, sliding on our seats part of the way, our squeals echoing coldly.

We had to build a wall against the fury of a north-west wind, something we should have done instead of poking around in the snow. It had been a hard day, and we were tired. Chores of cooking, cleaning dishes and teeth would take more discipline than I thought I could muster.

Our enthusiasm considerably sobered, we lugged stones to

pile up on the windward side of the tent. Jason, who had been my water-boy since he was seven, set out for the lakes without protest. There had been times in the past when he'd had to search some distance, but he was persistent. I'd watched him disappear in the pouring rain and seen him go out in the dark to supply me with water when I was sick. Today, my offer to accompany him on a wild and windy run was rejected with, "Of course not, that's my job."

I was glad when he returned. My usual dark imaginings were making me jittery. We were supremely insignificant here. As always, there had been the tug between the safety of traveled routes and the excitement of the lonely mountain. From the valley, in the daylight, the choice had been easy—we shunned the tourist atmosphere. But now, in the bitter cold, with the ice cracking and groaning on the glacier in our back yard, I wanted the warmth and safety of lamplight, of human voices. But this was what we had worked toward. How could it have seemed so desirable?

We put on sweaters, down vests, and booties, and pulled woolen caps over our ears. Jason took one of the bottles of ice water inside his sleeping bag to keep it from freezing. Our outer boots were filled with rocks and left outside, the lighter, inner ones were stuffed into the bottom of our bags.

"That was the worst dinner I ever had in my life," came the muffled complaint from the bundle next to me.

"It was pretty bad. It tasted like sick worms."

"It looked like sick worms. It tasted like dead ones."

"What did you expect, Quiche Lorraine?"

"Healthy worms. But less crunchy maybe."

"Go to sleep. You make me nauseous."

"Crunchy worms, crunchy worms...." he chanted deep in the down.

Though I curled up and doubled-over the bottom, my bag still did not provide enough warmth. The wind whistled, the glaciers boomed—strange, primordial calls.

For hours I kept my eyes tightly shut against the reality of our ice cave, but at last I opened them, and it was bright as day. Still bundled in my bag, I unzipped the fly. Before me a white landscape gleamed under a paper lantern moon. Though the wind whipped the tent, beyond, all was dead still. I contorted myself to look over the top of the tent at the glazed scenery without actually stepping outside.

"Jay," I whispered. Even a whisper sounded out of place in this unblemished world. "You gotta see this!"

"Mmm."

"Wake up! There's a full moon! A hundred million stars!"

"I'm freezing."

"C'mon...." He wiggled to the door and then forgot the cold. His bag slipped off his shoulders. Crouching on his knees, hands on the frozen rock with only his feet left inside, his eyes swept over the mountains in front, then behind the tent.

"Wow! Dad should see this!" He slunk inside his nest again, rattling with cold, but still watching the mountains. "We could have slept right through it...."

"Certainly. If we hadn't been so miserable." I fished out the camera and balanced it on one of the boots. With stinging fingers I cleaned the lens and attached the cable release for a time exposure. The moon and stars would streak the sky, but the shining peaks would be frozen on the film.

It was the coldest, most miserable night we ever spent, and it lasted interminably. We had misjudged the night temperature, thinking that if we slept in our down coats and sweaters we would be fine. We awakened unrefreshed.

Waiting for the sun to clear the peaks, we lay back to back, reading. The skin of my face felt tight and my eyes felt gritty. After a time, I closed them. There was an overwhelming sense of peace here in the untrampled snow with the wind tugging at the tent. It was another state of being, outside desire or compulsion.

Jason began to hum Shostakovitch. For him, at thirteen, being at peace wasn't yet so extraordinary.

When the ice crystals that had formed on the ceiling began to drip, it was time to get up and deal with breakfast and bulky layers of clothing that had to be aired.

Looking around, I sighed dejectedly. The chaos was absolute. Half-empty backpacks, clothes, food bags, the stove, a dirty pot with spoons, a lost teabag, all these items were lying about like a Klee composition. Again there was no hope of lighting the stove outside. I felt tired and grouchy.

"You," I punched the heap on the pad next to mine, "Are you going to read all day? We might as well have stayed in Guarda then and been comfortable. Gimme the water."

He tried to drag the bottle up with his feet. I got impatient and fetched the one we'd kept outside—it was a solid block of ice. The orange cap had popped off and a blob of ice had been forced out.

"C'mon, stop clowning. I'm not having a good time here," I said.

The bottle emerged then, and Jason, catching sight of me, tumbled over with laughter.

"What's got into you?" I was more than annoyed.

He pointed at me, tears rolling down his face. Peeved, I began to pour water in a clean pan.

"Mom, you should see yourself. You look like a.... some sort of....creature! Hahaha."

I threw my *Book of Laughter and Forgetting* at him.

"Oh Mom, you look crazy! Like one of those weird Jacques Cousteau animals."

"Next time, I'll bring my blow dryer and a lace nightie," I said. "Why don't you clean up this stinking mess? How can I cook in this?" I tossed him the first aid kit. "C'mon, stop that stupid giggling. Make yourself useful."

"Where would you like me to put it?" he asked sweetly, and burst out laughing again. "Sorry." More snickering.

From the corner of my eye I saw him slip the first aid kit under his sleeping pad. All of a sudden he sobered up.

"Oh no, I have to pee!" He started to rock vigorously, trying to put off going out into the cold.

"Go!" I said with satisfaction, "and make sure you face south."

This was a good time to have a look in the mirror I kept in my fanny pack. I hastily rummaged through the jumble, wiped the mirror on my sleeve, and stared horrified at the strange face. Sprigs of stiff, yellow hair stuck out of a cock-eyed woolen cap. That wasn't the worst of it. Swollen eyes peered suspiciously back at me—the eyes of a prize fighter. The lips were sausages, fleshy and decidedly lecherous. Was it caused by the cold, the altitude, or the reflection of yesterday's bright sun? Would it go away? I pasted snow on my face, hoping the swelling would go down. Then I changed my clothes, brushed my hair, and put on goggles.

Packaged in our sleeping bags, we lingered over breakfast, passing the homely pot of porridge back and forth. Our standards of hygiene and protocol had plummeted—when we accidentally spilled the gooey oatmeal, we spooned it back into the pot without hesitation. By nine-thirty the tent was toasty, though the wind had not abated. This, we decided democratically, wasn't a good day for beginning mountaineers. We would try for the peaks another day, after the wind had passed. A sudden gust could make us lose a precarious hold, and then, as Jason put it philosophically, it would be all over. I was surprised at his reasonable acquiescence.

"You must be disappointed," I said.

"Aren't you?" he looked at me suspiciously. I hastened to say of course, but in reality I was grateful for a day of loafing. I chewed my fat lips.

"So what do you want to do now?" asked Jason, killing my hibernation scheme. He answered his own question. "Let's hike to the next valley." Already he had the map out and started to trace the route. "There's a high valley maybe a thousand feet down from here. Where we crossed that river, remember?"

"I'll pack some food," I said, suppressing another sigh.

We cleaned up the tent, and while Jason filled the canteens, I put crackers, dried fruit, nuts, and hard candy in our packs. As an afterthought I added the toothbrushes, clean underwear, cosmetics, passports and traveler's checks. I left the plane tickets behind in my sock bag.

"You're not chickening out?" asked Jason, when he noticed things unnecessary for a dayhike piling up to be taken along.

"Are you crazy? It's just in case we're forced to stay in the valley tonight if the wind...."

"Oh Mom, you are chickening out."

"What's wrong with bringing a few extra things?" I zipped up the tent and checked the anchors. He waited impatiently, the rope slung over his small shoulders. After all the preparations, the ice climbing lessons, the waiting, only extreme weather would prevent us from climbing those peaks, from foiling his dreams.

"We'll come back here tonight and start out early, before the snow gets soft," I said. But I wished I were braver and stronger.

At the glacier, we roped up and separated a hundred feet or so. I was nervous and insecure. Crevasses gaped on the sides of the ice river, but the wind had swept off the snow, and we could see where we put our feet. It was safe, wasn't it?

Our heads were crammed with the experience of others about avalanches, glacier travel, mountain weather, lightning storms, first aid. But now we were on our own and that was my son ahead of me on the glacier and there was too much I didn't know.

And yet there wasn't a place I'd rather be.

"Were you scared?" I asked Jason when we were across.

"We didn't come here to sit in the tent all day," he shrugged, but I could see that he, too, was still tense. We'll learn, I thought, the more we do this "hands on" stuff.

Early in the afternoon we reached the alpine valley. The sun had grown hot and the wind tame, but dark clouds were forming. Far below us beckoned green pastures, but we didn't dare descend any more as we had to be back at the tent before the sun set. In the meantime, it was a relief to hike in tee shirts and feel the sun.

"How about lunch by the river?" I asked. "And then I think we should head back."

"Okay, I'm bushed. Can we have a siesta?" He finally had the right idea. Walking toward the river, we passed some cows who began to follow us ponderously.

"Don't they have cute faces?" I said.

"Adorable. Mom! Look over there!" A clan of some thirty cows led by two bulls came thundering down the mountain.

"You don't suppose they're interested in us?" I asked incredulously. We watched the lead bull make a beeline in our direction. "I don't think they'll hurt us, do you?"

"Oh no?" he snapped, "Then why do you suppose they're running this way and have their heads down like that?"

"But they're cows!"

"Can't you see the bulls!"

As the animals closed in, the small herd we'd passed earlier joined their compatriots.

"Don't run, head for the river," I said. With what we hoped passed for "cool," we strolled on, but it was too late—they were upon us. One of the bulls nudged me with his horns. Ten yards away Jason was getting the same rough treatment. I was terrified. If we tripped we would be trampled by the mutinous beasts.

Jason was in the river first. He waded in my direction, thigh deep in the swift current. I stumbled in and lost my footing on the rocks. The glacial water was numbing. Jason took my hand and pulled me to my feet. The cows stopped at the water's edge, gazing benevolently after us.

Then the bulls entered the water, and Jason cried, "They're coming after us. They want to kill us!"

"They're just cattle. Let's keep going."

The bulls decided we weren't worth cold hooves.

A quarter of a mile downstream we recrossed the river. While we were pouring the water from our boots and wringing out our socks, I tried to make excuses for our unglamorous retreat.

Jason said with chattering teeth, "At least now I know what it's like to be in mortal danger." Judging from his still dilated pupils, the cows might have been a gang of rhinos. I kept quiet, so as not to cheapen the experience.

"There's supposed to be a refuge nearby, Jay; I noticed it on the map. We should find it and dry out."

"I saw a sign for it earlier. We can get there in two hours. Three at the most."

I loathed my wet socks, and the absurdity of our situation wasn't lost on me.

"How are your feet?" I asked Jason.

"Not too bad. Cleaner."

"Don't tell anybody about the cows. Nobody'll believe it, you know."

"Who cares? Just be glad there was a river nearby." He was disgusted with my concern about our image.

"It was a regular Wyoming stampede, huh? Pound for pound, we were in no position to argue."

The sky promised a thunderstorm—something else for me to fret about. That and my blisters. But the rapid changes in the weather made it quite possible that tomorrow would be a sweet summer day; that cheered me up.

"Let's have a look at the map to make sure about the hut," I said. Holding down the map with our knees, we twittered with cold. The hut was there all right, but where were we? He was sure of the ridges, our approximate location between them, but I hesitated. If we got lost, wet as we were, we would be in grave danger of hypothermia. Jason stayed calm. "Rational," I thought, remembering Lentini.

While we sat guessing the map, a figure approached. Ha, I thought, it's true after all, in Switzerland you're never far from civilization.

"*Gruezi mit 'nand!*'" The familiar Swiss greeting came from a big man in grey woolen knickers, tomato-red knee stockings, and the obligatory felt hat with a colorful feather. An orange and green rope and an alpenstock were fastened to his pack.

"*Gruezi,*" I said sheepishly, rising stiffly to my feet. Not for anything was I going to tell this imposing person that we had been chased into a river, lost our way, and left our gear behind on the mountain.

The man smiled. "There's a storm brewing, we'd better get to the *Matratzenlager.*" He walked off without paying any further attention to us. I felt enormously relieved; we would be taken care of, I was sure. "Lucky huh?" I whispered to Jason.

He shrugged. "We were on the right track." I looked forward to a hot stove. We could dry our clothes and be like new tomorrow.

The mountaineer hiked on and on while the clouds closed in. My blisters were burning. I looked back at Jason. He walked with his head down and his hands thrust under his jacket.

"Are your hands very cold, Jay?"

"I left my gloves where we looked at the map," he said miserably.

"Use mine, my hands are warm."

"No. We're almost there anyway." Our guide seemed to have forgotten us. He tramped with long strides down the slope, trying to outrun the heavy drops of rain splatting down. I saw no sign of a hut.

To my relief, Jason had been right—we rounded a bend,

and a Swiss flag waved half a mile away. Here, the mountain man stopped and waited for us to catch up.

He said pleasantly, as though we had been socializing all along, "Did you two bivouac last night?" He'd sized up the situation without seeming to notice us particularly. "Bloody cold night." That ended the conversation again.

Then all at once there were friendly faces and hot drinks. The hut master brought thick, woolen blankets and draped us like Bedouins. We were given rosehip tea in steamed-up glasses. A woman climber lent us dry socks. While we were thawing I looked around the refuge. Axes were left at the entrance, along with crampons, boots, and several pairs of skis. Ropes were hung on pegs. The room had long tables with benches, tiny windows, and a squat coal stove with silver lion's feet. One wall held a huge topographical map of the Engadine Mountains.

There were eleven other people besides us, climbers all from the looks of them. The woman who lent us the socks was named Inge. She was a large woman with short, grey hair and strong-looking teeth. The rest were men. I was grateful we weren't asked why we had gone swimming. In fact, we were ignored after the initial welcome. On our way to the outside privy, ducking to avoid getting doused by the overflow from the gutter, Jason commented on the misplacement of the flush. It's all or nothing, he said. After choosing a bed in the bunk room, we hung our clothes out to dry over the stove, then put on the blanket capes again.

Over soup and biscuits as big as hats, we played a word game while rain lashed the window panes and lightening shot over the peaks. Some people paced up and down holding beer steins and watching the weather show from the warm safety of the room. I wondered if our tent would be snowed under, or if it would rain up there as well. I couldn't imagine lying on the icy rock again. Ever. Jason, with flushed face and sparkling eyes, looked a king in the drab blanket.

The hut master, who spoke a Swiss dialect, came over to our table with the guest book. We had a hard time communicating in a mixture of French and German, a situation I tried to exploit when he asked how we had gotten so wet. *"Kuhe,"* I said, *"Les Vaches."*

"Kuhe?" He raised his eyebrows. The ruts of his crows' feet were white from squinting against the mountain sun. He looked to Jason for an explanation.

"Bulls," Jason said emphatically. I handed back the book with a "thank you," telling him how we had enjoyed the soup.

"Na ja." He took his leave with the guest book pressed to his heart and then made an about turn, *"Ach so!"* he exclaimed with the triumph of Archimedes' "Eureka."

Now I had to fill in the details with the other guests lending interested ears. Since they all seemed to speak English, I took the easy way out when one of the guests offered to translate for the hut master.

"Never, never to turn your head to a male cow!" said he. "Just threaten him with the alpenstock and he'll go forth." This quaint rendition came from the translator. Jason loved it with his whole body, the way children do.

"We didn't run," I said, while everybody was laughing at us.

"Sometimes they get, eh, peppery, when thunder is coming. And also the hard wind yesterday. It makes them springy, *verstehen Sie*? But they will not hurt you." The hut master was decidedly patronizing.

"Yes, I see. They get springy," I mumbled. People returned to their friends, shaking their heads, chuckling.

"They weren't there," Jason told me.

"Darn right. But maybe we should brandish the axes next time. See what happens."

"Or you could talk to them," he said with disdain.

"Let's face it, darling, we did the wrong thing! Fortunately, because I sure enjoy being here. They serve breakfast at five I noticed. You want to get an early start?"

His face lit up again. "Sure!" Just then our former guide joined us.

"You like the mountains, yes?" he asked Jason. In his knobby white sweater the man was less formidable, especially with the hemp-colored head freed from the hat. Jason seized the moment.

"Could you show me which mountains to climb?" he started out for the map. The man nodded at me, his brown eyes full of laughter.

"Cows, huh?" he winked, and followed Jason before I could think of something snippy to toss at him. From a man of so few words the mockery felt like a tribute.

The two of them concentrated on one section of the map. Jason, at five feet ten, reached to the mountaineer's shoulder. I put up my feet. The syncopated flow of voices, rain, and the wheezing gas lanterns shut out a world of horror.

Done with the chart, the mountain man and Jason were apparently having a lively discussion.

I wrote in my diary, "Thanks to a bunch of cows, we had another splendidly full day. Maybe tomorrow we'll climb a mountain. Who knows? There are surprises around every corner. I'll not forget the paper moon, the biscuits, the funny little dog. Nor the rose snowbowl. But mostly I'll remember my Jason at thirteen."

I closed the book and hoped for a sunny day tomorrow.

Some People Have Seen Amazing Things on an Empty Stomach

By age fourteen Jason had formed friendships that would last through his school years and beyond. He played soccer, joined the swim team, fell in and out of love—to judge by mementos treasured and discarded. All his growing energy had been directed upwards; as yet he looked out of joint. Although he was spared a teenager's conspicuous symbols, storms were gathering. His disposition was fundamentally introspective; these days he appeared to see himself as if inadvertently deposited on a foreign planet. Paradoxically, this sentiment caused him to see things with unusual clarity, while at the same time his confused sense of identity obscured his judgment.

I learned about his state of mind from his writings rather than from observation. He put on my desk sheets covered with dark poetry and prose of obscure allusions. We didn't talk about it. He left the lined sheets and that was all. Sensing the fragility of his trust, I always feared the door between us would slam shut. When we did talk, it was he who picked the time and set the terms. Needless to say the terms were "hands off my life."

Many Sunday afternoons we took long hikes with Thor; on full moon nights we walked to the Quabbin Reservoir where we made small fires to roast apples. These were magic times, when deer came out on the opposite shore to drink of the black water with its highway of moonlight. Even then, conversation not sanctioned by Jason was apt to be met with hostile grunts. But suddenly he might jump up and begin skimming stones across the tight surface of the reservoir with the glee of a six-year-old, before launching into a passionate debate that would last the long tramp back to the car.

Although there were compensations, the tenor of the moon walks changed when, on rare occasions, others came along. Then the raucous play enjoyed by Jason and his friends and the unceasing chatter of the adults tended to trivialize the tangled forest with its abandoned stone walls, its Indian ghosts.

Jason had always been a reader. He had a habit of strewing books on the floor, and I had to pick my way between musical scores and volumes on Zen Buddhism, Hinduism, Islam. He read several translations of the Tao Te Ching and began serious efforts at meditation. I flunked meditation, but the scope of his interests changed my stale reading habits. As my European schooling had failed to give me research skills equal to his, I plowed doggedly through tomes while he managed to gain more sophisticated knowledge in less time through cross referencing. Later, when it became clear that I had missed or forgotten facts, he would look at me skeptically, as if suspecting me of nodding off over my book.

Joe mediated the dinner table philosophizing, but claimed that if he did any of our yoga exercises, he would not walk again. A few times he joined our chanting—I suspected more for its musical harmony than to gain spiritual awareness—and was surprised at the deeply satisfying effect it had. But as always, finding time away from his study appeared to be an insurmountable obstacle. As for me, no matter how hard I tried, or tried not to try, I was incapable of achieving anything resembling relaxation. While chanting I was apt to be planning supper or to remember the car's inspection sticker had expired.

"It's because you're not serious," Jason said.

"It just doesn't come naturally to me to do nothing. To think nothing. It makes me feel as if I'm playing a part."

"You can learn. You don't want to enough."

"Oh, but I do!"

"It's really very important, Mom. Some day I'm going to India and live in an ashram."

"I thought you were going to be a violinist. You won't have time."

"Right. Go to school. Study music. Practice day and night. How can I be a good musician if I don't know who I am?"

"You'll find out in an ashram?"

"I don't know. But once you're done with school you're expected to work for the rest of your life, right? We should all go to India. I guess that'll never happen."

We should all go to India? As time passed I began to think the proposal had potential. The culture shock alone would shake things up! As academic groupies we tended to slip into complacency. With the exception of the outdoor ventures with Jason, my life was taking on a robotic quality. Maybe we could make the journey, the three of us.

After prevailing on several icy peaks in the Engadine the year before, we began to read accounts of climbs. Photographs of Mont Blanc steeped in pink and amber light were not only tantalizing, but climbing the giant appeared to be a realistic objective. At the time we were innocent of the greatly increased difficulties that altitudes higher than we had so far experienced presented. We set out to lay the groundwork for a June expedition.

During the winter we threw a short rope in a daypack and headed for nearby cliffs where we donned climbing harnesses and practiced scaling the ice and belaying. These sessions were not without embarrassing defeats that we kept to ourselves. During free moments we made neat lists of equipment needed. Soon, mail order packages began to arrive from mountaineering companies. A hundred-and-fifty foot, high-tech, brightly colored rope came in a formidable coil. Were we really going to use this intimidating thing?

I sewed woolen knickers for each of us and a collection of red, blue, and yellow climbing slings. We could hardly keep our fingers off the spanking new carabiners, ice screws, and pitons, and enjoyed demonstrating their use to Joe and anyone else tolerant enough to put up with our strutting.

The planning of summer trips may have had more to do with our continued friendship throughout Jason's adolescence than their actual execution, which tended to be brief. It was logical to follow climbing practice with a review of our progress over hot chocolate and then to finish the day listening to Mahler.

Still, most of the time we saw each other only at the supper table; it was easy to overlook a boy who simply caused no trouble.

That Jason was an "A" student was taken for granted. His teachers found him "bright" and "interesting," and we more or less took the attitude of, "if it ain't broke, don't fix it." I suspected Jason felt alienated from his peers; he was bored in school. Aside from his music he didn't seem to get truly absorbed in anything, though he made the effort. Loneliness was in his bones; he could never quite forget its reality.

Joe, who had Reason, shrugged at my assumptions—his son was a normal teenager; some kids hung out, some took drugs, his boy just went around looking baffled. That he did.

At last June came with its fanfare of blossoms and bountiful green. We bought plane tickets and Eurail passes, and filled our packs.

The night before departure I stayed awake with my usual reticence when facing something new, my superstitions about splitting up the family.

Joe was to drive us to Boston, but when he got out of bed in the morning and bent over to put on his socks, his back went out. Pale with pain and with his body implausibly skewed, he observed that it would be difficult to drive the car. That was true enough; for some time he was unable to uncoil and get back into bed.

We outdid ourselves with sympathy for pain suffered and travels thwarted. Jason hung the beautiful rope on the ceiling beams in his room. We took the sticky packing tape off our crampons and put the gear away in the attic, where we stored things in cartons. For several days I hung around drinking coffee with Joe and eating oven-hot chocolate chip cookies. It was much easier than climbing Mont Blanc, and the sudden windfall of leisure wasn't a bad thing for our family at all.

It was the first summer since Jason was seven years old that we didn't go backpacking. Jason never questioned Joe's need for our support and practical assistance, though his disappointment was acute. Brett, I knew, would have thought of a thousand ways to try and make Joe believe he was better off with a good cane and plenty of peace and quiet than with our nursing ministrations. I identified with such a position, but was shamed into magnanimous conduct by my younger son.

I can't remember now why we never again mentioned climbing that particular mountain. It had given much indirect pleasure; perhaps there was wisdom in leaving well enough alone.

Jason spent the remainder of the summer making music in the Berkshires, and when Joe recovered, he and I left for our favorite inn on the coast of Maine. At all hours we sat on the grey painted porch with our clipboards, but no mathematical symbols appeared on Joe's blank sheet, nor the makings of a short story on mine, held captive as we were by the slapping breakers, the salt-heavy air. Every once in a while one of us went in to get coffee, and while sipping we resumed our contemplation. On chilly days the innkeeper brought blankets. With our feet on the banister we slumped in the wicker chairs, holding hands under the plaid covers. After a few days I felt about as generic as the fog.

The stray hours of synergy among gliding gulls and plain-tive buoy calls briefly aligned our days and perhaps our thoughts.

But just in case, we always brought clipboards.

During Jason's sophomore year, his violin studies became more demanding. In addition to a grueling schedule of practicing and schoolwork, he was concertmaster of the Young People's Symphony and sang in the school chorale. He won his first violin competition.

As the mother of a talented musician and the wife of a research scientist dwelling in an arcane universe of theoretical mathematics, I often felt my own life was insignificant. I was the resident Girl Friday. In my more perceptive moods I was content as a cat and aware of my blessings. But on ordinary days I stored up resentment at the burden of never ending chores, at my status as family sergeant, book-keeper, facilitator, organizer, mediator. Joe offered no opposition and little help. Although he was usually accommodating, it never entered his mind to offer suggestions for a vacation or even to propose dinner and a movie. It made me feel that, at best, the kids and I were an afterthought in his life. When my fuse did blow, he would say with genuine consternation, "Why didn't you just ask me?" Followed by my: "Are they only my kids? Is it my lawn? My trash? Should I clean the gutters before I iron your shirts and cook your dinner? Huh?"

I was creative when I hurled my grievances at him. It wasn't just my frustration with the labor. It bothered me that he never noticed anything. I could have painted the house orange, and two years later he might say, "Hey, did you ever notice that our house is orange?"

Also I was jealous. My career turned out to be seeing to it that the rest of the family could have theirs.

Jason's dream of going to India kept smoldering. After reading *The Snow Leopard* by Peter Mathiessen, I began to imagine myself as a speck on immaculate fields of snow, searching for the elusive leopard—a metaphor for the meaning of life. I asked Joe if he'd ever considered going to India.

"Never," he said.

"Jason is very drawn to India. He wants to spend some time in an ashram."

"That's not so surprising; he's interested in Hinduism and Buddhism."

"Yeah. He seems to be discontent with the way things are in the West."

"Well, he's still idealistic. I'm sure he would find the situation no better elsewhere."

"What situation?"

"Whatever. Morality. Politics."

"He doesn't know anything about politics. As for morality, I think he's flexible."

Joe laughed. I said, "Just kidding. I think he's big on morality."

"He's too smart for labels."

"You think? Anyway, what are the possibilities for spending your sabbatical in India?"

"We just had a sabbatical. So I would say 'none.'"

"What about some kind of grant? Or a leave of absence?"

"Forget it. If I'd go anywhere it would be to E.T.H. We all liked Zürich and it's an excellent place to work. You could brush up your German and Jason could go to school there."

"But we've been in Zürich, and anyway, school isn't the point. I would love to see India, wouldn't you?"

"Are you two plotting something?"

"Cross my heart!"

And then he said, "The Indian Statistical Institute is in New Delhi. It's world-class. But I don't know anybody there. Anyway, I've no desire to go to India."

"Too bad," I said.

The subject wouldn't rest. We had a dear friend, a colleague of Joe's, who spoke of his homeland with passion. Ram was a devoted father who had often gently berated Joe for not spending enough time with the family. He used to tell us that when all was said and done, the only thing of real importance in life was the relationships people had with friends and family. In India, he told us, the family is everything. The pace of life there would, well, generate togetherness! Joe listened skeptically. Ram was adept at circumventing objections. There was a brilliant young mathematician in Joe's field at the Statistical Institute. We could get housing on campus. We would love it!

The longer we talked, the less outlandish the undertaking appeared. Joe warmed to the idea. We went so far as to inquire into what we would have to do about Jason's high school credits. I wrote a letter to Zubin Mehta, who was born in India, requesting information about the chances of finding a violin teacher in Delhi. At last Joe sent a proposal to the Fulbright Foundation; we sat back and waited.

Many months later he received a grant; the die was cast. The following year we would spend six months in India. We had a year to get used to the idea.

In the meantime, Jason and I had our summer hike in Yosemite National Park to look forward to. As he grew older and the load of his pack began to exceed mine, his company became ever more interesting. He was very much at home in the wild, more than I would ever be. It was a rich childhood legacy.

Partly because of the frequently trying circumstances of our times outdoors, we had come to trust each other completely. We could let off steam without fear of repercussion. Indeed, a good deal of our bickering was in jest, even if it was a game only we understood. With the shared obligations and responsibilities, the minor unspoken irritations of daily family life were set aside. Whatever problem came up was direct and urgent enough to be dealt with on the spot. It added to our sense of total freedom.

Good thing too, for the trip got off to a shaky start. Right away we were stymied by a major swamp.

The topo showed the trail crossing a river, but exactly where was anyone's guess. We asked a couple of other confused packers, who finally turned back in frustration. Through tenacity and good luck Jason located it after many false starts and lost miles. The river was swollen from glacial water and fording it was nearly impossible. Jason had to make separate trips for each of the packs and then help me across. The water was so cold, it burned.

Another time a bear cub stumbled into camp just as Jason staked out a proper tree from which to hang our food. Knowing the cub's mother to be close by, I panicked and was ready to head back, but Jason put his foot down.

"I thought you said you felt guilty about buying all the gear and then not using it," he said.

"But we're all alone here; that baby's mom could make a mess of us!"

He had tied one of the food sacks to the line and was hauling it up. Now he let go of the line. The bundle came crashing down. "Maybe we should run!" he said with nasty sarcasm. "She'll have more fun that way."

I said nothing. If we happened to be between the mother and her young, it would be dangerous.

"So? What do you want?" he looked disgusted, and gave the pack a kick.

"I'm going to pray," I said. "And I'm going to take a picture. Your father might like to know what happened."

Before I could focus the camera, the cub swaggered off. I helped pull the food bundle up again. We tied a second sack to the other end of the line, balancing the load so that the heavier of the two sacks hung highest. A loop was left on the lighter one so we would be able to retrieve our food in the morning with the help of a long stick.

During the stick search, Jason marched around with exaggerated competence as if to compensate for my uselessness. I figured he wished I were fifteen and unrelated, and told him that, after all, I was responsible for our safety, that you got more cautious as you got older. He rolled his eyes. The more grown up he acted the more tender were my feelings for him. I wondered when I would be able to let go. Not only publicly, but in my heart.

Our tent was some distance from the food tree in a lovely clearing with scrubby cover. Jason lay with his arms under his head. I could see only the outline of his profile, but I imagined he looked angry still.

"You found a good bear tree," I said.

He jumped up. "Jeez! I forgot the damn toothpaste!"

"Uh oh!"

"I left it with the pots 'n pans. You think they'll find it?"

Bears are attracted by all smelly things humans tote around, but the cooking place where he had left the toothpaste was far from the tent.

"It's no worse than food in a tree. As long as it's not near us they'll leave us alone."

"You don't say," he grinned.

Every evening, at the end of our hiking day, Jason looked for a tree with a high, long branch while I set up the tent. At higher altitude there were no trees, and most likely no bears either. To be safe we put everything under a plastic cover at a good distance from the tent. We had met a man who told us he'd been too tired to string up his food, and a bear had come into his tent and rummaged through his pack. He had stopped breathing until the animal left. All his supplies were gone; this was his second day of hiking without food. We gave him enough so that he could make it out.

On the fifth day the weather deteriorated. We were then high in the mountains where the snow was still deep so early in July. It made route-finding problematic as the cairns were buried under snow. A fresh layer would cover our tracks, and we wouldn't be able to find our way back. We decided to head down to Half Dome. Jason wanted to see the enormous monolith, El Capitan, anyway, and there would still be time left to return to the back country.

It took us two ten-hour days to hike down. By then the weather had cleared, and the falls at the foot of the granite walls were teeming with visitors. Too late we realized this lovely spot was in close proximity to a road. After gorging ourselves on the spectacular views, we turned in early, and the next day hightailed it as far away from the crowd as we could get before nightfall.

We pitched the tent at a ghost campground along a swiftly running river. Although there were several other tents, no back-packers were to be seen. Food bags were strung up all right, but close to the tents and not very high. Some dangled close enough to tree trunks that bears could plunder them without tumbling down themselves. Obviously we'd been too "by the book" with our bear defenses.

A quick dip in the river explained the absence of people; hordes of vindictive mosquitos were holding them captive inside their tents. Without drying off, we hurried back into our clothes, then ate a meal of granola bars and gatorade while pacing to and fro on the path. Our rules forbade cooking in the tent in bear country, and doing it outside was intolerable.

We still had to find a tree. Ignoring rattle snake warning signs, we strayed farther away from camp. The forest was largely evergreen and conspicuous for its lack of proper branches. I was so frazzled, I no longer worried about snakes or bears. Jason persisted in the tree search. Rather than admiring his determination, I wondered if he was just willful. When at last he found a stately tree I thought perfect, he said, "We're wasting our time. It's no good. I'll stay up and guard the food."

"Oh come on," I said irritably.

"Mom, you can see that, can't you?"

"See? It's bloody pitch dark and the mosquitos are snacking on my eyeballs. Any moment I'm going to step on a snake! Why don't we just forget it? Nobody fusses with food the way we do. You're just being elitist!"

"I'm what?"

"You think you know every damn thing better than anyone else! You can't even keep the stupid rock tied on!"

That was true. Every time he flung the line, the rock flew off, and I had to grope around for another one with the proper characteristics.

He explained patiently that if we lost our food the trip

would be finished.

"You mean we would be forced to live like sane human beings."

"Would you please go get the flashlight?"

"Sir! One torch coming up!"

I lingered in the tent, free from bugs for the first time in hours. Then I got the idea that if we tied the rock in a kerchief, we could tie the whole business to the line and it wouldn't fly off. I jogged back to Jason, hoping he hadn't actually managed to toss the line over the branch. I would show him how one does such things.

It worked. Jason claimed he still had misgivings about the tree, but within minutes the guardian of our livelihood slept like a stone.

Usually, when I awakened at daybreak, I lay quietly for a while, listening. The morning sounded quite different from the evening, and both were boisterous compared to midday. I loved inhaling the rich dankness of the woods. But today I was thirsty. We had strung up our plastic water bottles as they smelled strongly of Gatorade.

"Hey Jay," I poked him.

"In a minute."

"I'm dying of thirst. I'll get the food down."

Though he knew I was too short to reach the loop, he didn't move. I unzipped the tent. With my feet outside the door, I began lacing up my boots, baiting him. Where was his sense of honor?

"Call me when the coffee is ready," he mumbled.

"You're a riot."

Still sleep rumpled, he set off in search of a stick while I snuggled back into my bag, gloating a little.

It was always a big job to recoup the provisions; he stayed away a long time. To do my share, I deflated the pads and was stuffing the down bags into their sacks, when he crouched in front of the tent.

"It's all gone," he said in a funeral tone.

"What is?"

"It's all gone." He shrugged. "That's it, I guess. Even the knife that Dad gave me."

"What knife? How.... Oh no! All of it? Absolutely nothing left?"

He looked like a ragamuffin with his sad, unwashed face and tousled hair. One of his knees was cut. "I'm starved," he said woefully.

"Oh my God!" I giggled, and soon worked myself up into a painful laughing fit. "Jason! You should hear yourself! You should see yourself!"

The dour expression on his face changed, and he began to describe the circumstances in detail. Under the tree were the wrappers of our most prized morsels—things we had hoarded for the latter part of the trip when we would need them most. The soap and toothpaste were eaten, our water bottles crushed. One daypack hung in tatters high in the tree, presumably with the hunting knife still in it. The other nylon sack was destroyed. Jason had looked for his knife underneath the tree, that's what had taken him so long. "I brought you a memento," he said, handing me the empty soap box with its claw marks.

"Wow!" I said respectfully.

Before shouldering the packs, we drank our fill from the river as we had no bottles to carry water. Everywhere, the remains of torn food sacks were dangling from trees; our fellow hikers barely managed a good morning.

Since we were on the trail by seven with considerably lighter packs, it was likely we'd reach the car before nightfall. Unfortunately, our map was up in the tree.

At first we kept ourselves occupied with tasteless jokes about food. I had five Tic-Tacs that would have to nourish us for at least twelve hours of hiking. We speculated as to where we might find water.

As the sun climbed higher, we stopped wasting energy on talking; I pondered our predicament in silence. Jason had been right about the food—we should have guarded it. Now we'd lost the opportunity to camp in the high country. Like his father, he hadn't stooped to "I told you." If he'd been the cause of my empty stomach, I wouldn't have been so generous.

By mid-afternoon we still had no idea how far we were from the car. We trudged through a wasteland left by a forest fire;

the sand mixed with ash was as dry as my throat. Jason was way ahead; he had become very worried about the lack of water. I was afraid we'd get an electrolyte imbalance. Every once in a while he waited until I almost caught up, then turned without saying a word. My legs and hands were grey from sweat mixed with soot. I was no longer hungry and was about to succumb to depression.

Jason came walking toward me without his pack. Taking mine, he slung it over one shoulder. "There's a river up ahead," was all he said.

We drank, and washed without soap. Then lay on a ledge to rest. Afterwards we were restored, and I knew I could walk a few more hours if most of it were downhill.

"We'd better get going," I said.

"We could just stay."

"All night? No. We need food with all the energy we're spending. It would be too risky. We don't know how far we have to go...".

"I guess so. And no fish in the river. Would be an interesting experience though. Some people, like Indian holy men, have seen amazing things on an empty stomach."

"Like what?"

"Dunno."

I tightened the straps of my pack and stood looking at Yosemite National Park while waiting for Jason to get back on his feet. Birds were singing. The river was singing. The early evening light cast feathered patterns through a giant spruce.

"I think maybe we could," I said, dropping my pack.

We didn't set up the tent that night, but lay on the ledge, close to the river, close to the night, looking into the deep mountain sky.

In the morning, miraculously, we were born again.

-13-

Looking Toward the East

Joe had never slept on a mountain. He'd never carried a pack.

"Try it just once," I said. "It's fun! We'll do the works—campfire, marshmallows, hot dogs, ghost stories."

"Okay, okay," he said.

One fine spring evening, we scrambled up a mini mountain: fabulous view, great fire. When the sun went down, he snuggled into his sleeping bag, not in the least affected by a growling raccoon, creepy crawlers, and jutting roots under the groundcloth—which kept me up all night.

Therefore, it shouldn't have surprised me that Joe took to India as a fish to water, while Jason and I, the crusaders, barely survived. But it did. I was especially impressed when he returned to New Delhi for three consecutive years while I remained Stateside, nursing my intestines back to health with the help of acidophilus.

In anticipation of our stay, we tried to educate ourselves about India by reading the Upanishads, commentary on the Upanishads, and elucidations of the commentary. We spoke with Westerners who had visited the country as well as with Indians, and chewed through a glut of information assembled by the Fulbright staff. And arrived at the feast in the emperor's new clothes.

When the six months were up, we were no wiser, hadn't found India or ourselves, but with all probabilities briefly suspended we'd relearned to look about us with child-like wonder.

Much has been written about India though to define her presents difficulties similar to catching an elephant with a butterfly net. Without tasting the dust, smelling the stench and the exotic fragrance, or feeling the heavy monsoon heat bear down, without absorbing the colors that burn deeply into the psyche, words skid off the essence of India. An attempt to describe her would parallel the courage of the Venezuelan artist who painted the portrait of God.

What follows are mere fragments from a six months' journey, symbolic of my impressions of India, which, though vivid and intense, never coalesced into an integrated whole.

We departed in February during a white-out. Gaia was in Germany; we arranged to meet her in Frankfurt. Brett and Karen were to be married in June while we were eight-thousand miles away. I couldn't imagine that we would all be together again in one place on the following Christmas.

When we finally arrived, Delhi lay blurred under an early morning haze. We looked for transportation, climbing over broken people with expressionless eyes and asking hands. Like our luggage, we were pummeled, shoved, compressed, and loaded into an ancient black and yellow taxi. The exhaust fumes came up through a hole in the floor, clogging our lungs. The sprawling city seemed to exist in several historic periods at once. The airport and the wide avenues of today were façades superimposed on antiquity. Things appeared recognizable on the surface, but then, suddenly, time warped back a thousand years. I was crushed by the poverty and the heat and the dust. Not to mention the loss of two bags and Joe tight with worry over his missing books and research papers, but not saying anything.

In my head lived an image of the Statistical Institute: low white buildings, palm trees, red gravelled avenues. Learned professors in robes drinking afternoon tea under the arbor of a banyan tree.

When the taxi stopped at the gate, a steaming mountain of rubbish reeked vile enough to shatter that illusion. Round-bellied pigs snorted through the pile; a pregnant cow lay dozing, her half-closed eyes jelled with flies. Farther down, a wizened woman was setting up a tea stall: two mugs on an upside-down crate, a clay vessel of water, an aluminum kettle over a dung-cake fire. Across the street, merchants arranged carrots, cabbages, and onions on the unpaved sidewalk amid animal droppings and muddy puddles of urine.

"We can't live here," I told Joe.

The guard at the gate ordered two sleep-drugged men to carry our luggage to a two-story, brick building that resembled a low-security prison. We were ushered to the canteen to drink tea at a long, vinyl-covered table with the manager of the Guest House, a man with a somewhat unctuous manner. We would take our meals here. The metal chairs rasped the stone floor; I felt the gritty sound in my teeth. Drab, mud-colored curtains sagged on each side of a row of windows; all but four of the rings were missing. On a stand in front of an open window, a towel-draped cooler chugged away, its loud vibrations transmitted to the metal and stone of the room. I tried to wash my hands at the sink, but the faucet was broken. Still, at five-thirty in the morning, the cook's smile gave me solace.

The flat consisted of three rooms and a bathroom; Jason's bedroom was between ours and the kitchen. Standing by his lumpy bed, I watched as he lay sleeping under his mosquito netting, exhausted from the long trip, days without sleep. The shadow under his eyes was the color of the stone floor. A ceiling fan chugged haltingly overhead, its blades flopping under their paste of crud. The room was empty but for the bed and a wobbly table. His violin lay on the table, with some sheet music: Bach and Bartok. Skins of wall paint hung in brittle yellow husks, balanced between gravity and cobwebs. I looked at Jason's face behind the net, and unaccountably tears began to mix with the sweat on my face. Damn, I sniveled, where are we going to find a music stand? Damn! Nothing was the way it was supposed to be. I longed for home where soon the lilacs would bloom; where Thor's coat shone blue in the sun.

I peered out of the grimy window. There was a wall with barbed wire around the campus. Within, on the far end, sat a row of shanties that housed the Rajasthani construction workers who were building another floor on the Guest House. Already, slow moving women with regal bearing piled bricks on their heads—eight at a time—to be transported to somewhere above my line of vision. The Rajasthanis belonged to their company much like indentured servants.

"They're used to it," the Manager had told us with his slick smile.

I took off Jason's sneakers; his legs were dead weight and his socks smelled. I wanted to hug him, but he was far away in sleep.

Joe wasn't in our room. I sat down on the bed and hurt my tailbone. The mattress, on inspection, had the consistency of Wonderbread. Supported by a plywood platform, it was less than two inches thick, covered with stains of human living. We had brought backpacking gear, but I hadn't planned on using it at home. I dug out my sleeping pad and bag. There were going to be as many layers as possible between me and that mattress.

In the bathroom, I, the toilet, and the wash stand were showered at the same time. I would have to figure out a way to keep my towel and clothes dry. After flushing the toilet, water streamed over the top of the tank. I quickly flushed again, wasting precious water, and examined the innards of the tank, which were held together with pieces of string. I closed the valve.

"How was your shower?" Joe asked, standing in the middle of the room with the spray can of Black Flag we'd brought from home. It was time for me to say something positive; he seemed to feel responsible for the squalor.

"Nice and cool." I didn't warn him about the flood.

"That's good. You'll have a good sleep."

"Whom did you poison?" I asked listlessly, expecting him to correct my grammar.

"Just some roaches in the kitchen."

"Many?"

"Well, yes. Many."

The kitchen was defined by the absence of a bed and the presence of a sink against one wall, a counter against the other. There were no cupboards. Earlier, I'd been startled by a bird that came zipping in with a beak full of sprigs. She was building a nest inside the kitchen door. That explained the white splats on the floor.

While Joe was in the shower, I lay on top of my bag, watching two lizards scoot along the angle of wall and ceiling. They were beautiful and funny. I named them Dillard (after Annie) and Durrell (after Gerald).

Joe was fighting with the toilet tank and losing his cool. "Sonofabitch," he growled.

On impulse, I got up again and put a tape of the Grosse Fuge on the boom box we'd lugged along. I turned up the volume, and drowned myself in Beethoven.

For the first time I realized I was a Westerner through and through.

-14-

Riding the Ganges at Dawn

At first there was only the sound of the oars pulling through
the water, slicking against the polished rim of the boat. It was
dawn. We were drifting on the sacred river Ganges, Jason and I,
overwhelmed again by India. A timeless sun swelled above the
river, and liquid light rendered a metaphysical perspective suggest-
ing a place without beginning or end.

Far on the eastern shore the land appeared to be void,
fanning out to where it met the horizon. Bands of gauzy mist
concealed stretches of shoreline, wedding river to land to sky. I
imagined the unseen space to be the Elysian fields, home of the
righteous dead. India nurtured dreaming.

Our boatman guided his boat along the west bank. Broad
shallow steps, or ghats, led down to the river. For the outsider this
was one of the most exotic sites in all of India. Though the sun had
not yet colored the morning, the ghats were rich with people.

Hindu pilgrims submerged themselves for ritual cleansing.
Many had traveled far to wash away the sins of the living. Men,
naked to the waist, and women, modestly hidden inside dripping
sarees, formed a wailing wall of apology.

Funeral pyres were burning at ghats reserved for cremation.
The day's bodies lay wrapped in white muslin, lined up and waiting their turn one last time. Nearby, children swam; their high
voices cut through the seasoned air of burning flesh—life and
death being points on the same circle.

The Ganges had many uses. Laundry was done at its designated place. Backs bent in a cadence of rinsing, beating, kneading,
rinsing, the way it had been done yesterday and would be tomor-

row. Fields of wild-colored sarees were laid out to dry.

A barge passed like a mirage, filled with pilgims mumbling prayers, or mantras. Cupping their hands, they raised the blessed water to their lips.

Houses and temples on the haphazard waterfront tilted capriciously toward the river. Among the drab decay, a few streaks of bright colored paint remained—reflections of peacock blue and hot pink bled into the water.

My attention returned to the people. A Brahmin priest traded blessings for rupees, and there, in front of a small altar strewn with sunny offerings of marigolds, a young man did yoga exercises, dissolving the disparity between mind and matter in the contortions of his body.

We looked into this world but did not see beyond the unfamiliar ceremony, beyond the awesome poverty. It was a world of ritual and continuity, and these were concepts we had long forgotten. Or had we? What then was it that stirred our souls and stilled our tongues? And was our western wealth just compensation for what we had lost? Perhaps these pilgrims thought our ceremony strange, our poverty awesome.

Suddenly, while gliding through the morning haze, our boat collided with another and immediately took water. The Ganges would neither cleanse nor carry us if the boat sank, for we were trespassers in another time; no one would notice our going down, Indian ways would perpetuate untouched. In my mind's eye I saw the river close over our heads without a ripple. Jason seemed oblivious of the rising water drenching his pants. We were strangely passive, as if not to interfere with destiny.

On a razor edge of time I saw myself outside myself watching him, framing his form, detaching him from these ephemeral surroundings. Distant eyes and curve of petulant chin imprinted on my brain with precision. Sun-bleached lashes, pale slope of neck, timid whiskers, back erect with brittle confidence, he was my fixed point of reference within abstraction.

The oars were tossed across the benches with a thud. Water cooled my feet and the sun burned the nape of my neck. Our oarsman began to bail out the boat, hastily returning to the river what was hers.

Fortunately he had many cousins willing to rescue us; they rowed their small crafts toward us. No problem, they laughed, and maneuvering alongside, hauled us aboard.

15

A Blessing

To save gas, the driver turned off the air conditioner. Suddenly he sped up, turned off the engine, coasted until the car nearly came to a stop, and then repeated the procedure. This system worked pretty well—we kept moving, though the needle on the gas gauge dropped through the red zone. Joe leaned forward, willing it back to safety. His tension over the gas situation made the car even more stifling.

"Stop worrying, Joe. Sit back, will you? Desh knows what he's doing." Here the engine died. We climbed out of the car. The white noon light was blistering, the silence sinister.

"Great," Jason said. "Now what?"

Desh opened the hood, offering hope.

"Out of gas," he said, with the air of an expert. He slammed the hood shut.

Joe asked, "How far to the nearest gas?"

"Only ten or fifteen." Desh scanned the surrounding plain nervously. He shook his head. "Not good," he said. For fear of marauders, neither he nor Joe had been keen to take the back roads. I had belittled their wariness, in spite of the fact that in India people are more dispensable than an old car and an American wallet.

"He must mean kilometers, huh? That's not far, why don't we walk?" Jason suggested.

"Christ, I bet he has no idea where to get gas," said Joe.

I snapped at Jason, "Walk where? He's just *assuming* there's gas up ahead. We'll get a heat stroke!" I slammed the car door shut. "And I'm wearing these stupid shoes!"

"You'll have to go and find help," Joe told Desh, whose English suddenly failed him. Joe took him by the shoulders, pivoting him in the right direction. "Go. Get help!" he said. Desh stood shrunken in the dust. He was twenty-three, but looked like a frightened pup when not behind the wheel of a live car. Joe threw up his hands.

"I think we should push it. We'll be okay, we had a Coke not too long ago," said Jason.

I shrugged, "Might as well."

We put wads of Kleenex under our hands, so they wouldn't fry on the blue metal. Desh was subdued; maybe he was surprised we could be useful. Already we were too dry to sweat. Who could possibly live in a thirsty place like this?

Camels, that's who. A group of camels and their keeper came shimmering down the road. The dark-skinned herdsman had a fetching carmine cloth wrapped around his head. He cautiously positioned himself behind one of the beasts and told Desh there was a farm with a truck just up the road.

The "farm" seemed to be waiting for the right moment to capsize, but we spotted an old green truck. Behind the hovel the toothless, scruffy owner lay snoring on a *charpoi,* a rope bed.

"Namaste," called Joe. Scrambling upright and straightening his garment, the man bowed sleepily to each of us in turn. Joe looked on intently while Desh negotiated in one of India's two hundred languages. There was enough gas in the truck to siphon off what we needed, but, "very expensive." The deal was sealed with nods and hand shakes.

The gas gauge still registered below empty when we drove off in a cloud of dust. Nobody mentioned the likelihood that there might be no gas at the next stop.

This was a small market town boasting a gas pump. A crowd of children clustered around the car; older folks watched gloomily from a distance. Last summer's monsoon had failed, causing this year's extreme hardship.

The children were becoming ever more aggressive, demanding candy and money. We rolled up the windows against too many poking hands. After a time they lost interest, except for a serious looking boy of about twelve, with long, tangled lashes, who studied every detail of the inside of the car.

"We could give him my book," Jason said.

"What would he do with it? Besides, you're not done with it," I said. (He was reading *The City of Joy,* by Dominique Lapierre.)

"I'm sure he'd like it," Jason insisted. "Give it to him, Mom."

I held the book up for the child, who broke into a radiant smile. "I guess you're right! There it goes then."

Like crows on carrion, the flock of children landed on the hapless boy before he had a chance to open the book. He ended up at the bottom of a pile of tearing arms and legs. When it was over, he looked in not much better condition than *The City of Joy*, which was divided among the best and bravest, while we looked on helplessly. With bleeding nose and torn clothes, he shrunk away.

Jason was miserable; there was nothing we could do for him, either.

Desh started the engine with his old bravado. The gas gauge read about an eighth of a tank.

"Oh no, you're not!" Joe said. "Fill the tank."

Desh gave him that distinctive Indian head waddle. "Cheaper," he indicated some vague spot up ahead with a flutter of his hand. Since the trip had been prepaid, it was to his advantage to husband the rupees.

"Yeah, well I don't give a damn. Fill it up here," Joe handed him the money.

With the anxiety about the gas alleviated, extreme lethargy overcame me. When our knees or elbows accidentally touched, we pulled away irritably. Joe asked me to photograph a cluster of shacks by some starving shrubs, but I said no, because all I saw was the drab misery that I wouldn't love. I felt the anger rising between us. Jason pushed deeper into his corner.

Late in the afternoon, the car sputtered, and Desh eased it into a village. "Carburator again," he grinned. We walked down the road, leaving Desh to do his usual pounding and lubricating.

The village was plain, its inhabitants oblivious of dirt. The houses were of mud construction, designed to protect against the heat and afford maximum ventilation. Garishly green, blue, and pink paintings ornamented the doorways. Women sat in their courtyards, surrounded by kids and animals. An old woman was husking grain, shaking her sifter with even movements of her arms, her silver bracelets clanging softly; another raked her hands through a basket of beans. The clear voices of the children fused with the braying of a donkey. I felt a curious yearning to belong, to be rid of the restlessness of my life.

A holy man dressed in a sepia tunic came toward us and asked if he could be of service. He had a supremely dignified air, heightened by his formal manner of speaking with a public school accent. Joe explained that we were looking to buy soft drinks.

"We would be honored if you would be the guests of our family," the man said. I couldn't take my eyes off his face. There was a bridled wildness about him. He was dark-skinned, had full sensual lips, and tranquil, somewhat detached eyes.

After protestations, we followed him into a stable where an ancient woman sat in an equally ancient chair. The sadhu knelt in front of her and kissed her feet. She touched his head and shoulders, blessing him, while he spoke to her softly. Her face lit up; she extended her hands.

"The mother will bless you," said the sadhu, and each in turn we knelt before her. Her hands were heavy on my head and shoulders, pressing into my skin. With a quiet smile she caressed Jason's face. Then Joe knelt in the dust, awkwardly, apologetically. I thought my heart would break.

"The mother wishes you to know that she is greatly honored. She says you are our brothers," said the sadhu.

"It is we who are honored," Joe mumbled. "Please thank the mother." Standing on the path, we spoke of village life. The sadhu was educated in Britain, the only person in the family ever to receive an education. After leaving London at age thirty-three, he wandered fourteen years in the Himalayas before returning home to teach the village children. Jason asked him if enough food could be grown to sustain the people.

"When there's water, there's food," the sadhu laughed. "It depends. We live one day at a time." The clarity of the distant summits was reflected in his eyes.

Women began to gather in the street, and suddenly everybody was running over with joy. Children carrying younger siblings on their backs paraded before us, the babies relishing our "oohs and aahs," the older kids giggling at our whiteness. I became self-conscious about my yellow-haired head that looked like a spotlight next to all those demurely covered heads. My loose summer dress and bare legs looked outrageous.

We were shown into a room with western style furniture. The sadhu urged us to "sit for some time" and then disappeared. We would not see him again. Soon bowls of rice, tea, bananas, and a stack of *chapatis* appeared. The women bade us to eat and stood in the doorway to coax us on when we stopped chewing. Jason was especially watched over as the upcoming head of the family.

After the meal, people crowded around again. A blind woman touched our faces and hair, partaking of what had turned into a celebration. And so we "sat for some time," bound by our sameness. It was one of those Indian non-events with powerful implications. The villagers in their earthy wisdom knew they needed each other to survive individually. If that was a fringe benefit of hardship, luxury wasn't quite so desirable.

Joe said it was time to go, but didn't stand waiting impatiently for me to catch up with his hurry. I was sipping the last of my tea when one of the women presented me with a gift. She put her tough-skinned hands over mine, pressing a piece of fabric between them. I unfolded a billiard-green shawl with metallic gold borders and stars. The woman shook her head when I thanked her; she steered me outside to the actual donor, who shyly draped the shawl over my head. I thought I looked presentable at last, but the women burst into good-natured laughter. I was irredeemable.

"I think you look great," Joe consoled me, but Jason joined in the ripple of laughter that rose above our heads. I felt like the blind man in Blind Man's Bluff—a component of the game, but with a disadvantage. I wished I had something to give in return.

"It's probably the finest thing she owns," I told Joe.

"I'm sure it is, but you have to accept it." He took a corner of the shawl between his index finger and thumb, and pulled it across my face in the style of the village women. I put my palms together, causing more amusement.

At last we walked toward the car, and still the people

flocked around, as if they needed us for blessing, for giving. It was nearly dark now. The air was hot and thick, mixed with a rich odor of dung.

"I'm glad you're so singularly irresponsible at times," Joe said in my ear.

I kissed his cheek. "Sometimes you just have to get off the main road, you know?"

We hung out of the windows waving goodbye until all there was left was the dried-up land.

16

Forty Rupees Allowed Our Skins To Touch

"Give me four rupees, and I'll take you to the Ritz or the Siddharta," said the rickshaw wallah, looking up at the darkening sky. He moved alongside, his motor percolating seductively. "Hot," he smiled at our red faces, "Only four rupees."

"We like to walk," I assured him. The Mysore railroad station was close to the city center; we could easily check out hotels on foot.

The rickshaw wallah began to whistle; he had plenty of time. He knew more about human nature than the hard sell hordes at the station. I stole a sideways glance at him; mockingly he pointed a finger toward the sky.

"Maybe we should go with him," I told Jason.

"I'm sick of these people," he said uncharitably.

"Don't talk that way. They're trying to make a living."

What had a few months in India done to his loving heart? My son who was going to dedicate his life to the poor. As soon as I know enough, he told me, I'll form a choir of orphans in Bombay. You'll see.

Rain began to pound the cocoa-dry dust; the beads rolled on the road like newborn jellyfish. The driver told us that, actually, neither the Ritz nor the Siddharta were very good.

"I know of a place that is special," he said, holding my backpack while I climbed into his contraption. The road was already flooded. Resigned, we rode along a wide avenue, leaving the center of Mysore. A few miles later, the rickshaw stopped in front of a three story white building. Our bags were carried in and the fare settled at eight rupees while we stood dripping in a cool marble foyer.

Our room looked out on a sultry landscape brushed with the broken tones of an impressionist painting: scarlet, orange, yellow. Long graceful arms of trees bowed under their weight of color.

Except for raspberry-red bedcovers, the wide room was decorated in muted pastels. Wall-length mirrors reflected the milky marble of the bathroom. We opened the glass doors to a balcony, sank into cream satin chairs, and watched the rain wash the tiled roofs of Mysore. Before going down to dinner we bathed with sandalwood soap, and I put on the one dress I brought, a sleeveless black linen, only moderately wrinkled.

For the moment we erased the pain of India from our minds. The lights were low in the dining-room. Three musicians sat on a platform strewn with flowers. The one in the center played the melody on a sarod; to his right sat the tabla player. A two note drone was held by an instrument Jason told me was a tampura. The red silk of the musicians' garments flowed like heat.

Indian music was at first as perplexing as Indian society. Something like synergy without harmony. The players went their own direction in improvisation within prescribed limits set by raga and rhythm. Then they seemed to crest a wave of creativity and converge, sweeping the audience along in the fulfillment of the music. Jason tried hard not to blink the tears from his eyes. In my heart the music, the incense, the colors, and the exotic aromas mingled with my love for him.

"What a relief this place is after last night," I sighed.

"Hm." Jason served himself from my dishes after finishing his. It was our first meal that day; he was a hungry sixteen-year-old. "How much does this place cost?" he asked, tearing off a piece of *naan* and using it to scoop up the red-hot gravy of a vegetable dish.

I confessed I had no idea and wasn't going to let anything spoil these almost forgotten comforts that were, I argued, for the soul as much as for the body. "We did penance in Bangalore," I added, reminding him of our rat-infested hotel there. "The contrasts are so extreme in this country."

"That's what makes it exciting. Of course we're not

stuck in one of the extremes. We can move from that dump last night to this place. We'll never really understand what it's like. We shouldn't stay in these places."

"Maybe not. But let's enjoy it while we're here. You want to try and arrange transportation to Somnathpur for tomorrow?"

It was a fine morning when we met the driver in front of the hotel. The age of the car was as ambiguous as that of the man—both appeared to have been around a long time. He greeted us with the conventional folding of palms and touching the forehead, but twice—too servile, especially for an older man.

After the clamor of Indian cities, the quiet of the country was tangible. Vegetation rose richly green from red soil. It was the first time in months that we were away from crowds and the foul air of fleets of motor rickshaws. Children playing around the clay cottages waved at us, carefree in their bare-footed poverty—so unlike the sickly urchins of the cities. Young girls pulled shawls across their laughing faces, bringing their heads together and ogling Jason, who pretended to be neutral to virginal charm.

We had seen so many temples in India, including those in Khajuraho with their overt erotic sculptures, that I was not overly excited to view another one. I regretted it when the hour-long ride through the countryside came to an end. The driver sauntered off, his body insubstantial inside his clothes, like a marionette.

Drawn to the shade of a tree, we sat down as if by prearrangement, soaking up the serenity. How we'd been invaded by pandemonium, the constant swell of bodies!

After a while Jason whispered, "This is what I miss the most," and began to walk slowly toward the temple.

The surface of the building was covered with stone carvings. We circled it several times before looking more closely at the friezes. I had read that the stone, though soft when quarried, turned hard as ivory by exposure to air. That explained the good condition of the seven-century-old temple.

In my mind's eye I saw hollow-eyed sculptors squatting among fragments of stone, their bare legs grey with dust, ten, twelve hours a day, a whole working life long. What had it been like working stone in the burning sun three centuries before Michelangelo painted the Sistine ceiling?

"Here's one from the Bhagavad Gita," Jason called. "This has to be the most beautiful building in the world...."

I didn't think of myself as blimpish, exactly, but although the structure was stunning, the carvings didn't really move me. I said, "You're more eclectic than I am."

"You've got a closed mind." he said, "Sometimes I don't understand you at all."

Almost certainly blood and tears lay frozen in the stone. Today the chisels were silent, the sculptors forgotten. Only the ancient stories lived on in the carvings, and the temple had become an oasis of peace. For now at least.

I sat on the cool stone, concentrating on one small group of carvings, until the figures began to take on meaning. Slowly, I was pulled in by the star shaped sanctuaries. From the beginning of time, people everywhere had wanted to leave something behind that would endure. Asking why made me sad.

Back in Mysore, we bought slices of watermelon and mangos, and a few bananas for the bossy monkeys darting about. A one-legged boy was sorting a tin of rusty screws—reverting chaos to chaos. He quickly shot out a grimy hand, a reflex set off by white skin. A goat was slaughtered; blood ran in a sinuous stream that puddled in front of a diner where tin pots of wonderful smelling food were bubbling. Farther down, people had their hair cut. A small mirror hung from a tree; the ground beneath the chair was padded with dark hair. A man was ironing a stack of *kurtas* on a bare plank, using one iron while another was heating on the coals. Flour was ground. Mechanical sewing machines whirred. Manuscripts were typed. A man asked us to send him jeans from America. "Come with me, I give you my size." The door to the abortion clinic—a one room shed—was shut, but at the hemorrhoid surgeon's, people were waiting their turn. I tried not to dwell on the contents of the bucket peeking from beneath the sheet that shielded the operating table.

We spent hours at the bazaar of small miracles. You could buy fish, get a tattoo, have your shoes fixed, your teeth, or your bicycle. You could have your ears irrigated. American rock screamed from the radio shop. We were boomeranged back and forth in time—pots of psychedelic dyes, shimmering sarees, strings of hot peppers, a thousand tired feet, children worming in and out of the light. A cow walked by, stole some greens, dropped a pie.

At last the afternoon burned out. Oil lamps were lit and the bazaar became an enchanted place as daylight dirt and poverty were muted by the lanterns. This was the moment the players met in their intricate improvisations of life. The men huddled together, smoking and gambling while women's tired faces softened in this the best of possible worlds.

We walked the three miles back to the hotel. The rain had cooled the city but not slowed its throb. Lives were lived on the streets in packs. Wearily we brushed off beggars and dope peddlers and money changers. In horror we turned from the stink of the deformed bodies of lepers slumping on the sidewalk, their leg stumps oozing through grey-brown rags like rotting prunes.

"God, why don't they take care of these people," said Jason. "This isn't a poor city!"

"There're too many of them. We should go back and give them some money."

"That's insulting."

"Yes." I dug up two twenty-rupee notes and put the money into the gnarled hands.

I thought about the untroubled eyes of the lepers as we lay on our raspberry beds with the doors to the balcony open. Perfume of sandalwood and wet grass wafted in, and strains of a flute accompanied the call of a nightbird riding the scented air. Another Indian day had ended. A day of peace and mayhem, spirit and body. Time that went too fast and yet was filled to slowness.

Forty rupees for the leper. Less than we had spent on beer.

17

From Hollywood to Disneyland

After a bone-jolting two hour bus ride, we arrived in the market town of Alleppey, braced to dodge vendors and beggars. But the tourist trade was non-existent during the monsoon, and we walked around undisturbed. The stalls were filled with fresh fruit and vegetables, which gave the town an appearance of prosperity.

We had come to Alleppey to take a boat through the backwaters to Kottayam, from where we would travel by bus to Kumily, and on to the Periyar Wildlife Sanctuary. Our itinerary was apparently written on our faces, because a young man who had been trailing us called out, "It is too late for the boat. I will show you a nice hotel."

"That's okay," I said, pulling Jason along toward the waterfront.

"You were rude, Mom. He was trying to be helpful."

"We didn't ask for his help. You're too trusting of strangers." But the man was right about the boat, and therefore confident we weren't going anywhere. Though I thought we'd discouraged him, he turned up once more to offer his services. He volunteered that he was a student and very interested in America. His name was Matthew. While I was plotting to get rid of him, he fell into an animated conversation with Jason.

"May I offer you a beer?" he asked me, and before I could articulate a reply, "Tea perhaps?"

"You must excuse us, we're very tired. Here's our hotel," I said, for we happened to be in front of one.

"I will call for you at eight o'clock to have dinner at my mother's house," the man said.

"Thanks!" said Jason. In the lobby he reprimanded me for

being unkind. "I suppose you won't want to go to his house tonight," he said angrily.

"Are you nuts?"

"You mean we can?"

"Absolutely not! And, furthermore, we're not staying here, just in case he shows up."

In the terrible heat we lugged our heavy packs to the Allepey Prince, four kilometers out of town. Jason didn't speak to me. Already I regretted I'd been surly. Perhaps it was better to err on the risky side than to insult a well-meaning person.

While Jason read, I dozed, and we didn't get back to the center of town to look for a restaurant until nine o'clock. Before we had a chance to read the menu, Matthew materialized, gushing joviality. "Our meeting is most fortunate. It is a sign!" he said.

I waited coldheartedly for an opportunity to dismiss him, but instead found myself inviting him to join us. He would have just a bite, to be sociable.

Jason tried to make up for my lack of enthusiasm by encouraging Matthew to talk about himself. To our surprise we learned that he was studying for the priesthood, which was bizarre for an Indian, but perhaps not for one named Matthew.

"Are there many Christians here?" I asked. There were a few, he said, all Catholics. After his second beer he got down to business. "You see, I have read about Hollywood. It is the ideal way to live."

"Hollywood?"

"Yes! It is my dearest wish. If I can make a lot of money, I can force people to do what I want. I'm willing to study for the priesthood, so I can come to America."

"Big of him, don't you think?" I asked Jason, who was stunned into silence. Matthew explained that if I would write a letter, his "contacts" would tell me he was well suited. Then I could convince the authorities in America. It wouldn't be difficult. He wrote down the address. He needed a little help with his plane ticket, but I shouldn't worry, he would pay me back.

When we parted, Father Matthew asked for a rupee so he could make the one-hour bus trip back to his village.

Jason's defeated comment was, "He must be at least thirty."

At the dock, early the next morning, I was greatly relieved that Matthew was nowhere to be seen. The boat was crowded, but, oddly, the two foremost seats were unoccupied, and we had room for our backpacks and Jason's long legs.

"We're probably not allowed to sit here," he whispered.

"I think it's okay for barbarians," I said, wondering how serious a gaffe we were committing.

The boat passed through narrow canals where luxuriant vegetation closed over our heads. Tiny thatched cottages, cashew and coconut trees lined the shore where brilliant red blossoms dotted the green. At times the waterways opened up into broad lagoons. Cantilevered Chinese fishing nets were silhouetted against an horizon fringed with palms, like delicate etchings in silver.

The many islands were only a few meters wide. Here, people raised children in isolation, and, perhaps, innocence. The few feet of land held a vegetable garden, a cottage, a cow or two, chickens, and ducks—another Indian miracle.

The atmosphere on board was hushed—the passengers were under the spell of the timeless wonder of light and form, our common response to the radiance of the day.

On arrival in Kottayam, the reverent calm of the waters was replaced by the usual brouhaha; we thought it serendipitous that we spotted the bus for the refuge immediately.

The bus had no shocks, but worse was the driver's habit of leaning on the air horn to herald our approach to villagers and livestock. It would have taken more than that to dampen our good spirits, though Jason moved to the back of the bus and stuck his fingers in his ears.

On the slopes of the Nilgiri Mountains, barefooted women were picking tea leaves on plantations belonging to magnificent estates. Bananas, coconuts, jackfruit and cardamom grew in abundance.

More than four hours of bumping and blasting brought us to the Periyar Sanctuary, which bordered a man-made lake. Our hotel, the Lake Palace, was deep in the reserve and reached by ferry, but we found the launch jetty deserted. We asked at the nearby Nivas Hotel at what time the next ferry would leave.

"There is no ferry."

"Well then, how does one get to the Palace Hotel?"

"It is closed. There is no electricity at the Sanctuary." The clerk seemed annoyed with us.

"No electricity," I said.

"Maybe we can walk. Do you have a map?" asked Jason.

"You can't walk, and anyway, there's no electricity." Another man explained the situation patiently. No electricity meant no food, no water. We would have to stay at the Nivas, which had a generator.

Our room was the V.I.P. suite, drab but palatial in size, with a wide verandah. A bucket of water from the lake was carried up to flush the toilet. Undaunted, we signed up for a boat trip in hopes of seeing the wildlife: elephants, boar, bison, and perhaps tigers.

Besides us, there were five Indians on board, four of whom immediately went to sleep. It was "a good time to see the animals," shouted the captain over the deafening roar of the engine. However, the lake was bordered with tropical flora, and we knew that among its tangles lived the great beasts. Now and then the captain cut the engine, and all we heard was human snoring. During these quieter times, we did spot two herds of bison, an enormous boar, a herd of sambar, two otters, a water snake, and a few exotic birds.

"They must think we're idiots," Jason said indignantly when we dismounted. "Why don't they advertise it as Disneyland!"

"Disneyland without a flush? Tell you what. Let's plan a hike into the jungle tomorrow, early. Maybe we can hire a guide. Hey, how would you like to go by elephant? I saw a notice at the desk."

"Let's go!"

The same dour fellow was at the reception desk. "We'd like to make reservations for an elephant ride into the jungle tomorrow, early if possible," I said.

"The elephant is sick."

"You have only one elephant?"

"Yes."

"In that case, do you have a guide available?"

"No guide."

"I see. No guide, no map, no elephant, no lights, no water, no animals. What does one do here I wonder. Are there trails we can follow?"

"It is forbidden for guests to go into the jungle without a guide, and we have no guide."

The generator wouldn't be started until eight o'clock, so we couldn't bathe. We decided to walk to the village of Kumily. On the way, we met a real priest who carried his altar boy on the back of his bicycle and a basket of vegetables on the front. He stopped to invite us to tea, at his home behind the church. The bicycle swayed dangerously when the priest pedaled away, his long white robe trailing like angels' wings and enfolding the little boy.

With some trepidation we left the road and followed a path through the woods for several kilometers. I had a strong sense of unreality, brought about by the unusual vegetation, the semidarkness. To think that the sequence of life's events had led me here. Just one missing link and I would not have known this fabled forest. Things followed each other inevitably; sixteen years ago Jason was born so he could walk here next to me. Wherever here was.

I started when a huge jackfruit fell with a thud, exploding next to my foot. Our laughter sounded as crass as the monkeys' screeching.

"They warned us for snakes and scorpions, but missiles are the true danger," I said. "Let's get back to the road."

"Which way?"

"That way."

"I don't think so."

"I'm sure."

"So am I. It's that way, remember? Where the road turned right and then....or was it left?"

"Damn, Jason, you're confusing me. What turn?" We argued some more and, in the end, agreed to backtrack.

Closer to Kumily, children were still playing outside; we obliged them by answering the usual questions about our comings and goings. There was no begging here. No "give me a rupee, give me a pen, give me a candy."

"What luck to meet that priest," said Jason. "I'm glad we

have something interesting to do."

"You must get bored hanging out with your old lady."

"Yeah. I'd much rather have a summer job in Amherst, bagging groceries."

"But that's not the only option, and at least you'd be with people your age."

"Then who would be crazy enough to do these wild things with you? You need me!"

"Wild things? We're visiting a priest!"

We stirred up a bunch of flying foxes as we groped along a narrow footpath to a clearing. A tiny church was almost entirely camouflaged by ivy. Perhaps the priest's quarters were hidden among the green maze.

"Spooky as hell here," Jason said irreverently, and then tripped over a vine. He sprawled face down and upset a metal bucket that went clanging down the incline. We got back to the road in a big hurry, and that was it as far as our having tea with the priest went.

It was a long, eerie walk back; we were glad to see the orange-yellow glow of the hotel through the trees.

"The generator!" we whooped at the same time.

"You can go first," Jason allowed, falling on his bed with a book.

I coaxed a trickle of water from the shower and warped my body under it. Just as I had my hair foaming, the water stopped and the light died.

"Shit," came from the V.I.P. suite.

"Get me some water, Jay, I'm all sudsy."

"I can't find the door."

"Get the...."

"I can't find the flashlight either."

A boy walked in with a candle in one hand and a bucket in the other as I came towel-wrapped and foam-haired out of the bathroom. He could have knocked with his foot, but at least he brought water.

"Please get us two more buckets, would you?" I asked. He smiled sweetly. I kicked at the bucket, holding up two fingers. "Two!"

"Okay, memsahib, no problem!" and away he sped.

In the morning the generator was fixed, but the pump was broken. No surprises here. We got our buckets filled, ate breakfast, and checked out.

"Where will you go?" the clerk asked maliciously.

"Go? Oh, back to Cochin." I noted with annoyance that our bill was steep.

"There's no bus."

"Why not?"

"This is the slow season. No bus until Thursday. Maybe not even then." Today was Monday.

"In that case, please make a call to Kumily and hire us a jeep." I refused to stay another night here; who knew what would break down next.

"I can't call. The telephone is out of order." At that remark, Jason's appreciation for the ridiculous reached its zenith. He threw himself on one of the deep chairs in the lobby, convulsing with laughter and holding his stomach. Tears rolled down his cheeks. "Oh my God!" he wheezed.

I watched uncertainly, but one look at the stony-faced boy at the desk, and I was lost too. We laughed until we were dry, and even then Jason relapsed from time to time.

"Sorry," I told the clerk, "you were saying the phone is dead." I could feel my face twitch on the verge of hysteria, but I hardened myself. "Can you send a boy to Kumily with a message? To rent a jeep?"

"Hee!" came from the chair. "The boy broke his leg!"

"This I can do," said the clerk. "No jeep, but maybe a car and driver."

"No, wait. We'll walk to Kumily and hire a car ourselves."

"It is too dangerous. You can travel more safe with a driver we know. The boy will be back in a couple of hours."

"All right."

"Eight hundred rupees."

"All right."

And so it happened that, two hours later, we drove through the Nilgiris with a fearless nineteen-year-old boy, too nauseated to appreciate the scenery. We were tossed from side to side in the back seat of a car that would have refused to run anywhere but in India. Our "Slow down, please!" was encountered with, "Okay, okay, no problem!" while the car continued to gun down the mountain.

The seven hour trip was over in four-and-a-half. The gung-ho driver was rewarded for his bravery and left us weak-kneed in the lobby of our hotel.

-18-

A Game of Chess

Jason expected to be treated like the indigenous people, but
soon learned that in India the color of his skin was synonymous
with affluence. Raised in a New England college town, he was
faced with a loss of identity—suddenly he stood for a concept, a
preconceived idea. He couldn't tolerate the Indian poor humiliating
themselves, and he objected to being taken for a fool. His method
of handling daily negotiations was often impractical and rigid. I
had no qualms about excusing the merchants' mini corruptions and
preferred to let them take me for a ride rather than exert myself
over a few rupees. But he had his principles. Which was why we
got entangled in a rickshaw war.

We'd just gotten off the plane and begun hiking toward
Trivandrum, flanked on either side by high-pressure rickshaw
wallahs. As usual we bucked when pressured, and plowed on. The
temperature was too extreme and Trivandrum too far to walk, but
the question was, who would take us there in the dignified fashion
Jason demanded. We were offered a ride for forty rupees. Jason
shrugged and kept walking, which brought down the price to
twenty rupees.

"That's fine," I said, but he continued to stall.

"Hotel Luciya? Fifteen rupees," said a fat wallah, grabbing
my pack. Things happened fast then. The fat fellow was surrounded by angry wallahs and couldn't move. Everybody was
yelling at once and a few men were shaking their fists. Our driver,
who had kept his motor running, managed a clever maneuver
through the mob, and away we roared. The other men jumped into
their machines and with militant expletives got on our tail. One by

one they fell behind, but four hung on. We were on the open road, veering in and out of traffic at top speed—that of a well maintained lawnmower. Our driver appeared more afraid of his colleagues than of cars.

"Stop!" I whacked him on the shoulder. "Let us off!"

One of the adversaries thumped into the side of our buggy, and although we sustained a couple of dimples, we couldn't be toppled, what with the heavy driver and backpacks. Nevertheless, we got our heads banged, and fear reached another level. Behind us a bus seemed bent on running us off the road. Our beleaguered driver headed straight for a gaggle of pedestrians and at the last minute corkscrewed between a taxi and a non-participating rickshaw up the embankment where he was intercepted by the competition. We were completely surrounded. The adversaries recycled their abuses and threats. When we attempted to climb out, the driver yelled at us to stay put "for our own safety." Droll counsel, considering the fact that it was he who brandished a knife. In the end the vigilantes allowed us to proceed; a civilized agreement seemed to have been reached. The driver took a swig of whiskey to soothe his nerves; we cruised on at a moderate clip.

"I'll be damned," Jason muttered.

"We nearly got killed over thirty-five cents. You think we contribute to social order by causing cock fights?" I said angrily.

We passed through a shanty town on the outskirts of Trivandrum. Children ran behind us, laughing, thumbing their noses.

"Fook you, Yankees!" they shouted bravely. Jason looked at me, and suddenly we laughed behind the driver's thick back. We put our arms around each other's shoulders and sang "Summertime and the livin' is easy" while the gods and mascots on the dash bobbed merrily.

"Forty rupees," the wallah demanded when we stopped.

"You said fifteen," Jason handed him the bills.

"They will kill me! Forty rupees!"

We figured the driver would have to go back to his brothers and share the fare. Jason paid up. After a perfunctory visit to the hotel lobby we decided to continue on to Kovalum Beach, sixteen kilometers south. The machiavellian driver was still waiting and shamelessly offered his services! Jason said "Fook you," under his breath. We took the bus, which satisfied all our expectations of Third World transportation.

From the half-circle balcony of our room at the Rockholm Hotel at Kovalum we looked over the crowns of palms to the Arabian Sea. The monsoon waves sprayed the already saturated air with a piquant mist, and the room was as perfect as the view— bare and white, clean linen, good reading lights, and a modern bath.

After a yukky meal we explored the gorgeous coves and the town itself. Although Kovalum had one of India's most famous beaches, there wasn't a tourist in sight. Clouds gathered toward evening. We swam in a rainstorm in the fiercest rip I'd ever seen. I washed back to shore some distance from where I started, and Jason, who was a strong swimmer, rode in behind me, smack under the "No Swimming Rip Tide" sign.

Our days at Kovalum were the stuff of dreams. We swam, napped, and took hikes, but mostly we looked. At the furious afternoon skies, the scarlet hibiscus, the paddies and the groves, and at the maze of ropes drying on the white sand, like a secret code. We roamed the narrow lanes of the fishing villages and watched the dugouts being pushed out to sea and the flexed bodies of the men as they hauled in the nets. In the shade of a thatched parasol we cut pineapples and mangos to share with the beach children, the sticky sap running down our arms.

Some days the waves were as high as cathedrals. Jason chose one such day to go for a swim.

"It's too dangerous, Jason, with those breakers and the undertow...." When the water pulled back we saw three opposing currents.

"Ah, but so beautiful! I'll be careful, don't worry. Look at those waves!"

"Don't go too deep...." but he was gone already. I immediately lost sight of him—he was no more than a piece of flotsam in the vortex. I slumped in the sand; my stomach snagged into knots. When I thought I spotted him, I started waving and shouting, but I couldn't even hear my own voice. I began to imagine Jason drowning. I would call Joe. "Joe, I'm sorry, but Jason is dead. Drowned

in the Arabian Sea. What do you mean why didn't I stop him." And
now I could never leave here. I would stay forever on this spot
where I saw him running long-legged to his grave....

Standing up to my knees in the churning water, I found
myself reeling with fear. I should have forbidden him to go. And
then he came running down the beach and dropped spumy-skinned
on the sand.

"It's incredible! You should've gone in, Mom."

"From now on, when you're with me, you'll play by my
rules. I was frightened to death! It's damned selfish of you to insist
on having everything your way." I kicked the towel. "Thanks a
lot!" My voice trembled.

He was stunned. He didn't remind me that I hadn't forbidden him to go swimming. I climbed the hill to the hotel, crying
over my angry words and over what could have happened.

When he came in half an hour later, I was sitting on the
balcony with my back to the room. I'd had enough time to realize
that one of the reasons we had gotten along so extraordinarily well
on our travels, was, that until recently, he had acquiesced to my
way of doing things. Now that he was old enough to disagree, we
were pulling against each other. How much freedom was I to give
a sixteen-year-old boy? When was my judgment more valid than
his? I couldn't stand tension between us; I needed to talk to him.

"Jay?" I banged the bathroom door. Silence. "Jason!
Answer me, will you?" I tried the door; it wasn't locked. "Can I
come in?" The bathroom was empty. What I had heard was the
maid bringing in bath towels. Again my imagination went wild. He
was so upset at my accusations, that he had gone back into those
waves....I knew how unpredictable teenage reactions were, how
exposed kids felt. I flew down the stairs like one possessed. He had
just returned and was asking for the room key.

"There you are," I said.

"Where're you going?"

"Looking for you. I was afraid you'd gone in again. Sorry I
yelled at you. Let's change, and take a taxi to the Ashoka," I
suggested.

"A taxi? Why don't we walk?"

"It's so dark, who knows who's out there...."

"Oh Mom, if you don't watch out you'll live forever and won't have any fun!"

The evening had become serene; a soft breeze touched our skins. A ship's call sounded far out to sea. The primordial sand that we curled our toes around lay abandoned under a starless sky. Gone were the fruit sellers and the children; an unnatural calm claimed the beach.

Suddenly, we were spooked by a group of men crouching in the sand. One of them began to follow us. We were going to have fun and not live forever.

The man blocked our path and said in a sing-song, "Ganja? Fenni? Very good Country Liquor?" He lit a match to display his marijuana. "Very good quality, you will like!"

"No, thank you." We stepped around him. He tied the weed back in the cloth and darted around us, singing "Fenni? Ganja? Special price for you!"

We couldn't actually see him, and it was creepy to have him hopping around in an insubstantial body. When he vanished at last we saw a dope peddler in every dark shape.

"What's fenni?" Jason had taken to whispering.

"No idea."

"Then how do you know we don't want some?"

Our dinner at the Ashoka was festive. We lingered over coffee and Indian sweets, uneager to leave the bright lights. This time it was Jason who suggested that we take a taxi, because he was too tired to walk.

"I'd rather sleep on the beach than walk all the way back," he said. I told him he'd had too much fenni.

No taxi was available. We started out in the woods surrounding the hotel, soon losing sight of it. Going around in circles, we got more and more disgruntled. We were so disoriented, that we didn't know how to get back to the beach, let alone to the road leading to our hotel.

"If only we had a flashlight," I said, but he silenced me.

"What would that do? We'd still be groping around like idiots."

In spite of his exasperation, or perhaps because of it, he soon zeroed in on the target road, and we had a pleasant walk back to the hotel, where, to our consternation, we found the iron gate closed. It was after midnight. Jason climbed over it and knocked at the door.

"Louder," I ordered, then, "Try the window!"

We spent the night we would have slept through on the beach, watching the tropical day grow toward morning with fresh clarities. Once again the strands of our separate lives ran in parallel lines.

That afternoon we were playing chess (I was losing big) in the lounge of the hotel when a local artist interrupted the game to show us his leaf paintings. The leaves were held intact by their intricate map of veins and desiccated paper-thin tissue. The paintings were of dancers and elephants, birds and lovers. We selected seven or eight, then we all took tea together. Mr. Kumar was an art teacher and well acquainted with western painting. He was barefoot and wore a white *longhi*. His eyes were narrow, almost smiling; his sleek, graying hair fell to his shoulders. I watched his broad, well manicured peasant hands holding the teacup, and tried to imagine him painting the delicate miniatures. I liked the soft-spoken painter immensely.

"Do you enjoy teaching art?" I asked.

"I do not teach art."

"But you said...."

"Art cannot be taught. Just as you cannot teach your son to become a good man." He smiled. "In the West many people think education is everything."

"Well, it may be a question of semantics then. If you don't teach your students, what exactly...."

"I give them an opportunity to see, that is all. If they have no imagination, they will not see. Art is in them or not—I cannot put it there."

"Are you saying art exists before its execution?"

"Not entirely. Art is, or should be, designed to open the eyes. It is like an acorn holding the secret of the crowned oak."

Jason said shyly, "When I first began to listen to music seriously, I used to hear errors in pitch or rhythm. I watched for the errors, I couldn't help myself, you know?" The artist nodded.

"But lately, when the music is beautiful, I listen....and I

think maybe I fill in what's not really there. Is that....is it something like what you mean?"

"What do you think?" was the maddening answer. "Let us finish the game, you and I. You are white, I think?"

Without waiting for an answer, he turned the board so that my side was facing him. They bent over the unfinished game, our guest toying with my fallen knight and bishop with his left hand.

"You're inheriting a mess I'm afraid. I'm not very good."

But his strategy made my losing army triumphant.

"I suppose you don't teach chess either?" I chuckled.

He laughed heartily. "Oh, you would have seen the solution. I have no doubt at all."

Calcutta

A political, social, and urban nightmare, Calcutta groaned under twenty million feet. Between the airport and the hotel all possible variations of suffering were on display. I looked around with grim fascination—oh beautiful, horrible world....

Our hotel, the Fairlawn, was run by a British couple. You turned your back on hardship once you entered the gate and crossed the terrace with its parasols and potted plants. You also left behind free and democratic India. They hadn't caught on here, the Raj was alive and well. We didn't immediately notice this state of affairs when we stood dazed in the lobby, delivering passports and signing traveler's cheques.

A bearer loaded our gear on his head, and with a whispered, "Sahib, Memsahib," bade us follow him up an elegant staircase. The second floor hall was an archive for memorabilia, symbolizing a time when British authority prevailed beyond this anachronistic establishment. On the walls hung portraits of family and horses. Well carved figures were on display, and a Delft vase —with plastic flowers. The chairs were re-upholstered in red vinyl, the magazines outdated. A moldy smell of times past permeated everything.

Our room was packed with shoddy furniture; a window was broken. There were echoes of Great Britain in the ponderous drapes, in a painting of a fox hunt.

"If they'd throw all this garbage out," I told Jason. "They could hose off the place."

"Just don't look in the bathroom," he said. "And please don't look under the beds." He turned on the fan, but the power was out.

"At least it's pretentious here, what with those dolled-up servants," I said. The employees wore turbans, stiff, white uniforms with gold braids, and white gloves—outfits ostensibly designed to make them sweat better.

"Mom," came from the bathroom, "the toilet doesn't flush, would you call somebody? There's a phone in the hall."

I sniggered. "What makes you think the phone is real?" and of course it wasn't, but one of the tip-toeing servants promised to send up a boy to fix the tank. Jason had, in the meantime, discovered a bucket behind the tub. The "boy," a man in his thirties, arrived half an hour later with a carafe of boiled water and two glasses. "Sahib, Memsahib...."

Later, in the pleasant dining room, the service of a watery five course meal was a comical pantomime.

Afterwards, outside the guarded compound, we were back in the real Calcutta. Near the gate, a woman, four children, and an old man lived on the pavement, their bodies emaciated except for the woman's milk-rich breasts. The man was asleep on a piece of cardboard. Only the infant in his mother's arms was ignorant of their plight. While we walked down Sudder Street, one of the children put his hand in Jason's and tagged along as far as the corner. When he turned back, Jason stared after him with the look of one who had lost something valuable.

"Cute little tyke," I said. It sounded banal. What I meant was, I'm sorry, I know how it makes you feel.

The road was scattered with animal dung and slime. Exhausted half-dead dogs vied with exhausted half-dead people for a place out of harm's way. Rats would have owned the street if it hadn't been for the traffic.

As we turned onto Chowringhee, pocket-sized children were nearly trampled by the slow moving mass of people. Countless feet stepped over a boy lying on the sidewalk. His left leg was folded behind his head grotesquely. Next to him sat his begging bowl. Western-style stores with expensive merchandise behind bright windows made a bizarre backdrop for the stalls of street merchants who sold everything from ballpoint pens to sweets.

"Let's bring the kid some food," Jason said.

He pushed me toward one of the food stalls where we

asked the wallah to put *samosas* and *gulab jamun* in paper contain-
ers. I couldn't imagine how the twisted child could eat, but that
immediate problem was solved by an old man who held up sorry
hands for us to fill with the child's food. The destitute must be
opportunistic—while the old man was inspecting supper, kids
crowded around. He quickly wrapped the food again and shuffled
off. But the kids knew they were on to something.

"This could take all night!" I felt somewhat panicky at the
numbers.

"Let's go in there. They'll follow us," Jason indicated a
restaurant.

"Great! I'll order dinner for three thousand!"

Jason asked the proprietor to fill several platters with fried
chicken, rice, and dal, enough for the little kids who followed us in
and now sat by twos and threes to a chair, filling their dirty little
hands with food and eating as fast and as much as they could. We
ordered *lassi,* a yoghurt drink, for them, then sneaked away.

"That was fun," I said. "I hope they're not shooed off
before they're done."

"We still have to buy something for that kid."

"Listen, how about tomorrow? I'm dead on my feet. We'll
start another swarm."

"You want him to wait until you're rested?"

"Jason, you're not being realistic."

"Realistic?"

We bought a small amount of finger food and offered it to
the child. He fell on it greedily, never taking his eyes off the
drumstick in his hands. He was about five years old and naked
except for filthy, torn drawers. He ate lying down, as the leg that
had grown behind his neck prevented him from sitting upright.
Jason supported his body so that he could drink a little, and guiltily
I feared that the child might pass on an illness to my son. I was
also in a squatting position, handing pieces of food to the little boy.
He never once looked at me. I stroked his cheek. He'd been dealt a
bum hand, but his problem was too big for me.

We had become the conspicuous center of a large crowd.

"Leave us alone!" Jason yelled. "Haven't you ever seen a
kid eat?" Some people giggled; they kept watching. It was as

though we were putting on a show.

"Mom, I bet you could get them to give him money."

"You want me to take up a collection?"

"I want you to beg," he said earnestly.

"Jason, you've flipped. You do it."

"I will, if you hold him. At least then they'll leave."

"What the hell." I picked up the begging bowl and got out of my crouching position. There was an almost imperceptible backing up of the onlookers.

I held up the empty bowl. "Well? How about a few rupees?" The money began to leave the pockets. The poor gave to the poorer. There were only coins, but there were many givers. The bowl filled up quickly, then the spectators dispersed. But now a funny thing happened. I took out a five-rupee note and put it near the child, on top of the coins. At the sight of paper money the little contortionist unwound, grabbed the money and hid it in his crotch! He sat perfectly straight, looking a little dazed.

"Gotcha!" I laughed, happy things weren't quite as bad as they seemed, but actually it was he who had gotten me.

"They don't stop at anything here," Jason said, horrified. He knew children were used for motives worse than survival. But knowing and seeing weren't the same thing.

"In a way I feel even more sorry for him now. Let's get out of here, Mom."

A few minutes later we were curious to know if the boy had looped himself again, and retraced our steps. We found his mother with him, taking charge of the finances.

There was pathos in the intensely human quality of the city. At night its pulse slowed, its breath cooled, and its tears changed to jewels in the glow of kerosine lanterns. With the softening of colors, reality turned to dream, the vendors' shouts changed to chants.

We eavesdropped on the miracle of human endurance in the slums but remained outsiders. The dramas taking place behind closed doors were in the paper the hotel provided with "bed tea" in the morning. Gruesome stories of brides set afire by inlaws demanding ever larger dowries. Dowry deaths transcended economic status; both the poor and the rich wanted more. The rich bought off the law; nobody bothered about the poor. And the girls burned. There were stories of women sold, two, three times, while bribed policemen looked the other way; of widows kicked out like dogs; of children sold to foreign countries; of people who sold a kidney for hope, for one more chance....I read this and I thought humanity has no future. For although the nature of our crimes changed from continent to continent, the size of our greed was the same.

We awoke late and in a stupor, with nausea and pounding head aches. Outside our door the bed tea had been left to grow a gray film. I thought it time to leave Calcutta. In the few days that we'd been here, we'd had to have the toilet tank and the cold water faucet replaced and a rat executed; we had coped with endless power outages; and now we were sick. We were aware of smoke coming in through the window, but since we avoided our room as much as possible and dropped off to sleep as soon as we hit our beds at night, we had accepted the smoke as another British quirk. Now Jason sat on the edge of his bed, rat colored. I leaned out the window to try and discover the source of the fumes. There, in the alley, smack under our window, I saw an open boiler smoking away with a pile of smouldering coal ashes next to it. We were being gassed!

"God Almighty, Jason, there's an open furnace here. Get up, we're checking out. We're breathing carbon monoxide!"

"Oh Mom, you can't smell carbon monoxide."

"We smell the smoke. It's the carbon monoxide that knocks us out. No wonder we have headaches."

Furious, I stumbled downstairs in my robe and demanded to see the proprietress.

"You have missed breakfast, but the boy can bring up tea and toast," she said graciously. I told her politely about the boiler. She nodded sympathy, all the while comforting her poodle while my son was getting brain damaged. They needed the boiler for hot water, she told me. How else could they run an efficient hotel? I must have noticed that the Indian government was incapable of keeping the power on for more than a few hours per day. She would give us another room away from the alley, but unfortunately everything was full. Perhaps tomorrow. We should sleep with the door open.

"It is absolutely impossible to wait for oxygen until tomorrow; we're checking out."

"I'm afraid you won't find anything better today; it's after eleven already. As for us," she kissed the little dog on its nose, "we're always glad to be home. Do you know we haven't set foot outside the hotel for two decades? Other than in the car, I mean. It's intolerable out there. Disgraceful! Unfit for decent human beings."

My head was bursting. This woman was crazy. Everything was crazy. I was crazy.

We hired a taxi and did the rounds, looking for another place to stay. Calcutta traffic offered about the same chance of survival as another night with the boiler. Our driver felt harassed by the frequent stops at seedy hotels without parking space. He got into a fight with another driver about a spot and after that told us to take our problems elsewhere. We tried a few more hotels and guest houses on foot; everything was full.

"We could go home," I suggested.

"You know we'll never get a flight. And we'll miss going to Mother Teresa's Mission. I thought you were so anxious to go there tomorrow."

"I'm just trying to stay somewhat alive."

We returned to the hotel and pleaded with the owners to kill the fire under the boiler after eleven at night, but instead it was decided we would sleep out in the hall until a room became available.

There were places in Calcutta where you could get away from the pressure for a while, as on the wide and grassy Maidan. Haughty English architecture and nice lawns were an escape from the sweltering masses, but didn't hold our interest long. We returned to the underworld of slums, walking hot miles in yellow-fouled air, courting the downside of life. In an alley, we squeezed through a wall of stench past a man up to his waist in a sewer, his arms pasted with excrement. Flies sucked the pathetic blood of sleeping babies—small curled-up bundles that would be the brides and grooms of tomorrow, making more babies. Life raged in the slum; as we strolled among the people, it was not only poverty that we saw, but strength and energy and affection as well.

Later that afternoon we found ourselves at a ghat on the Hooghly river. Numbed into silence, we watched a legless boy moving down the ghat with speed and bright laughter.

The river received all human waste; along its edges sludge rippled in tired patterns. Discarded altar blossoms bobbed madly downstream and vanished in the haze. A headless human cadaver rode by, another of a million untold stories.

To avoid sickness, we made it a point not to eat or drink anything away from the hotel, so around supper time we returned there. Delicious smells wafted over Sudder Street where food was prepared in sidewalk cauldrons. The hotel food invariably smelled of turnips. We sat on the terrace drinking beer, waiting for the gong to announce dinner. Frequently, other guests joined us for an hour of make-believe under the blooms of bougainvillea, catered to by the white-gloved waiters. Not surprisingly, there were no Indian guests staying at the hotel.

Evenings we bought food for the family living on our street. The mother was sweet and dignified as she received the greasy bags. We never saw the children's father, and the old man was always asleep. She awakened him and fed him first. It was certain that soon she would have one less mouth to feed. Why, after the grace of our first slender breath, were we compelled to struggle for the next?

That was evidently not a question Mother Teresa presumed to ask. She was too busy keeping house for God. And what a house! It was quiet at the Mission, cool and clean. Nuns in white, blue-trimmed sarees dispensed medicine, scrubbed floors, changed diapers, taught school. We went up a stone staircase and entered a room with about twenty cribs. Some held more than one child. These were thrown away children, suffering from "failure to thrive" syndrome in addition to the usual diseases of neglect. A few cried but without the passion my own babies had put into their crying. Hesitantly at first, I picked up a frail body and walked up and down the room with the tiny warm face leaning in my neck. The crying stopped. A triumph! Jason held a dull-eyed girl on his knee as if he'd been an uncle all his life. His whole being was concentrated on the anemic little heap on his lap. I looked on with satisfaction.

The nuns went about their quiet routine, tolerating us. We touched and smiled and changed nappies. No Pampers here, but remnants of colored cotton. And no washing machines. How did they manage? In the dining area, volunteers fed infants and toddlers with that same mystical calm. A young English girl sat, tailor fashion, on the tile floor; a tin bowl with a mixture of rice and dal stood near her. She had the pure skin of English rains. Light leaked in above her head, casting pearly accents on the blond spirals that had escaped from her braids, as in a Vermeer painting. The severely retarded boy in her arms couldn't hold up his head. She pushed the food back into his mouth, over and over, until it didn't dribble out anymore. She kissed him.

"You are such a good boy," another kiss, "Annie loves you so much!"

The child was out in space like an orphaned bird. Annie filled his belly, but his eyes remained empty. She took another pinch of mush between her fingers and guided it between his miniature lips.

"He's doing so much better," she bubbled "You should've seen him when I first came, two months ago. I say, why don't you come 'round tomorrow? Mother Teresa will be here, you can meet her."

Later, we stopped by the chapel; the mumbling of the kneeling nuns followed us out into the merciless Calcutta streets.

Jason wanted to take the training course for volunteers and work at the Mission in Delhi. "Then I won't have to wait ten years before I can be useful," he said.

I answered, "Uhuh."

What was the point of nursing these human remnants? To help them grow up so they could breed another generation in their image? And who decided which child would get that chance? My feet fell into a tempo, "he loves me, he loves me not, he loves me...." Chance and luck. He loves me not.

"Can you believe we'll meet Mother Teresa tomorrow?" Jason said excitedly. He was full of purpose now; he didn't need my sighing. "We should go early; maybe they'll let us help a little again."

"Maybe."

"You don't sound pleased."

"Well, it's the magnitude of the problem. Bracing the Tower of Pisa with a toothpick."

"I try not to see it that way," he said in his superior manner. Snotnose. He was wearing a kind of Indian pajama that made him look even taller and thinner. He kept walking a step or two ahead of me, so that I was constantly trotting in his wake.

"Slow down, will you? I'm getting sick of you setting the pace and me struggling on behind. I should have taught you manners."

"You're free to go as fast or as slow as you want. Don't blame me. And besides, manners are a meaningless middle class idea."

He slowed down though. We kept a stubborn silence. My irritation slowly changed to sadness. It was true we were moving at different paces now. He was ready to take on the world and I was withdrawing. Well, he would find out all too soon. When I was a kid I used to bury dead sea gulls. I spent hours in the dunes after North Sea storms, looking for them. Give them a decent send-off. Now *there* was something useful. I took Jason's arm.

"Life is ridiculous," I said, "when you look at the big picture."

"Which you can't." He was still angry with me, didn't want me hanging on his arm.

"You're trying to bludgeon your emotions to death, Mom, you and Dad. You think you're being so rational and clever. Dad's always pontificating about education and he doesn't even know what it means! I've learned more here about life and about myself than I can learn from some—some professor!"

"You're here because of your professor father, kid."

"Oh gimme a break!"

Big silence. I let go of his arm. He was half a step ahead, conscientiously keeping that distance between us. Then he mumbled, "Don't do it, Mom. It'll make you old."

"I used to bury sea gulls."

"What?"

"I did. I used to cry a lot."

"You're still crying."

"What makes you so smart?"

"You did. You made me look at things up close. Bugs and leaves. Poems."

"Oh...."

"Don't get soupy. So we'll do babies tomorrow?"

"We'll do babies."

We were small creatures suited to small deeds. I liked boundaries, small gestures. What could I have been thinking of?

"We can be there by nine," I said.

-20-

Magic Happens

The evening after our visit to the Mission we had dinner with an American family, a mother and two daughters. Their ample femininity was restrained in too tight jeans and bulging tee shirts. When the watery soup arrived, the pretty, bored-looking teenage girls stuck their gum under the table and ladled listlessly.

Jason wasn't eating, his face was flushed. He excused himself and went upstairs. After dinner, I found him on his cot in the hall, burning with fever, contorted with cramps. He had vomited and had profuse diarrhea. I called the doctor who was astonished to hear we traveled without antibiotics or even a thermometer. There wasn't much he could do tonight, but he would call early in the morning.

"Keep him hydrated," he said.

A few hours later I was violently seized by the same symptoms. Somehow we got through the night, cruising between our old bathroom and our cots in the hall. If possible, we were sicker in the morning, and weaker.

The doctor came to our room before eight. He was a reserved man in his forties, wearing dark slacks, a white shirt open at the collar and with the sleeves rolled up. His expert hands touched us with great delicacy. There was an elegance about Indian physicians I had noticed before. After some probing and blood pressure taking, he whistled through his teeth.

"Very low pressure indeed. Do you have an antiseptic?"

Jason carried rubbing alcohol with him to clean his violin strings. The doctor broke a small glass vial and filled two syringes.

"Do you have any cotton?" We had Kleenex.

The examination was interrupted by trips to the bathroom to have what the doctor referred to as "motions." He would arrange a quiet room for us and set up laboratory tests at his clinic. We were to take a taxi there immediately.

I fainted at the clinic and woke up on a stretcher. Later, the doctor showed up again at the hotel, in our new room, with the necessary drugs—Crocin, Balargan, Maxeron, Flagyl, Bactrym, Lomotil, and Megcid. We were to keep a chart of drug taking, temperature, and motions. He gave us injections of vitamin B-something and got a boy to buy coconuts, of which we were to drink the juice.

This routine continued for several miserable days: doctor visits twice a day, vitamin shots, coconut juice. The lab tests showed we had amoebic dysentery as well as a bacterial infection, and that Jason was in worse condition than I was. Initially. After four days he stood up like a newly born foal, thin as a stick, and remembered we were supposed to fly to Ranchi that very day.

"We've got to find someone to go to Indian Airlines to cancel our flight," I groaned.

"I'll do that myself," he said.

"No, Jason, you can hardly walk. You haven't eaten...." I didn't have the energy to care about a refund or anything else. I was nauseous and still had a fever. "Maybe Doctor Chatterjee knows what to do." I'd been infantilized under the doctor's paternal care.

"Come on, Mom, we're not the only sick people in Calcutta! We can't bother him with a stupid thing like that. I'm feeling okay. I'll just cancel our flight and book for Delhi. When do you think you can travel?"

"How should I know? I can't be away from a bathroom...."

"In two days, okay? We've got to get home, no matter what. This stinkhole only makes us sicker."

I turned away, on the verge of tears. I had difficulty walking as far as the bathroom. How did he expect me to get on a plane? He sat on the edge of my bed; the rocking of the spring made me dizzy.

"Come on, Mom," he said, running the back of his hand

over my face. "We're leaving in two days. I'll be back as soon as I can."

He put the bottle of lukewarm water within my reach, looked down at me, and shrugged. I heard the door close softly, his footsteps fade away.

When I woke up, my fever had broken and I was drenched. Groping for my watch, I knocked over the water bottle. I raised myself a section at a time, watched dark flecks racing around the room, got things into focus, and stumbled to the bathroom. I began to sponge myself under the thin trickle from the faucet. How could I have gotten so thin in only four days? I put on fresh underwear and a tee shirt, then lay down on Jason's bed, as my sheet was soaked with sweat. It was four-fifteen; Jason had been gone for three hours instead of one. I knew about Indian bureaucracy, it was slow. But three hours? Maybe he hadn't been able to find a taxi. Maybe....no, Jason could look after himself, he'd be okay. I tried reading. One of the people from the kitchen brought coconut juice and a piece of toast.

"What time do you have?" I asked, hoping my watch was wrong.

"It is half past four, exactly."

Jason had been gone for three hours and fifteen minutes.

By six I sat hunched in a miserable heap. Anything could have happened. I was too fearful of the truth to call the police to tell them my son had been gobbled up by Calcutta. My fever shot up again. As in a dream, I was unable to answer when someone knocked. I stared wild-eyed at the door as it opened slowly to admit Dr. Chatterjee.

"What's wrong?" he said, dropping his bag and taking me by the shoulders. I was still in suspended animation. He shook me gently.

"Where's Jason?"

That was the magic word. I succumbed to full-blown hysteria, slobbering all over the dear doctor. He sat down on the bed, stroking my back while I sprung another well of tears on his white shirt. Then he lowered me gently on the pillow, gave me two shots and told me to rest. He would wait for Jason. "Be not concerned. Nothing has happened to him. He's been detained at the airline office and couldn't secure transportation during the rush hour."

"But he's still ill...." I felt the sedative taking hold.

"He's young. You Americans are strong!"

My muscles were limp now, but my mind couldn't let go of Jason. I closed my eyes. Dr.Chatterjee was reading *India Today*.

"Do you think we should call my husband," I asked, but the doctor didn't answer, so maybe I hadn't really asked him. I wondered if he was still in his chair, next to the bed, but was too tired to check.

Now I heard whispering. I saw Jason's blue shirt. "Jay?" He didn't answer. I bit my tongue and tasted the metallic taste of blood. I was awake, I did see him.

"Jason!" I said as loud as I could. The sound came from a great distance.

"Sh, go to sleep, Mom, I'm talking to the doctor. I'll tell you everything when you're out of your fog."

"Don't leave."

In the middle of the night he told me his story, lying belly down on the bed.

"First I stopped at Dr. Chatterjee's to get a note saying you are too sick to fly."

"You thought of that?"

"Uhuh. I took a rickshaw to the airlines. For the next hour I was bounced back and forth between the circulation desk, the duty officer, and the reservation manager. Finally the duty officer told me he would cancel the tickets. The penalty was a hundred percent, because of "no show.""

"What would be the point of that?"

"No kidding. I pleaded with the reservation manager, who wrote a note regarding the refund and sent me back to the duty officer. He studied the note and the tickets carefully, and came up with the notion that only your ticket was refundable, as the note didn't have my name on it!"

"Good God! Then what?"

"Luckily the reservation manager happened to pass by; he told him to refund both tickets."

"At last. You must have been exhausted!"

"Well, it was pretty hot there. Anyway, the reservation manager made me write a formal letter of application—in triplicate of course—requesting the refund. I wrote a stupid note that will no doubt stay in the active file for two hundred years. Then a clerk began to work the computer in earnest, asking the other agents about the all important "procedure." Then she disappeared. I was terrified, because I still had to book for Delhi, and it was ten past six. Finally someone started to slam stamps on everything, and I thought the end was in sight. But they'd made a mistake and had to start over."

"No!"

"After that, all the papers had to be approved by a supervisor, who read them as slowly as he could, hoping to find a snag."

"I'm proud of the way you handled everything, Jay."

"I didn't get the refund."

Surely he was joking? I couldn't see his face in the dark, but he sounded too tired to make jokes.

"And one more thing. Somebody forgot to install cooling systems in the computers, so every desk has a huge fan, and papers are blowing all over the place. The doctor said you were upset." He yawned.

"It was boring to be sick alone. I missed you," I said.

On the day of departure, Jason set his jaw in that way he has when he's unstoppable. I felt obliged not to whine though my heart broke with self-pity.

The taxi got stuck in a traffic jam. The heat and the fumes were almost unendurable. Out on the street the agony of the Indian poor was unmitigated. My own tribulations helped me relate to the defenseless people scurrying about; it was easier now to grasp the tiredness in their bones, the hollow in their bellies. But I couldn't imagine living my life this way. The taxi moved on.

While waiting for the plane at Dum Dum Airport, we caved in on a bench. The lounge was clean, modern, uncrowded. From my supine position, I saw silk sarees brush the floor and bare feet in sandals scuff by. There was a soothing hum of disembodied voices. Then a pair of Nikes stopped before me, and another, larger pair. My eyes traveled up jeans, I sat up, and was vexed to recognize the Americans from the hotel. They were in a jovial, back-slapping kind of mood. The mother's bikini underpants were visible through her dress. They were all masticating. They'd had a great time in Calcutta and were now going to see the Taj Mahal.

"Right," I said. "That'll be nice."

Jason took no responsibility for these women; he pretended to be asleep. The women's warmth was genuine; I kept myself decently upright for a friendly conversation until they sauntered off in search of drinks.

My seat in the plane was next to the mother. The weather was unstable and the aircraft leapt through the sky; each dip left my insides in worse condition. I felt close to swooning, an almost pleasant escape, since I had stopped fighting my karma for the time being.

"Do you mind if I put my hands on you?" the woman asked.

"Not in the least," I said politely.

She leaned toward me and put her hands on my stomach. Laughing inwardly, I wondered what people might think. I thought it pretty weird, but became so tranquil, that even the bobbing of the plane didn't matter any more. My stomach began to glow and I was saturated with well-being. The warmth spread, comforting, soothing. I lost track of time.

The woman removed her hands and leaned back in her seat. My relaxation was complete.

When the glowing began to fade, perhaps after twenty minutes, I realized I had to thank her, because miraculously my sickness seemed to be gone. A biblical event! Or was I dreaming again?

"How did you know I was sick?" I asked, and at that moment realized she also knew I had judged her and her daughters meanly. I felt the blood rise to my face. She smiled.

"My whole body was glowing, how did you do it?" I touched her hands. They were cool. "But your hands, they felt like the sun!"

"Everybody says that," she laughed.

"But...."

"How do you feel now? How's your abdomen?"

"Well, I can't believe it! I feel great! What did you, I mean, why did you, what I mean is...."

"You'll have no more problem now. You're a very strong person, but not physically."

Her rich voice seemed to be amplified by a vast chamber, like chords on a cello, when she told me about her "healing hands."

"Calcutta was a privilege. It went very well. Jenny's getting very good. She's only fifteen, you know." Rolling r's, deep vowels.

"I never heard of healing hands. When did you know you had them?"

"I always knew. But I had to teach the girls."

I was going to hate myself for not asking more questions, but it didn't seem the right thing to do. Besides, my very words lay languid in my throat.

"You're very kind," I managed.

"People are so good to us! We travel all over the world, working our hands." She held them palms down on her knees, spread her fingers, curled them, then linked them together.

"There was a girl in Norway. Cancer all over her body. Metastasized to the liver. Bald like a new-born mouse. They try to cure with sledge hammers. I sat with her for three days. Seeing her as she was before she became sick. Then I slept. Yes. She's getting married next month."

Joe was not going to believe this. You were already getting better, he would say it was coincidental. Of course her hands felt warm against your stomach, what's so odd about that? Or maybe you imagined it. After all that fasting. But I would never forget. Not ever.

I saw her once more at the Delhi airport, sitting patiently on her baggage, chewing. I didn't even know her name. When I related my strange experience to Jason, he only shook his head. He was too saturated with impressions to take in one more wonder.

We were back where we first met India. The beggars looked almost like old friends now. I felt my own pockets bulge with invisible, lasting treasure. As we drove along the sultry roads, I saw the same things differently. There was a familiarity in the snake charmers, the nattily uniformed school children, the rag pickers, the bathing at neighborhood wells. I was meeting India on its own terms.

In front of the Institute, life at the piggery was going on as before, except that the family had grown. A healthy sow was nursing a row of piglets with the usual brood of birds picking her back clean. When the taxi turned into the driveway, the smiling guard waved us on. Faculty children sat on the steps, and a group of graduate students played ping pong. Pink and white blossoms softened the severe outline of the guest house.

"Hello Sir! Hello Sir!" we were greeted by Arun, the cook. "Go tell Sir!" he ordered another man, taking our backpacks from us. Someone ran to alert Joe of our arrival.

"Arun, when will you stop calling me 'Sir'?" I grinned.

"Guests is Sir!" he beamed, slapping Jason on the back. "Sir is getting so narrow! He did not eat?"

"I'm so glad to be home," said Jason.

And then there was Joe. He came running down the path, book in hand, half the staff on his heels.

Under the approving eyes of the onlookers, the three of us bundled into a complicated embrace. Coming home was always the best part of the trip.

-21-

Earth, Air, Fire, Water

Three weeks after our return from Calcutta, we managed to get together the necessary visas and trekking permits for Nepal. It took several days of cruising Delhi by rickshaw and waiting in bureaucratic lines, but it got done.

Under the circumstances I was surprised that Joe had not protested what promised to be a rigorous trip; we had barely regained our strength after the Calcutta debacle. Probably we had caught him off guard, immersed as he was in research. I mentioned to Jason that we were lucky to have his father's support for the undertaking. He grunted something.

"We'll be out of touch for over a month, you know," I insisted, thinking this kid's getting pretty jaded.

"Uhuh."

"And he has to stay home alone and work. And worry about us all the time."

"He doesn't. I don't think he cares where we go or what we do, as long as it doesn't interfere with his work."

"Of course he cares. He's just no dictator."

"And he knows when you have something in your head you won't let go."

"He never complains about the money we spend, Jay."

"He'd rather pay up than waste time arguing."

I wasn't pleased that Jason thought his father didn't worry about our well-being. Joe had always left the care of the children to me—ostensibly, as long as things got done for them, it didn't matter who did them. That didn't translate into indifference; he'd gotten used to my arranging things, and gave too much credence to my common sense. Of course, to Jason he gave the impression of being detached. Jason knew full well that I would have badgered him with every possible calamity that could befall him in Nepal if I were staying behind. He knew I would stand weeping at the gate with a thousand last-minute, useless words of wisdom. And deep down, he knew Joe cared, but he needed to hear it.

I thought it ironic that when Joe and the staff saw us off, the cook reassured me: "Don't worry about Sir, we will take care of him good." Goodness sakes.

The sky was of the purest blue when we flew into Kathmandu. From the air, one could behold the entire Annapurna range with its fathomless chasms and soaring galleries of frozen wilderness. The sheer magnitude of the Himalayas was beyond human conception. My brain, at least, felt incapable of keeping pace with what my eyes were seeing. It's what separates us from other animals, our response to the glories of our planet. How very privileged we were to be in this magnificent place! What could Jason, at sixteen, do for an encore?

Outside the small friendly airport, we were overwhelmed by eager entrepreneurs, though not with the frenzied prodding we'd come to expect in India. The taxis were strikingly ancient. We put ourselves in the hands of a dignified, albeit tenacious, young man who delivered us to the modest hotel we'd requested.

Our room was rather more humble than I'd had in mind; still, we were in Kathmandu! Our first task was the hiring of a porter for our trek. We had to carry most of our food for a month as well as cold weather gear. It would be difficult to carry a heavy load at high altitude, and it didn't take much of a sales pitch from the trekking company to convince us to hire two porters. It was less clear how we became the employers of a guide and a cook as well, but eventually we were grateful for them.

The guide's name was Sambhu. I believed Sambhu had his doubts about the success of the expedition though he didn't exactly say so. He came to our hotel room to inspect our gear, and it was obvious he had more confidence in its utility than in mine.

"How old you are?" he asked, and shook his head. "Mother very old."

"Ha!" I said.

Two days later, we set out with reasonably light packs, twenty to twenty-five pounds. Sambhu had a small bundle of his own belongings. Ranked highest, he wasn't expected to carry a load. Badri, the cook, was responsible for the mess paraphernalia, and the oldest men, Sanu and Manoj, piled their baskets high with food, mountain boots, crampons, tent, sleeping bags, down parkas, stove and fuel, as well as with their own equipment.

Three pleasant days of trekking through the lush, terraced farmland of the Kathmandu Valley brought us to Jiri; the sun had already sunk behind the mountains. Bashed up oil drums and heaps of tires flanked the bleak road, adding to the air of neglect. This would be the largest village until we reached Junbesi, in about four days. We hoped to be at our destination, Cho Oyu Base Camp, three weeks hence, and planned to hike from there to Lukla, where we would take a bush plane back to Kathmandu.

The porters helped pitch our tent, then left to look for their own accommodations. A stream of children, menacing as mosquitos, squashed their snotty noses against the screen and poked their small hands into the nylon, trapping us inside.

Jason lay down without inflating his pad. His hat slipped backwards and, in the moonlight, the curls spilling from it made his head resemble a potted plant.

"I'm too tired to eat, but we should get something to drink," he said. He raised one leg and tried hooking his toe in a ceiling loop, but the bulky socks made it impossible. The gesture got on my nerves.

"We'll have to wait for the porters; we can't leave our stuff unattended," I said.

"I need water," he dropped his leg.

We'd hiked for nine hours on one meal and were dried out from exertion, sun, and wind. Dehydration was an immediate threat and the likely cause of our lethargy.

"Better get the filter then," I told him. While he sat list-lessly rummaging through his pack, Badri squatted in front of the tent with mugs of steaming tea.

Jason sometimes had difficulty justifying the many tasks the porters performed for us. He disliked being privileged. But now we slurped indecorously with Badri looking on, his teeth gleaming like frozen snow. Sambhu was doing a St. Vitus dance to keep the children at bay.

"Maybe not safe here," Sambhu said then, stooping next to Badri. "Better put values in bottom of sleeping bag." He was uncomfortable with the word "stealing" in connection with his countrymen, and gave his crooked smile. "Hotel is better."

Since he had chosen the camp site, this came as a surprise, but we crawled out docilely.

"Tonight, everybody eats in restaurant," Sambhu announced, yanking out the stakes. Two jackals paced nearby, and watched the collapsing tent nervously. The porters helped us carry everything to the Sagarmatha Lodge, where they left us to fend for ourselves. We tossed down our gear and set out to look for vittles.

At the restaurant, we were joined by three Danes; together we waited for our spaghetti in a windowless room above the basket shop. A bald dog and some chickens scurried about; the other trekkers in the tiny restaurant nudged them with their boots. We passed a bottle of Indian beer around, another, then another. Every time I picked it up, it sucked at the grime on the table and made a squelchy sound.

We had introduced ourselves when we sat down with the young men, but I had already forgotten their names. One of them was straw blond and on the brink of tears—reminding me of Jason's first day of kindergarten.

Each of the four makeshift tables in the *bhatti* had a candle rooted in a mound of wax that looked like old city snow. We kept putting our fingers in the soft part near the wick and rolling grey balls between our palms. Jason stuck the caps of the beer bottles into the mound—for fortification, maybe.

The spaghetti was slow in coming. The blond boy was getting more depressed, and with justification. He and I faced the pantry where the cooking was going on. The cook was choking over an open fire, grunting, and spitting on the floor. A girl of seven or so washed the tin plates and glasses, seated on her haunches among chicken droppings and food spills, her greasy dress tucked between her legs. Every once in a while she moved the strands of hair that had fallen over her eyes with a dry part of her arm. She moved slowly, as if in a trance, pushing the leftovers onto a piece of green plastic. Then, dragging the plates through the water in a bowl placed between her feet, she daintily scraped off food with her fingernails. After some finished dishes had accumulated, she changed to a kneeling position and with a brownish-grey rag stuck into the sash of her dress, methodically, dreamily, dried them. A waitress picked them up off the floor to have them loaded with food for the trekkers.

Our waitress was an elderly woman with yellow skin and splayed toes. She had a small, silver ornament embedded in the side of her nose, and smiled proudly at the beauty of the food, showing a single brown tooth. That was when the boy next to me made for the door, mumbling something in Danish. I wanted to leave, too. The noodles smelled of sour milk; the watery sauce was bright pink. Jason looked at me defiantly. He twirled the pasta on his fork, and stuffed it into his mouth.

"It's cooked dead," he said. "Don't worry."

The Danes evidently enjoyed some in-joke; their faces were flushed with laughter. Picking at the pink food, I felt incompetent and spoiled.

Earlier at the Sagarmatha Lodge I had met an English girl who travelled alone with a minimum of gear. She lived like the local people, she said, and didn't need more than they did. I had confessed to our hiring of a four-man crew.

After dinner we creaked up the ladder to our dormitory where a chicken roosted on the top bunk. Jason found this inordinately funny, perhaps because of the beer. Getting crankier by the minute, I sat down on the edge of the bed.

"Can't you even catch a chicken?" I said. He didn't seem capable of grasping more than a handful of feathers.

High with laughter and the chase, he said, "Watch this!" He pointed a finger at the brown bird, commanding, "Down girl!" It fluttered its wings defiantly. "Sit!" he yelled, and, somewhat unfairly, I thought, threw his 150 lbs on the bird. He missed, and she strutted out of the room.

"I always do this before I go to bed," he said.

"I wish we'd stayed in the tent, damn it; this place makes me itchy."

I was up early, trying to avoid the latrine, but already people were about. I strolled down the sandy road and washed my hands and face at the village well, using my long skirt for towel. A girl dumped her laundry on the wet gravel near the well. Others filled earthenware pots and carried them home on their heads, hips rolling, bosoms high. I sat down on a low wall and started to write in my diary.

"Where you go, Lady?" asked a little boy. I pointed east.

"What you write, Lady?" I handed him the diary. He brought it close to his eyes, sniffed it, then paged through it slowly. He did this with exaggerated respect, as though the seedy little book were precious. Without a word, he returned it and hopped away, crossing and re-crossing the drainage ditch that ran through the village.

"We're going, Mom." Jason had already loaded up. "Guess what our landlord charged for the chicken coop."

"Hadn't we agreed on ten rupees?"

"He asked for twenty-five. I told him ten or nothing. He was so disgusted he took nothing."

"Why bicker over a few cents?"

"It's the principle. How many times do I have to tell you? The baskets and stuff were eighty rupees, Sambhu said."

The porters had needed new baskets, tumplines, and plastic covers to throw over the gear. Baskets are used to transport goods through the mountains. There are almost no roads in Nepal; the villages are supplied by "porter train." Tumplines are bands leading from the basket around the forehead, to shift the weight to the head. This way porters can carry more than half their weight over long distances.

Around Jiri the trail and nearby scrub were covered with human excrement; we had to be choosy about where to place our feet. After several hours of hiking uphill, we reached the summit of a minor pass, where we found three huts surrounded by rhododendron trees; Sambhu called a halt. As usual, he arranged with one of the housewives for a place to rest and asked permission for Badri to use the cooking fire. I photographed the children, who had clearly been through the routine before—they posed with coquettish professionalism. Never mind they were gorgeous with their sunflower faces and hot-pink dresses.

Inside the hut was a single platform with some covers where the entire family slept. A few metal cups hung on the wall and off to one side was a place on the earthen floor for a fire. Aside from a three-legged stool, there was no furniture. Most Nepali mountain cottages have no chimney, so that the small rooms fill with smoke. The women and children, who spend much of their time indoors, cough constantly. When I questioned Sambhu, he explained that a chimney would make the hut too cold.

After my eyes adjusted to the semi-darkness, I noticed a small altar in a corner. On a carpet of blood-red rhododendron petals sat a statue of the Buddha, its shiny gold and crimson robes illuminated by a shaft of sunlight every time someone opened the door.

Badri's porridge had not agreed with me. I kept having to run for the bushes. Always, when the porters saw Jason standing alone on the trail, they hung back discreetly.

"You'd better take a Bactrim, Mom," said Jason. "You probably caught something."

"I'll do a ten-day stint of the little devils, don't worry," I said. But I wasn't sure whether Bactrim was the right drug.What if I had picked up an amoeba?

Around mid-afternoon we reached another pass. We were at 8000 feet and had our first spectacular view of the peaks.

Sambhu said, "Half hour we rest."

The porters put down their loads and all of us sat leaning against our packs, looking into infinity. Jason and Sambhu identi-fied some of the peaks, Sambhu's voice happy and proud. He was only twenty-one years old, but he understood the mountains—their loveliness, but also their inaccessible, icy indifference.

We hadn't had much rapport with the porters. Except for Sambhu, they spoke no English. Since we shared neither food nor quarters, and usually walked some distance ahead of them, it was hard to become friends. But now, with all six of us under the mountains' spell, we began to sing. First Manoj, and then Sanu, the reserved one, chimed in with his rumbling bass. We sent our waves of celebration through the mountains, chanting a rowdy "Annapurna! Dhaulaghiri! Machapuchare-e-e!"

Jason and I looked at each other, satisfied that finally all of us had become a team.

"Ready to move on?" I asked him.

Every time we put the packs back on, Jason had to go through his checking routine: "Am I zipped up? My axe on tight?" Sometimes he would follow up with: "You sure?" if he suspected insincerity on my part.

On the downhill I kept track of my miseries: my left knee and queasy stomach. We passed through several villages of three to five huts, raising folded hands in greeting and exchanging the Nepali, "Namaste!" Sambhu was never far behind, keeping an eye on us to make sure we stayed on the right trail, which was mostly unavoidable, except when we got lost and he was nowhere in sight. He usually ended the trekking day before everybody was exhausted. Jason and I protested. As true Westerners, we felt obliged to move until we dropped.

"No," Sambhu said in his sing-song English, "Here we stay."

"The next village is only two miles away," I said, waving the map, "and it's only three thirty." All I got for that was a half-smile and a look at his back. We learned, slowly, to trust his judgment.

The village was Shivalaya and looked like a Swiss high mountain village with its stone and mud cottages, cheery verandas and porches. And there was a river! I dug up the shampoo and clean undies and set out with Jason along the edges of the gardens for a decent distance from civilization.

We had done so much camping together that we knew our respective routines. A dollop of shampoo on my dry hair would do for me, then he would take the bottle and look for privacy elsewhere, while I began to soap up. The icy water stung my skin, but I would have rolled in the snow to get clean.

The porters had everything ready when we got back; the tent was up and Badri was cooking the main meal of the day: *dalbhaat, chapatis,* and greens. I had a few spoons of rice, but couldn't eat more than that. We asked Badri to boil us some drinking water. Jason had noticed that the filter was leaking; he wanted to wait until daylight to try and see what was wrong with it.

"Please have him boil it for twenty minutes," I told Sambhu, the translator. Badri looked contemptuous at the request. I understood how absurd our ways appeared to him; why could we not drink from the river the way they did? Alone in our tent we felt isolated from their easy comradery.

For a few rupees, the local people opened their houses to travelers, but we preferred the cold tent to the stuffy, smokey huts. Sambhu always placed our camp close to his lodgings.

Without warning the wind came booming over the ridge, threatening to whip the tent to tatters. Jason shouted at me.

"What??" I yelled. I made out the word,"Hold."

"Sure!"

"What?"

I knew the porters were drinking *rakshi,* telling stories. It would be more fun for Jason to be with the young people, and without me he would join them, smoke or not. In the dark, I searched for his hand and received a bone-cracking squeeze.

Suddenly, I saw a light zigzagging in our direction, but before I had worked up a good panic, a voice shouted, "Hello!" Jason unzipped the front flap and more or less hauled Sambhu inside, out of the ferocious wind. He yelled something in Jason's ear, and then Jason cupped his hand around mine.

"He wants to know what we want for breakfast, omelet, soup, egg."

"Oh my God," I said, "That's what he came outside for?"

Jason started his "What?" bit again, so I said, "Omelet."

Sambhu, having read my lips, shook his head. "Too greasy for you!"

"Egg then."

"Hard-boil egg. Twenty minutes!" Sambhu grinned with good-natured ridicule at our fastidious water boiling. Jason poked him in the ribs in quasi-protest.

By the glow of Sambhu's flashlight I could see the aluminum poles of the tent bend with the force of the gale.

"No problem," Sambhu said, following my gaze.

At intervals, all through the restless night, his beam of light played over the roof of our tent.

Every day the terrain became more difficult. The trek we had elected to do, about 175 miles one way, followed the Everest trail as far as Namche Bazaar. We had decided not to go to Everest Base Camp because of its popularity, but instead to try for the foot of Cho Oyu at 18,000 ft. We would be well acclimatized by then, we hoped, especially after resting a day or two in Namche Bazaar, at 11,300 ft.

I was looking forward to a hot shower there. Namche was a busy trading town in the northern Khumbu region of Nepal and boasted a hydro-electric generating station. We would fit out the porters with warm jackets and boots, and take a trip to the monastery in Tengboche before crossing the high pass to view Cho Oyu. At 26,748 ft, Cho Oyu is one of the ten highest mountains in the world, eight of which are in Northern Nepal. Everest, or Sagarmatha, is 29,028 ft.

Since most rivers in Nepal run north-south and are separated by high ridges, our trek eastward was against the grain of the land. The great height of the ridges often made it necessary to spend an entire day either climbing or descending. People of all ages suffered from knee problems, known to porters as "sahib's knee," a malady with which they were not afflicted. We had no major problems—while in Delhi, we had jogged in one hundred degree temperatures and climbed the stairs of the Institute for half an hour each day.

My gut did not respond to several days of antibiotics. I changed to flagyl, which was supposed to cure giardia, a parasite, and amoebic dysentery. I had more or less stopped eating and was losing weight. A major worry was loss of fluids, a serious problem at altitude where one needs a minimum of three quarts of liquid a day to maintain hydration. Nevertheless, our mood stayed upbeat.

One afternoon, when we stopped for a short rest, Sambhu told us the story of his frostbitten foot. He gingerly rolled up his pants and peeled down his sock.

"Oh my God!" Jason covered his mouth with his hand in horror.

"Much better now," smiled Sambhu. We all stared at the black, swollen flesh. Sambhu caressed the foot, as if he were glad he still had it.

"Should he be walking on that, Mom?" asked Jason.

"I don't even see how he can." The sight of the foot turned my stomach. The fellow had been walking on a blood sausage for a few rupees a day, for our entertainment, and hadn't even mentioned it. Sambhu continued to stroke his foot tenderly. I wished it would go back inside the sock.

"Does it hurt much?" I asked.

"Of course it hurts," Jason snapped. "What do you think!"

"No hurt. Okay now," said Sambhu.

The frostbite had happened when an American tourist had insisted they cross a high pass on the Annapurna trek in a snow squall. It had been his first trip to the Himalayas and all his knowledge had come from a guidebook. Sambhu, who had inadequate footgear, had tried to reason with the man. It was dangerous, he'd explained, the mountain would not welcome them.

"You should have told him to go by himself," said Jason.

Sambhu put his boot on. "Okay now," he repeated. The other men's faces turned away. The gate between East and West, rich and poor, had again been bolted with heavy hand. The amber light on the peaks had paled, and I felt chilled.

"Let's go," I said.

We hiked in silence, Jason withdrawn into himself. He had become ever more private and more critical of me. I thought he blamed me for Sambhu's foot, for not being compassionate enough. He walked some distance ahead of me, probably struggling with the great issues of injustice.

Jason shared a meal with the porters that night while I lay licking my wounds in the tent. He was cheerful when he brought me tea and a few crackers.

"Eat one more, Mom," he kept saying, "They're so small you can always eat one more."

"What did you have for supper?"

"You don't want to know; you didn't miss much."

Sambhu came to collect my cup and stayed to chat.

"We make things easy for you," he said in an oily manner. "You pay all the money, then no more worry."

Jason said, "What exactly do you mean?"

It was his job to pay the porters for their daily expenses. In order to simplify his task, he gave them an allowance every three days, and Sambhu kept track of extras. One extra was drinking money. Rakshi soothed tired muscles and was something to look forward to. Their actual wages were to be paid by the trekking company, on completion of the trek. The porters received a fraction of the amount we paid the "boss" in advance.

Sambhu explained that paying them for the month would give us less to worry about. I was somewhat embarrassed, because, really, I didn't care one way or the other, and there was his foot....To my surprise Jason got quite worked up.

"No way!" he shouted. "Just get out of here! Go on," he waved his hand in dismissal. Sambhu didn't move—he looked shrunken. "Do you think we are fools?" Jason said coldly.

Sambhu shrugged, drooping submissively. "Not my idea," he said. "They, you know." He pointed toward the hut, keeping the accusing thumb frozen over his shoulder.

I said, "Tell them they were wrong to make you ask."

He crawled out of the tent. We watched him tuck his chin in his collar and shove his hands in his pockets. From the back he looked old and tired.

"They're in cahoots. You see they don't give a damn about us," Jason said. "You just can't trust them. We should stop buying them booze. They act so sweet when we're around, but they just want our money."

"They have nothing, Jay."

"If he would ask for it, that would be different, but he tried to trick us, Mom. They know you're sick, and if we have to go back to Kathmandu...."

Sambhu had wanted to secure the money for food and lodging for a month whether they would be portering or not.

"But we're not going back, we're going to Cho Oyu," I said.

"I was hoping we could be friends," Jason was obviously upset.

"Well."

"They act like servants. He made a fool of himself." He pulled his sleeping bag over his face.

After a while I said, "Good night, darling," but he didn't hear me.

The incident made everyone uncomfortable; the porters lagged well behind and kept to themselves more than ever. From Namche on, when the trek would become hairy, this arrangement would be untenable—we had to function as a team. Just as I was thinking that this childish squabble could cost us Cho Oyu, Sambhu came over and offered to carry my pack. Clearly he wanted to improve our chances of success by having me preserve my strength. What more generous gesture could he have made?

"Thanks, Sambhu," I handed over my pack, entrusting all our "values," as he called them, to him. I wanted to be a full member of the team and my pride was wounded, but without the weight on my back the going was easier. By noon, we were singing.

In one of the villages, a wedding, complete with music and dancing, was in progress, and we were able to buy a piece of goat meat for the porters. I wished we weren't vegetarians, because Jason's pants were sliding off his hips. At least he didn't have worms. I supposed the porters also had fleas and lice from sleeping under the covers provided by the villagers. We'd seen many people picking lice off each other.

The climb was relentless, but, oddly, I didn't feel particularly bad, though after several days on crackers and tea, I should have been hungry. I kept wondering, did we have to come this far, be this dirty, risk our health, and exhaust our bodies, to learn something new?

"Hey you with the baggy drawers," I called, "You having fun yet? How are you feeling, anyway?"

"I love it here. I could walk forever, except that my blisters burn and my underarms are growing moss."

"Maybe we could raise alfalpha sprouts in them."

"Yuk! You have a dirty mind, Mom."

"Think of the fresh veggies."

"Gross."

We passed a group of barefoot porters, a woman, and two men. Her basket was filled with kindling and topped with fodder.

The load was as tall as she and a good deal wider. Her *kurta* seemed welded to her body and smelled none too nice. One of the men had a metal desk and a brown chest strapped to his back. The others carried cans of cooking oil and Coca-Cola, the latter to sell to tourists. Their legs were sticks with knotted muscles, and the soles of their wide feet had deep fissures from portering over long distances.

"Namaste!"

The porters let us pass them, leaning back on their T-shaped sticks. "Namaste!" they chanted in return. Their grins would melt the icecap off K-2.

Sambhu caught up to tell us we were to stop at the next village. I knew he would stay within earshot now, in case we "forgot" to stop.

"How's your foot?" I asked. The trail was steep and strewn with loose rocks. My calf muscles were hard, my thighs ached.

"No problem." Sambhu's stock answer. He pointed to a valley, "You see?"

"That's where we camp?" I could just distinguish two houses on a tributary. Sambhu told us we were ahead of schedule and would put in a shorter day tomorrow.

Around a bend in the trail we came upon a little boy and his sister, a shepherdess.

"Namaste, Bahini," I said to the maidenly girl, "Hello, Little Sister."

She smiled demurely. Sambhu spoke to her with friendly authority.

"Namaste, Ama," "Good day, Mother," the girl said obediently. She was on the verge of a giggle, probably caused by the two young men who were looking her over. She had wide peasant hips, and her soiled dress was getting tight around her softly swelling chest.

"Ask her what she's knitting," I asked Sambhu. She wouldn't tell him. "Then ask her if I can take her picture."

The little boy was jumping around Jason, who playfully put his hat on him.

"Maybe that's not the greatest idea, Jay," I said, remembering the lice.

"He's so cute!" said Jason, "Look at him dance!"

"You can take picture—I think," Sambhu said uncertainly. I did, in spite of the girl's discomfort. Then I brooded about it and regretted having taken advantage of her shyness.

After Sambhu gave his approval to the site we picked to pitch the tent, all four porters helped level the terrain. They borrowed a shovel at their lodgings, which lay across the stream from our camp. Badri scraped away half-buried rocks with his shoe; Manoj had the shovel, and the others used their hands. This way they managed to create a fairly flat spot. By now the porters were familiar with the tangle of poles and stakes and the freaky-looking rainfly. The tent was up in a minute or two, in spite of the lack of coordination as the six of us snapped poles together and roped down corners. The tent was new for this trip. It had a corridor where we kept our boots and two nooks for sleeping. It was a luxury for Jason to be able to stretch full-length and for each of us to have a good-sized window. The maroon tent had an odd shape and was the object of discussion and head bobbing by the villagers. To the children, it was another foreign eccentricity; they giggled shamelessly.

When the porters left, we readied ourselves for the night; we inflated the sleeping pads, put on extra layers of thermal underwear, and washed up with Wet Ones as bathing would be impossible.

Nepalis are very modest, bodies are kept hidden. I never saw anyone relieve himself, unlike in India where this is regarded as a fact of life. Only the larger villages had latrines. With a chronic shortage of firewood, especially near settlements, every growth that could have provided privacy was burned. This situation made life laborious; I became mildly obsessed with scanning the territory for bushes, and sometimes had to walk a considerable distance in discomfort. Jason patiently accompanied me, for there were always children to keep away. I marveled at his generosity. He was like his father that way — you do what you have to, no point in making a fuss. After a strenuous day, I would have resented making these runs for anybody and certainly would have objected to the frequency.

Our chores completed, we crossed the bridge to the two-story building where the porters stayed. We expected to find Badri working on supper, but there was no one around. Climbing the ladder to their sleeping loft, we fished a package of Knorr soup from the supplies; I had a sudden craving for salt. A man came up to see what we were doing and beckoned for us to come down to the living quarters.

Here, we found a woman of perhaps fifty sitting in front of a fire. She immediately offered her stool. Under slightly drooping eyelids, her eyes resembled buttonholes in her round face. Her lips turned up in a soft pink bow and long braids under a tattered yellow head wrap added to her rag doll appearance. She blew industriously on smoking dung cakes; her husband opened the door when I had a coughing fit. We sat in a circle and smiled at each other. When the woman started tea preparations, I asked Jason to get our own cups.

"Isn't that insulting?"

"Please just do it." I couldn't risk yet another infection. The tea would be boiled, so that was safe enough.

Our hostess took the cups from Jason with a stream of words and put them on a piece of cloth on the floor. We went through a pantomime to explain our interest in the disappearance of the porters, but we weren't convincing. The man kept repeating *chiya* and pointing at the tea preparation.

Finally, Sambhu appeared in the doorway, happier than he'd been for a while. He had been drinking. Jason told him not to worry about supper just yet, that we were fine.

"If no problem, then...."

"No problem," Jason said.

"They must know all the watering holes on the route," I chuckled.

"They're having fun. I'd like to stay here for a while anyway, wouldn't you?"

The man grinned on cue. The skin of his face was stretched over fine bones, like canvas on a frame. He had a humorous twinkle in his small, black eyes.

The tea was thick with yak butter and salt, and probably too rich for my starved insides.

"Mmm, good!" said Jason, and got his cup filled again. I

sipped quietly, utterly content. The dung cakes were bright red, and shadows twisted like Balinese dancers on the mud wall.

Jason sat tailor-fashion, his hands cupped together on his lap as if taking holy communion. His lashes cast a spidery fringe on his cheek. The woman touched his arm.

"Logne," she said, pointing at her husband.

"Logne?" we tried, and they laughed at our pronunciation. She patted her chest: *"Swasni!"*

"I am son," Jason said, and she nodded.

"San. *Chhora.*" Then, targeting me, *"Ama?"*

"Yes," said Jason. "Mother."

Son, mother, husband, wife. It was easy. Earth, air, fire, water. We sat together for a long time, watching the dung cakes burn.

-22-

Sherpa Country

It was a clear day, and we had a good view of Gaurishankar to the north, which for Jason and me was like looking toward the Promised Land. The porters shared in our enthusiasm; it was easy to forget that we were on vacation while they were doing a job.

"Over 7,000 meter," Sambhu said with pride.

"7,150," said Jason. He knew the altitudes, first ascents, and by whom of the major mountains of the world, and could identify them by their contours. Maybe they were gigantic sculptures to him, holy, because of their perfection.

My mind was less orderly, one shape was not more aesthetic than another. What I saw were the shifting hues—violets, shimmering carmine. And the mystique. There were snow leopards in those palaces of ice, places where no human eye had judged, unimaginable secrets....

Heading south along a ridge, we crossed a pass at 8,900 feet after a steep climb. We were now in a region inhabited by Sherpas. Prayer flags fluttered around scattered villages like wings of doves . We stopped at a *chorten*—a Buddhist religious structure —to admire the Tibetan script carved in the tablets, or mani stones. The chorten looked like upside-down chalices.

"Can you read it?" I asked Sambhu. He shook his head. We knew his home region and guessed he was a Hindu. I asked him what he knew about Buddhism.

"All same God," said Sambhu, looking away from the earth, and drawing a wide arc over our heads. "Christmas too."

"Christ," I said. Sambhu realized his mistake, then proved his knowledge of the gospel to us. "Christ love everybody, Nepalese people love everybody. Is good," he said. He stayed behind to wait for the porters, and we began the descent, keeping the Mani stones to our right as the Buddhists do.

"All same God," said Jason. "Mom, he could teach my high school class something. They hate everyone who's different."

"I doubt the porters have accepted our differentness," I said.

"Or we theirs."

"Good heavens."

It was unpleasant to carry on a conversation while picking our way down the slope. I had to strain to hear what Jason said, and my thoughts began to wander. How spread out my family was! Joe in Delhi, Gaia in Scotland the last we heard, and Brett and Karen on their honeymoon in Mexico. We would need a week to get through everybody's slides! If only Joe were with us, I thought for the hundredth time. I hoped we would be able to send him a wire from Namche, as promised. "Having a great time-stop-almost reached destination-stop-your highnesses." He would smile at the highnesses and be proud of us, wouldn't he?

"Even my teachers," said Jason.

"Huh?"

"Forget it," he said irritably.

I backed up to the prejudice topic. He would be brooding, trying to figure things out. Why was I so flighty?

I kept an eye on the low sky; the weather was changing. The porters moved slowly under their loads; we waited for them at a tea shop where we ran into our drinking pals, the Danes. In spite of his abstinence from the pasta, the nervous one was ill with diarrhea. I was shocked to see how thin he had gotten. He slumped on a rock while his friends capered with young male energy.

"Perhaps you'd better fly out," I told him, ambushed by sudden rationality—clearly, the thought had been lurking in my head.

He echoed my own thin expectations: "I think I'll get better."

"I hope so. Keep drinking anyway." I could commiserate; my own symptoms pointed to dysentery.

Jason climbed into his pack. "Am I zipped up? Is my axe on tight?"

"Good luck," the Danes waved good-bye.

It was time for me to grapple with the issue of my health, but instead, I kept repeating the velvet names of Nepal in my head: Sangbadanda, Shivalaya, Chaumrikharka, Kenja Khola....I could walk to eternity, moving my feet, Sangbadanda, Shivalaya....It was like riding a train and rocking my mind to the rhythm of the wheels. We crossed a wobbly suspension bridge with some of the boards missing, and another. On the barren downslope, the porters followed close behind. Every once in a while Jason would look over his shoulder and ask, "Are you okay?"

Not really. My skin sagged and my eyes were popping. I had stopped combing my hair; my lips were swollen and bleeding from ultraviolet radiation.

We'd had good hiking weather the whole trip, but now it began to rain. Sambhu stopped for the night in Dakchu, a few houses at 9,350 ft.

We pitched the wet tent, then joined the porters at their shelter. Not that it was very pleasant there either, but at least the misery was shared. Sanu, who was a quiet man, sat near the entrance of the hut. His apple-red sweatpants failed to compensate for his melancholy features as he watched the fat, grey tears dripping off the roof. Badri was at the creek washing pots and pans, the usual cheery clatter muted by water-soaked air. Sambhu paced back and forth.

"At least it's not snowing," I said.

"Snow later," Sambhu declared.

The lady of the house put down a mat for us and moved her stool close to the smoldering embers, urging me to accept the place of honor. The wrinkles on her face ran in a circular pattern, except on her high cheekbones where her ivory skin was smooth. She was busily hospitable, symbolically rearranging cups, smoothing the mat to welcome us. The warmth relaxed the cold-stiffened plastic of my rain jacket. We smelled like wet animals.

Manoj found comfort in his cigarette, taking a puff, then warming his hands around the butt. Every time he exhaled the smoke, he threw back his head. Always, more smoke seemed to come out than could have gone in. At last he catapulted the butt out of the door and produced a gamy notebook.

"Bonjour. Guten Abend," he said seriously. "Good night, right?" He looked like a man of thirty-five though he was only twenty-eight. Just then, though, in the half darkness, he became a boy again. It was the first time he'd spoken directly to me.

Sambhu grinned, "Buenas noches!"

Manoj tilted his book toward the light and followed what was written with his finger. Among Nepalis, with the world's fourth highest illiteracy rate, these men belonged to the elite. All could read, and each carried a song book.

"How are you?" Manoj continued the lesson, "Merci, c'a va. Et vous?" His silhouette was outlined against the remnants of daylight. "Is right?" he said with confidence. The men had learned these phrases from trekkers. We sang "Frère Jacques" together while our hostess slapped the beat on her thighs with both hands.

I got up to see what a girl was doing in a corner of the room and found she was drawing letters by candle light, the tip of her tongue pressed over her upper lip. Her mother handed me the school paper, then waited for my reaction with her arms akimbo.

The child went to school twice a week, Sambhu told us. It was unthinkable. Here in this forlorn corner of the Himalayas, in a one-room hut without as much as an outhouse, sat a girl in rags, her eyes weepy from the foul air, lining up letters to form English words.

"Eh?" the mother said eagerly, waiting for congratulations. Her daughter coughed wetly, concentrating on her work again.

We chirped, "Wonderful! Unbelievable!" but there was something intensely pathetic about the pencil stub, the mushy candle, the coughing fits. What was she going to do with her English words? She didn't have shoes, a bed of her own. Yet, it was what humans did. I wrote down my story, Manoj learned his phrases.

I couldn't get warm that night, though I wore my down vest inside my sleeping bag and made myself as small as possible to reduce contact with the inhospitable mountain. "Do you realize we're paying for this misery, Jay?"

"Hm."

"Are you cold?"

"Am I alive?"

"Maybe singing will cheer us up."

"Go ahead."

"Let's imagine a hot bath, towels so thick and soft you want to live in them. Sheets smelling of mowed grass. Hot coffee...."

"Go to sleep, Mom, I don't like coffee."

"Cocoa then. Jay?" No answer. That's the way it is with males, I thought, they go to sleep.

Rumbling in my belly woke me; I too had dozed off. The rain no longer pattered on the roof, and deep silence insulated the tent. I leaned on an elbow, groping for the flashlight. I felt nauseous and crampy; I wished I were home. In order to preserve the warmth in my sleeping bag, I folded it over before I got into my frozen-stiff boots. Slowly, I pulled down the zipper of the fly, hoping not to wake Jason. Outside had disappeared. I faced a wall of snow and stared at it idiotically for a moment before realizing we were snowed in. Shoving a shoulder into the fluff, I emerged from the tent.

The sky had cleared. It was a Christmas sky with burning candles. I stood looking at this purified world, overcome with the beauty of it. I'll always have this, I thought, I've seen a Himalayan night.

Lifting my legs high like a heron, I traipsed through the snow, clutching a roll of toilet paper. The spot I so carefully picked turned out to belong to a yak, whom I had overlooked in my haste. I said "Hi," feeling rather silly, squatting with my hat on. His eyes were bulging with bovine profundity. "Excuse me," I said.

The tent had to be dug out. I could hardly get colder, so I swept an avalanche off the roof with my arm.

"What? What are you doing?" came a voice from below.

"Sh, it snowed. I'm afraid there's too much on the fly."

"I'll come and help."

"No. Stay warm, it's nearly done."

I moved my pad close to Jason's and put my hands under his jacket. Still I couldn't stop shivering. He rubbed my shoulders.

"I think I can't go on, Jay." The cramps were back already; I would have to go and see the yak again.

"I know. Do you think you can make it over the pass?"

The highest pass of the trek so far, at 11,582 feet, would

have to be crossed the next day. Then a hard several days lay ahead to Lukla, where the airstrip was. Our tickets would be the wrong date; I hoped we could get a flight out.

"I'll make it. We'll have to tell the porters tomorrow."

"They already know."

"But I just now...."

"I told Sambhu to count on aborting the trip. We have to get you to a hospital, Mom. You haven't eaten, you don't drink."

So now you're making the decisions, I thought.

"Pit stops" became more and more frequent; I had lost all sense of embarrassment. I was relieved the decision to get out of the mountains was made, and sad at the same time. It seemed extraordinary to me that I managed the pass without trouble. We changed to our double boots, which were inflexible, in order to accommodate crampons. The porters we met on the way curled their bare toes around the ice-glazed boulders. They wore cotton jackets and moved sadly through the snow, like Napoleon's retreating army.

From the Lamjura Pass we sloshed down to Taktor where we stopped for soft drinks and food. It was pleasantly warm there. I lay down on a bench to rest, free from worry or thought of any kind. A canticle of children's voices, yapping dogs, and forlorn rooster cries floated by. "No, nothing," I told Jason, who tried to revive my interest in food.

A young girl, who introduced herself as Amy, sat down on the free spot left by my pulled-up knees. She started emptying out her pack, dumping everything in the dirt. Out came a down jacket, which she put under my head. Next thing I knew, I had a straw in my mouth and was sipping Coke. With so many good people in the world, why must we have wars?

"I wish I could tell you how happy it makes me to see you drink," she said. "Please don't stop drinking. Your son is very worried. You've got to try."

Amy was a nurse and confirmed my diagnosis of dysentery while dabbing my lips with salve. Her kind concern for a stranger shook me up enough to begin to feel quite sorry for myself. Our group left before hers did. I didn't thank her for the Coke, but she is stored in my memory bank.

Descending from the alpine to a more temperate zone, the trail continued on the north side of the valley past beautifully cultivated fields of barley, wheat, and potatoes. Closer to Junbesi signs were posted: "Hot showers at the Yak Inn, first on your right." "Private rooms, breakfast, and laundry at Mountain View Hotel."

"Can you believe that, Jay? I wonder why Sambhu didn't tell us?" I was going to have a shower; it was enough to make me cry.

Junbesi appeared prosperous, with its white-washed solid houses. Though it was late in the afternoon, people were still busy cleaning, gardening, and repairing their homes. This was truly a Sherpa village. Thus far, the attitude of the mountain people had seemed one of acceptance. Why was it that in a similar geographic setting, these people lived healthful, comfortable lives, and without having lost their ethnicity, while poverty reigned in most other villages? We were on a main trekking trail—why hadn't everybody taken advantage of tourism? Through ambition and imagination these Sherpas had carved out Shangri La. The children were clean, with soft hair and crisp school uniforms. In spite of the lack of modern conveniences, there was indeed a hot shower. Water was piped all the way from the river, then heated over a fire and hoisted up by pulleys to a wooden platform, from which gravity led it to a shower stall. It was expensive and had to be specially ordered. I went first, groaning with pleasure.

The hotel had a clean bunkroom for us; the porters stayed in a dorm for almost nothing—a customary courtesy the Nepalese extended to their own. There was even a *chaarpi,* or latrine, at the end of the garden, with the usual bucket of water.

A few other trekkers had gathered in a large room downstairs. Lamps were lit and benches placed around the periphery. There was a chimney over the cooking area, so the room was nearly free of smoke. A young boy, alert as a colt, pranced among the guests, trying to keep up with their appetites. He was serving Swiss Miss when we came in, and Jason drank three cups in quick succession. There were potatoes too, more food than any of us had seen for days. To avoid confusion, the guests entered their consumption in a book; bills would be settled at check out.

The specialty of the house was Sherpa Stew, made of fresh garden produce. Trekkers and porters alike were intoxicated by the aroma drifting in from the kitchen. Cheeks were flushed, fish stories abounded. Badri and Sambhu sat with their arms around each other, a gesture of friendship between men. Jason was engrossed in conversation with a stranger reaching no higher than his chest. A lock of midnight hair fell over the man's face; they were gesticulating great guns. I noticed that Jason was barefoot, too. Perhaps the stranger was a famous Sherpa, one of the many who had distinguished themselves as mountaineers.

I paid for an evening of fun and comfort and my reckless eating of the stew by spending a sleepless night.

Early the next morning, while settling our account with the landlord, we discovered that he spoke the king's English. He had traveled, in particular to Singapore, a fact that clarified the village's prosperity to some extent. Evidently he had dealt with trekkers' tribulations. He offered the suggestion that we try to fly from Phaphlu, which was closer than Lukla and off the route, improving our chances of getting on a plane. We decided to follow his advice.

The trail led through a prickly-leaved oak forest, on a moderate grade. Jason seemed invigorated after the Sherpa Stew; there was more bounce to his steps. The porters were dallying in Junbesi, and we enjoyed being alone. School children passed in small groups, the boys shouting what we gathered were uncomplimentary remarks, the little girls giggling. I turned to them, feigning shock at their naughtiness. They ran down the mountain.

Inevitably, we got lost. Jason left me nursing my ragged body in a splendid pasture, while he scouted the area. The narrow paths seemed to lead nowhere in particular, or everywhere?

Three hours after leaving Junbesi, we came on a beautiful house with a private *gomba,* or temple. Sunlight flashed off the metal roof and lit up the white-washed facade of the house. Two black-timbered windows on either side of a heavy black door were partially shaded by a wood-shingled corbel. The upper story was intricately decorated with painted geometric designs—dark-green, orange, ochre, white, yellow, aqua, lilac, and brick-red patterns seemed to oppose the austere simplicity of the lower half of the building. The *gomba* lay directly behind the house and imitated its embellishments, though these were even finer. Its front portals were honeycombed. All the colors blended like a field of wildflowers.

"I wish we could go in," said Jason. "It must be beautiful inside, too."

"It's a private place, it seems. Nobody around, anyway."

A few minutes later we passed the airstrip of Phaphlu—our way out of the mountains.

Crystal Violets

"Royal Nepalese Airlines" was painted in big red letters on the corrugated roof of a deserted shack. We dropped the gear and settled down on the floor, hoping somebody would show up. I withdrew into my granny skirt, put my head on Jason's pack, and pulled the floppy green hat I had bought in Kathmandu over my face. The occasional remarks between the porters seemed to come from far away, much like the sound of parents' voices droning in a child's febrile ears.

"Feeling lousy?" Jason peeked under my hat.

"Just tired."

"Get up, Mom, he's here. Let's get the tickets."

Sambhu was speaking in Nepalese to an official who seemed unhappy with his job or with us. He never once looked up from his desk, but kept poking furiously at some scattered papers.

At last, Sambhu shrugged dejectedly, "Flight's fulled."

"Fooled? Oh! What about the next one?"

"Maybe two weeks, maybe not then."

"How far to Lukla from here?"

"Not far. Few days, but mother very old, very sick." Sambhu looked at me uncertainly. I resumed my fetal position.

"Look, tell him we can pay double. Maybe we can trade with someone?" asked Jason.

More negotiations. I tried to figure out how much "double" would be. And what about the porters? They were in our employ for a month, I supposed they could walk back. I propped myself up to a more dignified posture.

For some impenetrable reason, Sambhu didn't seem to

favor a more simple solution: about a half hour south, in Salleri,was the district center of Solu-Khumbu. We were to go there and ask the District Chief for permission to use the two seats that were normally kept in reserve for government officials. The next flight out would be in two days; as of now, the seats were unclaimed.

"Let's go," said Jason.

"Couldn't we call or something? Couldn't Sambhu and Badri go?" Now that I was about to be relieved from hiking, I was tempted to surrender to my sickness.

"You go, easy road," Sambhu walked out of the shack.

Earlier, we had noticed a sign for a field hospital built by Sir Edmund Hillary. It occurred to me that if I made one last effort at a quick cure, perhaps we could still continue the trek.

"How about if Jason and I check out the hospital first, and then go with you to Salleri, Sambhu. Badri can cook lunch, the others can watch the gear," I said with a spurt of energy, hoping to regain some authority.

On the trail leading to the hospital we met the doctor. He wasn't an M.D., but he was the only medic stationed at the clinic. After listening to my complaints he sat down on the path to write a prescription, which, he warned, might make me vomit!

If I started vomiting I would become even more dehydrated; I decided to stop all medication and try to drink more. We politely continued up the hill to fill the prescription before joining a surly Sambhu for the walk to Salleri. The airline clerk had assured Sambhu that our request would be a mere formality. Once we had the option of flying out, we could relax, and still change our minds if things improved.

"Sorry I blew it," I said to Jason.

"Don't worry about it, lots of people get sick. I don't feel too great myself."

"I may still get over it."

"We can come back to Nepal some other time, can't we? Besides, it's been an incredible trip."

"I'm sorry we didn't see Cho Oyu."

"Think of what we did see! It's going to be interesting to take off from that make-believe runway in those teeny planes.

They must have to pull up pretty fast to clear the mountains!"

"If the weather holds that is. Sambhu says sometimes they can't fly for weeks."

The village resembled a movie set. On both sides of the unpaved road were grim looking woodframe houses, a barber, some tea shops, a general merchandise shop. The unfiltered mountain light heightened the squalor of the street. I could imagine all props removed in an instant—the mangy dogs and flapping chickens, the store fronts with their painted signs.

It was complicated to find out the whereabouts of the District Chief. We were sent here and there, to little back rooms up pissy staircases. Heads were shaken, eyes shifted nervously. Sambhu fell into a "you asked for it" attitude.

At last we learned that the great man's residence was on top of a hill and that he had been informed of our impending arrival. The hill seemed an omen—we'd had enough dealings with the authorities to know that "a mere formality" might take an hour. Plodding on laboriously, I felt like a mechanical toy in need of new batteries.

The solid, white house had a massive front door. Sambhu knocked. Silence.

"A little louder," I told him, but he pretended not to understand. I rapped my wedding ring against the wood. A stone-faced, uniformed man appeared and without a word led us through a narrow corridor to a patio. Sambhu hung back; he was inordinately ill at ease.

We found the object of our search in repose, stuck in a molded plastic armchair, much like a muffin too puffed up for its tin. He was dressed in light trousers and a soft-collared shirt. His mouth was his dominant feature, well formed, but settled in a permanent sneer. We exchanged greetings, and I stated briefly the reason for our visit, ending with an apology for disturbing him. With a royal gesture he gave us permission to sit, his pastry face impassive. From the disdainful once-over we received, I gathered he wasn't pleased with us.

"You're Americans," he said. "Do you know Nancy Hart?"

He undid himself from the chair and disappeared into the house. Jason and I exchanged shrugs.

The Chief emerged with a stack of posters. "Here."

One for each of us with a black and white photograph of a young Peace Corps worker with candid eyes and a determined chin: Nancy Hart. A request for information concerning her whereabouts, or, from the vintage of the poster, (it was three months old) her fate. She had traveled alone and was last seen in Junbesi on Christmas Day, the Chief told us.

"I even went to look for her myself, something I don't have to do, but one has humanitarian principles after all."

"How awful!" I said. "What do you think happened?"

The Chief raised his hands. How should he know? Bandits, perhaps, or an accident. Had the weather been severe? I wanted to know. An accident was unlikely, even for a person less experienced than Nancy Hart, who evidently knew the mountains and spoke Nepalese fluently. The weather had been stable.

"It's a tragedy," I said, and Jason added, "Terrible not to know what happened." The Chief seemed to take that personally; he glowered at Jason.

"Well," I said, "I'm a little tired, so...."

"Lie down," said the Chief with sudden mental agility, "There's no hurry. Here," he handed us each another, identical poster, "take a look at this."

"Yes. It's tragic." What a weird guy, I thought.

"Awful," Jason said, parrot-like. The Chief glared.

"Read it!"

"I wish there were something we could do," I said, "but unfortunately...."

"Your President Reagan was very interested in the case."

"What did he do?"

"He was interested. Other people too, in your country."

"Of course. She was a Peace Corps worker. I'm sorry, Sir, our porters haven't eaten since six this morning. Could you consider our request?"

"How's your heart?"

"Eh, my heart? Fine!"

"How bad is your diarrhea?" So Mr. Doctor had spread the word. I preferred not to discuss the matter, but sensed the need for compliance.

"The doctor gave me some pills."

"How bad?"

"I'm very uncomfortable," I said, hoping the euphemism would suffice and he wouldn't insist on a demonstration.

"Just wait a minute," he handed us another poster from the stack on his lap, straining over his abdomen, "Are you sure you don't know her?"

"How could we possibly?" Jason was obviously vexed; he didn't handle irrationality well. Just like Joe, I thought, who would throw a disdainful "What?" at me for drawing an incorrect conclusion.

"What's your goodname?" the Chief asked him. Jason looked helplessly at me.

I said, "Your goodname."

"Can't you answer?" said the Chief. Jason whispered "Jason," which turned out not to be his goodname. He submissively corrected himself, giving his last name. For that he received another poster. I stared at the pile left on the Chief's marshy thighs.

"You're not going to help us, are you," I was about through with the charade.

"I thought we were having a civilized conversation," said the Chief.

To keep words locked up, I closed my mouth tightly, a habit I had cultivated as a child, and left the patio, followed by Jason.

Sambhu was waiting at the door, evidently without curiosity—he didn't ask for the results of our visit.

"What an unpleasant man," I said. Jason thought bonkers was a better word.

Halfway down the hill we were called back. "No way," I said.

"We need those tickets to get out of here, Mom, I'll go." I sat down on the gravel, and contemplated my boots. Farther down, Sambhu collapsed too. I felt drained; this hanging around seemed to have centered my fatigue. Damn, I thought, Jason is taking his time. Irritated at the delay, I scraped the Chief's gravel maliciously with the heels of my boots.

Abruptly, my impatience changed to a sense of foreboding.

My heart started thumping when I thought of Jason's defenseless boy's face encountering those puffy eyes and smirking lips. Scrambling wildly uphill, a wad of my skirt clutched in my fist, I ran panting back into the house, yelling "Jason! Jason!" The piercing sound of my fear echoed off stone walls.

"Shit!" I cried undiplomatically, "Where are you?" He emerged from a room and pushed me ahead of him.

Sh," he said, suppressing rage, "Just walk."

The man had slapped his face. Not hard, he assured me, but in a demeaning way, and had asked him inappropriate questions about sex. He wiped a stray, angry tear from his chin, ending his story, "Oh well, it was worth a try. Poor Mom. I guess we made the detour for nothing."

On the way back to the other porters, I spilled my sinking strength in useless anger.

Just as we were about to enter our guest house, four policemen armed with clubs appeared.

"They want passport," Sambhu translated.

Jason, brought up in the Land of the Free, said, "Don't give them our papers, Mom," more as a reflex than as an option.

I handed over the passports and trekking permits. Sambhu made his lips vanish inside his mouth, and Badri, who came humming out of the house with a hatfull of chile peppers, stopped dead. Sambhu motioned with his head that we were to go with the police.

"Do you know why?" I asked. Sambhu shook his head. "Ask them if I can see the doctor first." I needed time to think. The request was evidently not in the itinerary; the posse conferred, then one man motioned permission with a jerk of his head.

In the little hospital I tried to explain the situation to a nurse who was helping a woman who was giving birth. She rubbed the bulging belly. The baby was very low. The birthing woman looked resigned; her hair lay sleek and damp on the plastic covered table. The nurse smiled, not minding the intrusion. In my head, the drama of birth became confused with my own drama. I told my story, repeating my name several times, hoping she would remember; there was no comprehension in her eyes.

I felt we had to establish our presence somehow. Jason certainly was noticed by the man at the dispensary. My brain

slowly caught up with an uneasy intuition. We were totally isolated, had surrendered our identity papers, and were at the mercy
of a madman.

At the guest house, Sambhu was pounding his head with
his fists, repeating, "Very bad, very bad." The policemen,
nonchalantly talking together, waited up the road a bit. They
weren't worried; where could we go?

"You're coming with us," I told Sambhu. Hand in hand,
Sambhu and Badri escorted us back to Salleri.

"What do you think he'll do?" said Jason.

"I don't know."

"Are you scared?"

"Very."

"I wish Dad were here."

"Me too."

Back in the dismal village, the police left us and marched
the porters away. We kept falling into a western way of thinking
and made a pathetic attempt to reason with an official at the Court
House. He sat behind an empty wooden desk and looked over our
heads when he spoke. He thought things would be all right, providing. Providing what?

"Don't worry," he said, and encouraged us to leave his
office by leaving himself. We followed his lumbering figure down
the narrow staircase. There was no place to flee, no American
government to protect us.

Outside, a crowd had gathered. Untidy looking women with
children clutching at their long skirts were on one side of the street,
on the other stood a group of men. We were regarded with the
respectful curiosity afforded a man on the gallows.

"I wish they would buzz off," Jason said with uncharacter-
istic harshness. The attitude of the gloomy, staring villagers served
as a terror tactic; we had become accustomed to Nepalese hospital-
ity—suddenly we were a foreign diversion. With all our gazing at
the mountains, our brief friendships with the people, we came to
realize we understood nothing here.

But now a friendly face emerged from the crowd.

"Manoj!" Jason called, "What are you doing here?"

"Big problem," Manoj said, smoking furiously and spitting

out little soggy pieces of tobacco. We walked away from the
crowd, Manoj fidgeting with his cuffs, turning them up, then
changing his mind and allowing them to fall over his hands again.
He kicked at the small stones, adding another layer of dirt to his
sneakers.

Manoj knew more English than he had let on. "Very big
problem," he pointed across the street. "Telex," he said, "Yeti." He
had telexed the trekking company in Kathmandu. At least that was
something.

"Good idea, Manoj."

"Good idea, but man say no." He wrote with his index
finger on his left hand. "Chief writing."

Yes, of course. You had to have the Chief's permission to
use the telex. Manoj was very frightened—his friends were in
captivity: all of us were pawns on the Chief's board.

Luckily, the medic came walking up the road. Certainly he,
as an educated man, could give us advice? But he brushed us off
nervously; he, too, had been summoned.

"I don't think you have to worry," he said, and over his
shoulder, "How many porters did you bring?"

"Four."

"Good." He nearly ran away from us.

We also noticed the gentlemanly Sherpa innkeeper from
Junbesi in conversation with a group of men. He didn't appear to
remember us. What was he doing here? Was he in cahoots with....
no, I was getting paranoid.

Finally, the police reappeared and led us to a compound
where they left us in the yard in front of the barracks. Several
uniformed men sat at a small table in a corner, their faces expressionless, not acknowledging our common humanity. I felt naked in
my white skin and was glad I wore the cumbersome long skirt, a
concession to Nepalese modesty.

I concentrated on the shiny patches in the dirt, like snail
tracks, from dried up spittle. We had felt so close to the people,
squatting in smokey huts, pointing to each other, "mother," "son,"
and laughing with the joy of our understanding. Mother, son,
sharing the universal weight of it. "Nepalese people love everybody. Is good," Sambhu had told us, and we'd had no reason to

doubt him. And now this.

I looked at Jason's pale face. His chestnut hair was a tangle of unkempt curls. He had sky eyes with long lashes I had always envied. Not yet grown to manhood, he carried his six-foot-two frame indecisively.

Four men came to take us away. They didn't touch us, in fact, they seemed embarrassed. Once again, we climbed the hill to the Chief's residence. I felt little streams of sweat seeping off my breasts; my hands were wet. It was mid-afternoon and sunny, but I shivered immoderately. I put my arm around Jason's waist, he put his around mine.

"He's going to kill us," Jason said. I stroked his back, fighting tears. He was sixteen. He shaved just once a week....

"I have a pretty good idea what happened to that girl," Jason said.

I thought, what if we're tortured? "Jay, maybe, no, that's absurd."

"What?"

"I'm going to offer the cops a piece of gum and slip you a razor blade. Put it in your boot if you can. There are things worse than death." In my empty stomach, nails were churning. Jason stopped to retie his boot, I put my blade in my pocket.

"It works better if you cut your artery lengthwise, Mom," he said clinically.

In my mind's eye I saw Jason's blood flowing in a dirty back room. Oh God, please let us stay together at least, I thought desperately, "what ifs" flashing through my brain.

Jason, with the icy composure of extreme terror, said, "No one can harm us, just our bodies." He braced himself for what lay ahead.

We were nearing the house.

"Listen," Jason whispered, "he has the power, so we have to outwit him; it's all we've got." Straightening himself, he pushed me away. His courage made me realize that fear was an indulgence we couldn't afford. At the door, the four policemen let us pass. Jason, taking me by the elbow steered me ahead of him, the way he sometimes did when we entered a movie theater.

"Don't say anything, let me do the talking, Jay." An artificial resoluteness took hold of me. If that crackpot thought he could make us squirm, he was making a mistake.

The Chief was on his patio, plunged in his chair. Badri and Sambhu sat on the edges of their seats. Badri wept noiselessly and Sambhu's pupils filled his irises. The Chief blotted a trickle of blood dripping from his nose with a large towel. Smiling obsequiously, I bowed and offered my hand.

"I do apologize for my rudeness, I didn't mean it. I wasn't feeling well. Not that that is an excuse. Will you forgive me?"

He accepted my groveling without humility. "I'm used to a little more respect," he sulked.

"You deserve it," I agreed.

"Sit," he motioned royally.

I smiled at a weary woman sitting cross-legged on the floor. The Chief waved his blood-stained banner in her direction, "My wife."

"Does she understand English?"

"Yes. But she doesn't speak in front of me. The doctor tells me amoebic dysentery isn't fatal. You shouldn't worry."

The conversation returned to the Peace Corps worker. We were given a poster to study. My own dread allowed me to express earnest commiseration.

"What does your husband do?" The Chief's eyes were wandering over me. I assumed as relaxed a posture as I could fake. Joe was a pretty important fellow, I told him. Working for both the American and Indian governments. Science. He was waiting for us in Kathmandu. I hoped Jason wouldn't let slip, "What?"

"Are you a Buddhist?" I asked.

"No. I was in New York, you see. Also in Boston. Your country is okay, but it's more beautiful here."

I went over to his wife to admire her knitting. Standing between her and her husband, I searched her face. She shook her head imperceptibly, her eyes distraught with a lifetime of female suffering. We communicated without speaking, like sisters. My distaste for her lordly husband became suffocating. I felt exceedingly faint. When I passed Badri's bent head, I laid my hand on it a moment.

"You will eat," said the Chief.

"Thanks very much, Sir, but really, I'm not hungry."

He snapped his fingers and gave long instructions to a servant. Poison? Sedatives?

"That's why people get sick, you see. They think they know the mountains. They must eat!"

It was getting dark. We continued our idiotic socializing. More than three hours passed. The rice arrived with two plates, two eggs, two glasses of warm water.

The porters sat motionless. Jason fell on the food. I ate a few spoons of rice and gave him my egg.

Suddenly, the Chief stuck out the passports. "Everything's in order."

I stretched lazily, then retrieved the passports and nonchalantly dropped them in Sambhu's lap, indicating I expected all of us to leave together.

"Can you hang on to them, Sambhu?" I didn't dare look at Jason; I thought I could hear his heartbeat.

The Chief snapped his fingers again. An underling brought pen and paper, opened the pen, and, bowing, retreated backwards. The whole act seemed illusory, including my own responses.

"I made the decision. The boy must walk. You may buy one ticket." He thrust a note in my direction.

"I'm deeply grateful," I said. Did he think I was going to leave Jason behind?

"That's okay. I'm here to help people."

"Most kind. The rice was delicious."

"Yeah, great!" said Jason. The Chief's ego prevented him from noticing our mockery. I wished he would dismiss us; I felt I couldn't grin much longer. The dread of the porters expanded my own.

"Perhaps I could keep this?" I asked, indicating the poster.

At last stalling became unbearable; I had to know if he would let us go. I thanked him profusely once more, adding that I feared we had bothered him long enough.

"Come," I told the porters. They were petrified.

Jason gave Sambhu his hand. "Let's go, it's getting late."

No one stopped us. We were followed discretely on the return trip. Badri had to stop to vomit. Speaking in low voices, we bunched together. They had been threatened with jail, Sambhu told us. He shivered.

"Very bad business. When in jail—then finish."

I said I could well imagine.

"My God," Jason whispered. Sambhu blew softly through his teeth. We bent under the weight of our collective horror.

"Sorry," Sambhu put an arm around Jason. "Sorry."

"No. It wasn't your fault."

Sambhu's arm gave him the comfort he needed so badly. We walked slowly back to the guest house. It occurred to me that I'd had no problem with my dysentery all day. Like a wounded soldier crawling to safety by force of will, no thought had been given to the body.

Later, we sat on boxes around a sooty fire in the kitchen. Sambhu and I on one box, Jason and Sanu back to back on another. We were talked out and drooped, round-shouldered and exhausted.

A policeman took a dorm next to ours; we speculated about his mission. Nervously I tiptoed down the stairs and outside to visit the *chaarpi*. Looking along the road I saw a figure approach: Badri. I knew his distaste for backhouses; he'd been out in the woods somewhere. He was fastidious, washing himself in cold rivers, even scrubbing his hat clean in the rain. The other men hadn't bathed since Kathmandu.

"That you, Badri?" I didn't want to dive into the *chaarpi* in front of him. He carried his little *loTa* (a vessel for carrying water to clean oneself after defecating) in his left hand. I had never spoken to the reserved Badri beyond "Thank you," nor had he given any indication that he understood English. He was a handsome, wheat-skinned boy with proud carriage, who managed to wear clean shirts and was capable of cooking excellent *chapatis* (flat unleavened bread) under primitive circumstances.

With all vestiges of aloofness gone, he took my hand in his. "You good. Nepalese people bad."

I looked up into the beautiful face. What did he mean? He dropped my hand, and poking a finger against my arm repeated, "You good," then, pounding his chest, "Nepalese people bad, bad, bad!"

My held-back emotions were finally freed. "No," I choked, "Badri, no." Leaning against each other, we stood weeping in front of the *chaarpi.*

The night was spent huddled close on Sanu's cot. Manoj smoked, Jason slept fitfully for a while, then woke with a scream. Sambhu said we couldn't leave before six, because the bill had to be paid.

"But everything okay now, no more problem." He went to the window to peer down the road.

We left before the sun came up. Panch Pokhari was still hiding its treacherous glaciers in thick mists. When the porters stopped to munch dried noodles, I photographed the patches of gentians, also called crystal violets, knowing their frailty was deceptive.

"How far do we go today, Sambhu?" I desperately wanted to get to Lukla. I was afraid we'd be called back and kept looking over my shoulder, expecting to see the police. My whole system was in overdrive. I needed to keep going; I felt our lives depended on it. But Sambhu had decided we needed sleep before crossing the Tragsindho La pass. We stopped a few hours later.

The hotel was a two-storied building with stucco walls and baby blue doors and window frames. A sign above the door read: Fooding and Lodging. It was cold there. Jason and I spent the rest of the day in our tent, fearfully peering down the trail for uniformed visitors. Around midnight, we became frightened and stealthily joined the porters in their hotel. Sambhu woke up and quietly went out into the bitter night to gather our belongings for safe keeping in the dormitory. At age twenty-one, he looked after our whole trekking family.

When everyone was asleep, I squatted in the orchard, melting small circles of snow.

The next two days were a blur. Jason got giardia. Badri cooked *chapatis.* We climbed, descended. Sambhu said respectfully, after we came over the last pass, "American mother not so old."

I was in a state outside fatigue and mechanically moved my legs. I felt that if I stopped, I would be finished, and kept ahead of the team, making it tough on Jason, who was weak from his infection. The excitable condition of my gut made every separate nerve jittery. Later, in a secondhand bookstore in Kathmandu, Jason told me that my supercharged behavior had frightened him even more than my appearance.

In Lukla, the airstrip stayed fogged in for three days. On the fourth day, five bush planes arrived in succession. Our group was flown back to Kathmandu at midday.

In a cloudless sky, flying past Everest with its snow plume, Nuptse, Pumori, Ama Dablang, the wide expanse of snow and ice, I knew Sambhu had been right: no more problem.

The day after we left Lukla, a French-Canadian girl was reported missing in the area of Junbesi.

-24-

The Lost Mountain

In our house are many maps. Mostly topos on which we study the tiny brown lines. All the walls in the basement that can be penetrated by thumbtacks have maps on them. I especially like the astrosolar one of Our Milky Way—a hundred billion stars depicted as a pastel spiral of wind-born soap bubbles.

One day, when I came home through the basement after jogging in gray February snow and sat down on the stairs to untie my sneakers, my eyes were drawn to the map of South America. I wasn't conscious of any aspirations when I started tracing the Andes range alongside the Pacific at a thousand miles per second, sliding my finger northward past the equator into Colombia, where I got stuck in volcanic perplexities. Back to Patagonia. Well, I thought, it's too expensive to go all the way down there, and before I knew it a plan was hatching for the summer's backpacking trip. I ran upstairs for a magic marker to plant red dots on Aconcagua in Argentina, El Misti and Huascaran in Peru, Cotopaxi and Chimborazo in Ecuador. Jason would know if we could climb any of these peaks with our limited ice climbing skills. It would be the kind of graduation present he would want; I could hardly wait for him to come home from school.

"Of course I would!" said Jason. "Sure, we could try El Misti! Aconcagua's too high. Almost 23,000."

"It's too far, anyway, but Peru, we should think about it. How high is El Misti?" That was the one whose name appealed to me.

"Over nineteen."

I couldn't imagine lugging myself to 19,000 feet, but got excited none the less. I said, "We could see the Inca ruins, too."

We never did go to Peru. The Shining Path guerrillas were active at the time; the embassy advised against travel there.

Brett and his wife, Karen, had come to dinner when we discussed this obstacle. We went down to the basement with our filled wine glasses to see where the Andes went after Colombia. A major spur of the Northern Andes unraveled into Venezuela, the Cordillera de Merida.

Over dessert, Plan B waxed as Brett cooked up fantastic ideas for canoeing on the Orinoco and snorkeling in the Caribbean. While Jason lay on the floor with the encyclopedia, looking for Angel Falls, Joe had another piece of chocolate cake and looked bemused.

Karen said, "Brett, Brett!"—she often repeated his name to break through his preoccupation with things—"Are you thinking of going with them?"

Brett had been holding forth on tepuyes, tabletop mountains. Precambrian, he said, and not to be missed. He looked at his wife and said innocently, "No, but that's a good idea, Babe."

That's how we all ended up in Venezuela, Brett-Brett and Babe, Jason and I. The country was a vacationer's paradise. There was much to see and do, but we had only a little more than two weeks. The last week had to be held open for an attempt to climb Pico Bolivar—we had agreed on that. Nothing came of Brett's snorkeling plans. Instead we flew to the Guyana Highlands in Venezuela's wild interior, where we saw Angel Falls rage more than half a mile in unbroken fall.

One of the advantages of having Brett along was his vitality that inspired us to greater courage than we ordinarily would have had. I always felt safe with him. He was resourceful and had good judgment, as well as an unfailing sense of direction. It was thanks to Brett that we dared leave the beaten track to bushwack through the jungle. This risky undertaking was something Jason and I would never have considered. I wasn't crazy about swinging on a vine across a snake-filled river, but Brett could talk anybody into doing anything. He found a narrow Indian trail and we were fortunate enough to come upon an authentic slash and burn farm. Seated under a banana tree, we watched the pulse of the Indian family's life—the babies dozing in hammocks, the baking of large quantities of flat breads, the making of cassava.

Jason, for his part, happily regressed to baby brother. From the onset, we had designated Brett leader in order to avoid feuds. Accommodating four people instead of two had changed our routine, of course. Jason and I were so tuned in to each other— there wasn't another person in the world I was more at ease with. But it was good to see my sons walk the same road. With a nine year gap in their ages, and Brett now a married man, they had grown apart. We'd be a family of strangers if we stopped walking together.

From Guyana we flew to Merida, in the Andes. The old mountain city was nestled in a broad valley with snowcapped mountains to the south, Pico Bolivar being the highest at 16,427 feet.

We settled in at a luxurious hotel, changed to our city clothes, and went downstairs to the tastefully decorated dining room. Here we availed ourselves of the fantastic cuisine, keeping in mind that the near future wouldn't be so soft. Afterwards, we lingered over espresso, lightheartedly disregarding all tomorrows.

Although surrounded by mountains, we had a hard time getting to them on our first exploratory stroll. All roads through the outskirts of the city led to some insurmountable obstacle. We walked in a light rain on roads that led only to other roads, munching interesting pastries we bought along the way.

At last, two energetic little boys guided us through a maze of streets, darting ahead and signaling us onward. When they stopped, we were still far from the mountains, but the kids pointed down toward *el puente*, the bridge across the river that would lead to the mountains. We continued to zigzag down the highway until Brett, done with pavement walking, suggested a shortcut: the descent of a steep embankment covered with brush.

"Forget it," Karen said, to my relief.

"Don't be ridiculous," Brett said. "Come on, Babe."

"No."

"Mom's coming!" Brett spoke for me.

Since my hiking buddies were all under thirty, I felt an obligation to be enterprising. I made a symbolic inspection trip into the scratchy bushes. At the bottom of the switchback, toy-sized cars lined up for *el puente.*

"What about snakes," I said, more worried about the angle of the drop-off. "They're probably all over the place. There are thirty-two kinds of poisonous snakes here."

"I'll go with you, Brett," Jason said. Oh no you're not, I wanted to say, but held my tongue. I was glad they were wearing sturdy hiking boots, for now I had scared myself with the snake excuse.

Without assistance from male motorists, who tried to lure us off the hot road with *"Gringas, aqui!"* and seductive whistling, Karen and I made it down in less than an hour. The boys took somewhat longer. We watched them perched above us, cautiously searching for footholds in the final steep wall, Brett gesticulating and shouting instructions to Jason. We settled down comfortably under a black pine, shading our eyes to watch the progress on the rock face.

Brett's grin was of a classic shit-eating sort when they joined us, bloody and completely filthy after the completion of the shortcut.

"At least we're getting in shape," Brett said creatively, brushing off Karen's protests concerning his ruined shorts. "It was fun, wasn't it, Jay?"

"For getting mud under your skin and dying of thirst you couldn't beat it," Jason agreed.

The foothills were blazing with tropical flowers in fragrant shades of pinks and purples. Wending our way past an occasional small farm, we stopped to take pictures of shy children against backgrounds of sun-burned stucco garlanded with oleander. Although climbing steadily, we didn't get to an altitude useful for acclimatization that afternoon.

On our third day in Merida, we began making preparations in earnest for the ascent of Pico Bolivar. The problem was, nobody knew where to get permits. We were sent from place to place with reassuring smiles and total faith on our part that the last person we talked to had the answer. Karen was methodical and patient, Jason cooperative, Brett and I chafing at the bit, indignant at losing precious hours. We were lucky to have happened on a taxi driver who made our welfare his responsibility.

Even when the correct office was finally found, the permit remained elusive due to our inability to express ourselves in Spanish (in which I held an ancient degree) and the indifference of the officials. Karen repeated the name of the mountain we were interested in, using sign language to indicate the size of our group and the expected number of days of our stay in the mountains, with the rest of us nodding dumbly. After a sleepy inspection of the would-be expedition members, a permit was issued in Brett's name. Karen took possession of the precious document, given his proclivity for losing things.

The approach to the mountain was from the Parque Nacional. We engaged our friendly driver for seven A.M. the next morning.

After lunch we took a taxi to the Parque to see what the trail looked like. The driver, a small, taciturn fellow, dropped us off at a village in the foothills, promising to collect us at four o'clock.

There was no sign of a park headquarters, but Brett was convinced we were in exactly the right place. We waded through walls of impatiens swelling from soft pink through impossible shades of red to violet, to ask directions at a German-looking farm of post and beam construction. Brett crossed the courtyard and spoke to a man who was doing something with buckets. Knitting a few nouns together, like *direccion, montaña, pico,* he was satisfied that he had made himself clear. *"Bien. Muchas gracias,"* he said, in unlikely accents.

"No hay de que," the man smiled.

"How do you know he understood what you wanted?" I wondered.

"Mom, it's obvious." My children were always a step ahead of me.

At first the trail was well defined, albeit steep. There were no markers or blazes—this was not the Appalachian Trail. Flies the size of limousines swarmed around our heads. After about an hour of difficult hiking, the trail abruptly vanished, presumably because no one had felt the need to hack out a path beyond the stream. Sweat washed off our repellent as soon as we applied it. I kept getting tangled up and grabbed by the ravening growth. Brett was in fine fettle, finding his way through the thicket as easily as if he were in a country lane. The rest of us followed with mounting anxiety; how did he know where he was going?

"He's crazy," Karen observed, "There's no trail here."

"There is now, look behind you," said Jason.

"Damn it, Brett, wait up! Brett! Brett!" Karen shouted, "I'm going back! There's no path!"

"Yes there is! Here, look!" Brett waited for us to claw our way up. He stood on a fallen tree like a knight errant, indicating a track barely wide enough for a rabbit. Jason, who'd figured out his brother before he was three years old, either didn't wish to waste energy in protesting so obvious a fantasy or felt that with two women on his case, Brett would have to capitulate.

I understood the hunger in Brett; if he went back now, he would forever miss knowing what lay beyond. I remembered him, restless and eager as a child, and myself of long ago.

"Any spot you can squeeze one foot into you call a trail. Just look around; there's not a sign anybody's ever been through here," said Karen.

She was right of course, but Brett said the reason we didn't see it was because "things grow so fast in the tropics."

"It's here, but you just can't see it," I clarified.

"A no-see-um," Jason added. Brett plunged indignantly down the mountain.

We had been unable to find our way, and the next day, at seven A.M., the climb was to start. As far as I was concerned we couldn't go into the Andes without knowledge of the route. Our efforts to buy a map had proved unsuccessful; we would have to try to find someone who could give us information in a familiar language.

Back at the hotel we split up; Karen and Brett took a taxi to the Civil Defense Office while Jason and I spoke to a German travel agent. She was aghast that we planned to climb Pico Bolivar without a guide. It was too dangerous, too cold, and too high.

"*Aber,*" I said, "We know mountains pretty well."

"Doch!" she said, pursing her lips.

We left with an appointment to meet a prospective guide at eight o'clock that evening, and with that settled, went for an espresso at the cafe. Brett and Karen soon joined us, proudly waving a piece of paper. A map? Certainly. Brett had copied it freehand from the wall map at the Civil Defense Office. It showed several high lakes and shelters, but was necessarily grossly inaccurate. No scale, no date, no little brown lines to put my mind at ease. Nevertheless, the decision was made to go without a guide. I had more faith in Brett than in his map, and suspected that was true for him as well. Surely he knew his drawing was useless beyond its psychological appeal.

During dinner we were irritable. Karen countered any mention of difficulties by Jason or me with, "Then why did you come here," though she knew we had counted on finding maps of the route in Merida. I was convinced that she underestimated the wildness of the terrain, treacherous mountain weather conditions, and the extent of our ignorance. I kept my anger at her responses in check, aware we would very much depend on each other. Then, at the next table, a man lit a large cigar.

"That does it," I said. "Let's move."

Karen let out an exaggerated sigh and made her "what a pain in the ass you are" face, familiar to her husband.

"I don't understand why we have to put up with this heinous stink so meekly," I said.

"You don't have to worry about being meek, Paula," Karen snapped.

"Stay here then if you like," I said, and strutted off.

Though the altercations were minor, I was wounded by Karen's remark regarding my lack of humility. In our room Jason's judicious silence irked me. Didn't he know I was kind and tolerant? I started badgering him.

"Why didn't you tell Karen it wasn't a big deal to get away from that disgusting smoke?"

"You still thinking about that?" He didn't look up from his book.

"It seems to me that she was wrong, and you could have supported me. When you say nothing, you seem to agree with her."

"I didn't, of course."

"So?"

"So what?"

Men were exasperating. From the adjoining room came gunshots—Karen and Brett had turned on the television.

"That map isn't going to help us," I persisted.

"Probably not."

"Then why didn't you say so?"

"You know Brett. Stop fussing, Mom. We'll go back down if we think it's unsafe." He turned off his light. "Get some sleep. Brett's no fool."

Frustrated with my inability to be reasonable, I couldn't fall asleep. I regretted that I had organized the trip. Alone with Jason, things used to be simple: we just walked, ate, slept; I had taken our compatibility for granted. Now there were four people misreading each other. I'll stay at the hotel, I thought vindictively, but I knew I wouldn't.

The taxi driver was already waiting when Jason and I went outside before seven o'clock. We loaded our gear in the trunk, then scanned the sky to forecast the weather. The driver paced the lobby, rubbing his hands while chatting with a pimpled young fellow at the reception desk. Across the street, the military trotted around a grassy play yard, shouting aggressive syllables.

Brett and Karen, looking competent and strong with their spanking new packs and just-so outfits, came stomping down the stairs. I thought Jason and I appeared, well, vague by comparison. During the seventy minute ride to the Parque Nacional not much talking went on. I wondered if the others were still sleepy or apprehensive, too. Our kind driver shook his head in consternation when he heard I was actually planning to climb the mountain, as though I had come with my walker.

"She's coming too?" he asked Brett.

"*Si, naturalmente,*" Brett laughed. The boys had always been irreverent of my age. The driver took another look at me in his rearview mirror, and laughed with good-natured ridicule.

"*Mucho frio!*" he warned, pointing toward an invisible mountain summit. I was used to this attitude toward older women hikers outside Europe and the States.

This time we were delivered to the right place, but the ranger was still asleep. Our driver banged on doors and windows to no avail while we crunched through the gravel. We couldn't go on without signing in—bypassing the bureaucracy would scare me more than any mountain. At last a tousled ranger opened the door, pulling up his suspenders and squinting against the bright day. Our driver presented us as a father might his offspring. He waited until the inspection of our papers was completed, hoping until the last that I would be deprived of an opportunity to kill myself.

"Mucho, mucho frio!" he insisted, but then shook my hand warmly; perhaps the large tip was a testament to my sanity.

At first the trail snaked gently upward through the jungle. Howler monkeys screeched the last sleeping creatures awake while Brett eulogized hot peppers, coffee trees, and bamboo. Everything seemed to be sucking sustenance from everything else in an excessive appetite for life, clinging, clinging....Ferns spanned above, fanning shadowed patterns on our skins. Karen and I took close-ups of waxen blossoms, relishing the ginger-like scent, and of orchids, their dainty orange cups filled with sifted light.

As we climbed higher, the roar of falling water began to drown out other forest sounds. Powerful surges of white spray tumbled from great heights onto the green. We brunched in these mansions, on a riverbank. Brett made coffee. All of us were swollen with contentment. Jason and I, who had pared our packs down to the minimum, ate our last slice of bread, trying not to lust after Karen's peanut butter—a backpacker's fantasy. Somehow, Karen let the jar slip into the swift stream where it set sail with Brett in pursuit. He wiped the flotsam off the jar with a corner of his shorts, protesting, "Why do you always do that," as though Karen were a pathological peanut butter loser.

My pack always seemed more burdensome after a rest, for a while at least. Now and then we caught a glimpse of the alluvial plain of the Merida valley, already far below. The kids had me lead the way, so I could set the pace. I did my best to cache some of my reserves for the climb ahead without slowing down too much.

"Don't worry, Mom," said Brett, "I can't go any faster under this load." He was carrying seventy pounds against my thirty-five.

Every bend in the trail revealed another breathtaking view; the entire jungle looked like a giant frittilary.

The few minor obstacles we had thus far encountered hardly prepared us for a white-water crossing. It wasn't all that deep or wide, but it boomed vigorously toward a falls just beyond the only possible traverse. I hadn't the least intention of putting one foot in it, though going back on our first day was also out of the question. Unsuccessfully, Brett looked for another place to cross, swore, set his jaw, then ventured out. Large, slick-looking boulders protruded from the river, but they were too far apart for jumping. Deep troughs had formed between them, through which the water coursed with great force. In the middle of the river Brett appeared to lose his balance and mowed his arms like a novice tight-rope dancer. We held our breath. When he climbed ashore, he was drenched. What I'd had of courage washed downstream; if the water reached to Brett's shorts, Karen and I would be in it up to our waists, but that was the least of it. While Brett was doing his Leader thing, Jason sat on a rock, vaguely chewing a sprig of grass.

"We'll never get across," I told him.

"Well, we'll have to."

"How, pray tell, do you expect Karen and me to ford that thing? Or are you going to build a bridge."

"Brett'll think of something," Jason said matter-of-factly.

"Not this time, I'm afraid. If you slip down that drop-off, you'll be squashed to compost."

"Could be."

Brett had recrossed the river and was all business.

"Okay, this is going to be a piece of cake. Gimme the rope, Jay. All right. Now." He picked up his pack and hung his boots around his neck. "I'm taking the rope across. Tie your end securely around that boulder. Double-check your knots. Karen, when I signal, you go first. Hang on to the rope, go slow, watch where you put your feet. Mom, leave your pack and your boots, don't start out until Karen is across." (I suppose he thought I couldn't wait.) "You last, Jay, then I'll go back to get the rope. Here we go."

He set out again, and in spite of the load, seemed to have

found a way to stay upright. Karen stepped into the river, bent down to grab the rope. There was so much slack that it was useless. Brett climbed higher up the opposite bank, hanging back on the rope.

"That's great, Babe, you're almost there!" he shouted, before Karen had taken three steps. She suddenly looked very small amid that unharnessed power. I could hardly stand watching.

After a congratulatory kiss, Karen immediately disappeared into the bushes.

My turn. I changed my mind three times by climbing back onto the bank, aggravating everybody to death, but I was plenty scared. In the middle of the river I froze, unfit for more action. Brett talked me across.

"Now go through your knees a little. Lift the rope over your head, but for God's sake don't let go. You're doing great. Put your left foot...." I was rewarded with hugs from my oldest son who was nearly as unnerved by my performance as I was.

Jason came over without a fuss, carrying his pack, but leaving his size-twelve boots. I still felt shaky when Brett went back to retrieve the rope and the rest of the stuff. He swung my tied boots in a gigantic circle across the river. Jason's were so heavy, he had to spin them into an even greater arc. Bending backwards, he let the boots fly—and in midair they came untied. One fell close to the riverbank, where Jason barely rescued it in time from a voyage downstream. Alas, the other hit the water. I cried out, Karen grabbed her head. The boot tilted at a rakish angle, gathered momentum, then came to an ambiguous halt atop a rock.

With split-second timing, Brett sized up the quandary, contorted his body into a cat-stance culminating in a wiggle of his tail-end, and sprang swiftly from boulder to boulder, landing belly down on the boot that stood teetering on the brink of the waterfall. He reminded me of an eagle swooping down on his pray. Climbing ashore, he stood panting his nervous energy away, looking rather green under his tan.

Jason, pale as a winter moon and speechless, slapped his brother on the back.

"Next time, tie them together better, Jay," said Brett. Jason poured the water from his boots and put them back on.

"Good thing you learned pole vaulting in high school," I told Brett. We all talked at the same time, laughing with relief. "It's weird," I said, "but in a flash I saw us fashion slippers for Jason from bamboo!"

"That was the first thing I thought of, bamboo," said Brett. Jason said he could have hopped on a pogo stick, while Karen would have been in favor of building a dug-out canoe to go after the boot. Clearly we would have thought of something!

We camped that night on the paramos, the lands above treeline. The boys gathered dry brush for a fire and we warmed water to rinse each other's hair. While we sat watching the winking embers, I added allspice, cloves, and dried orange peel—nearly weightless luxuries—to the tea. The young faces, softer in the warm light, looked younger still. A small breeze teased Karen's long, dark hair into her face. She inhaled the fragrant tea with closed eyes, absorbed as a child with a lollypop. Brett, barefoot and busy, drew figures with a burning stick in the immense night sky, and Jason had his beautiful stillness. He sat round-shouldered, a little sad. He had forgotten to take off his wet boots.

We spoke of trifles, for neither our intimacy nor our isolation could be acknowledged. I cherished the tea and the clean wind, the mingling odors of spices and Brett's sweat.

Karen yawned, "We'd better call it a day." I gathered up the tea things.

"Would you get some water to douse the fire, Jay?" I asked, holding out the pot. "Why don't you go with him, Brett?"

"Let's do some bonding," Jason said.

Karen and I did our ablutions and had just gone into our tents when angry shouts came from the river. Brett seemed to be raging at Jason. I couldn't imagine Jason causing so much ire— Brett was in a real frenzy.

"Hey Karen! What do you think that's all about?" I shouted, but needn't have, she was suddenly right outside my tent. "God Almighty, girl, you scared me to death!"

"Sorry. Should we go pull them apart?"

We could now make out some rather basic vocabulary in Brett's monologue as they returned from the river. Jason carried both the pan and a bottle; Brett had something wrapped in his shirt, which he dumped with another expletive. Beer cans.

"Pigs!" he said. We stared at the pile of trash. "I'll have to pack that shit out." He put on his boots and trampled the cans.

"Can't we bury them?" I asked. Surely we had enough trouble carrying our own stuff.

"You know better than that. I'm going to bed," he said.

After we had bedded down, I asked Jason if he thought Brett had over-reacted.

"No."

"Did you offer to help him carry that mess tomorrow?"

"I wanted to, but I think he needs to do it. He's right, you know, we should never accept such disrespect." He leaned his head in his hands. "If you get used to ugliness you stop seeing beauty too, and you're—well, diminished, I guess. We should all be screaming about the desecration of the planet."

"He's so extreme!" I said in reference to Brett, but I thought Jason's rather formal discourse extreme too, especially when he added, "I think maybe it's part of a larger issue. Loss of innocence and all that."

"That's what he said?"

"He said it pissed him off."

"Oh. Well, he was pretty convincing. I'm glad you don't explode so easily." He scoffed. Brett's anger had been magnificent, he said. He wished things were so clear to him.

Over and out. I was left as though holding a glass of water that had sprung from a mysterious underground source.

During the night my head hurt. It was the beginning of the altitude sickness that was to get worse as the days passed.

In the morning, Brett took some of my load on the steep grade. After several hours of slow climbing, the trail ended at an unclimbable wall. This wall had to be traversed on a bridge made of planks resting precariously on rusty pegs banged into the stone. To get onto the boards one had to hazard a jump up and across a foot-wide chasm. The only way to avoid this passage was to undo the morning's climb, drop all the way back down to the river, then struggle up beyond an outcrop. That is, so far as we could guess from our position on the ridge.

"So let's go," I said, placing myself before the planks.

"They're not safe, even if you didn't miss the leap up, which you well may. No way are we risking our lives to save a couple of hours," Brett said.

"I think we can do it all right. Why else would they have built the bridge?" I was ready to jump, gauging the distance.

I have to admit that normally I wouldn't consider getting on a wobbly surface even if the drop-off were seven instead of seventy feet. But my reluctance to add to the climb was greater than my fear. Brett took my elbow and shoved me in the right direction—down.

Grand scenery made me forget my headache. The valleys were narrow and flanked by snowcapped peaks. A strong wind whisked the snow off a distant glacier into a sequined veil. The slopes were covered with alpine fur-covered plants called frailejones, or great friars. They hadn't anything friar-like that I could see, no mendicant tilt of the stem, though the fine yellow blossoms softened the barren rock.

Late in the afternoon we lost the trail, and Brett called a halt. He, too, was developing a headache and was exhausted from the weight he carried. We estimated our altitude to be about 10,000 feet. According to Brett's map, we should have come to a shelter.

Brett and Karen quickly took the only level, protected place to pitch their tent; we didn't see them again until morning. To Jason and me remained the slope and the wind. We struggled with our stove long enough to make a cup of soup, nibbled crackers listlessly, and went to bed. Again I spent the night semi-sitting against my pack.

Breaking camp in the morning was challenging, with a wind that threatened to carry off anything we didn't stand on. One of my teeshirts was raised to Cottonbird of the Andes; it billowed away. I thought, if we could stay for another day I would get used to the altitude, but the hike to Pico Bolivar continued. On the other side of a gully we spotted the trail again. For a while, the going was easy. Stopping only to don sweaters on descents and take them off again when climbing, we hiked for several hours with the promise of a coffeebreak.

At a small stream formed by melted snow from the peaks, we dropped our packs. At this altitude it took a long time for the water to boil, and when it did, it wasn't very hot. To stay warm we crouched together, drinking coffee while keeping our eyes fixed on the splintered horizon. Paths of shrill water-light streamed through the clouds.

Eventually we came to a gem-colored lake and a shelter. The shelter was well-placed in this cold and windy spot, but we rejected it after a quick inspection of its dirty interior. Nearby, previous campers had left two circular stone walls that gave the desolate terrain a prehistoric air. With stern application, we pitched the tents within these ramparts while the wind yanked at the flapping nylon. The corners had to be roped down, yet even with the weight of the gear inside, the gale crept under the floor. Jason and Brett went to look for colorless water. Karen sat in the front opening of her tent like the Queen of the Nile, with her snow-white Arab headdress (really a baseball cap with a skirt), and I took pictures in the last light.

While Karen and Brett knelt with a steaming dish of macaroni between them, we were still coaxing our stove to do something. Since their cheap stove outperformed our fancy high-altitude one, Brett teased us, "You guys better start your breakfast."

Actually, we felt too sick to eat and decided to forget the nuisance of cooking and dishwashing. Karen said it was no wonder we were sick, because we didn't eat.

"That's like blaming a person dying of emphysema for not breathing," Jason told her.

Brett and Karen were eating course after course of things from baggies, when suddenly we became aware that the shelter had become occupied. Someone stood outside the circular dwelling, swinging his arms to stay warm.

"Wait a minute, there're two guys!" said Brett. And then there were four. We eyed them suspiciously from our fortifications. They were young, dressed in baggy pants and sweaters. One of them sported a cute hat on his sleek dark hair; the others wore sweatbands. Strange rites were going on. Two of the men made four or five raids around the neighborhood, returning with bulging plastic bags which they handed to the others. At last they all disappeared inside.

"What the hell is going on?" Brett wondered, setting out

with his coffee mug to investigate.

"Hold it," Karen said, "Let's bring them something." We brought nuts and other snacks on our social call and were welcomed with enthusiasm. The four Indians, squatting around a small fire, invited us to join them. They were frying sausages in a rusty pan and eating them with what looked like pieces of matzo. The riddle of the bags was solved: when you travel without down parkas, tents, or sleeping bags, you use great friars for bed and blanket. The men had spread a bouncy layer of frailejones in one corner. I didn't have the energy to regret the language difficulty.

During the night I tested my reason by counting backwards and reciting my address and phone number, to check the status of my altitude sickness. If confusion set in, I would have to descend right away. I didn't take into account that I was my own, possibly unreliable, judge.

Our valley was in a cirque, any wall of which could lead to the continuation of the trail. There were no cairns or signs of human traffic. Brett had to admit our helpless position to the Indians, which he did the next morning with the least possible damage to his dignity.

"Right. Sure, that's what I thought," he mumbled, when the fellow with the hat pointed toward a steep talus slope.

Karen started the climb while the rest of us puttered around the campsite. She was a mere spot of blue and white from our vantage point, when we began to make our way up on the rock slide.

"Karen is really moving this morning," Brett said proudly. He had a headache and was sweating in spite of the cold. With most of their gear on his back, this was one rare occasion that we weren't left in his dust.

Jason had matter-of-factly taken responsibility for my well-being. On tricky spots, he placed his boot as an anchor for mine, or he climbed ahead in order to haul me over a slide. Halfway up the slope, Karen suddenly slowed down. When we caught up she sat on a narrow ledge, drinking from her canteen.

"It's getting really steep here," she said.

Below us, the sun reflected off the hut's metal roof, making it look like a dime lost in a vacant lot.

There was no place for anyone else to sit, so I pushed on. Jason wasn't revved up yet, apparently; he stayed anchored in the scree. I couldn't wait to see what lay beyond the top of the ridge.

Pleased with my progress I forged ahead; I wasn't about to be overtaken by those hotshots. The first summit was a false one. While I picked my way cautiously through a short couloir, a new horizon came into view.

"It's not the summit!" I shouted down. The angle now was about sixty degrees, but at least there was solid rock here. I leaned forward, causing my pack to scrape against my backbone. Every three or four steps I had to stop to gulp the thin air.

When, at last, we reached the crest, we looked down on another valley. All around were mountains beyond mountains with bands of silver clouds girding the distant peaks. The question once again was, which way? We spread out, looking for cairns or any sign of previous hikers. I followed the ridge since that seemed the most attractive way to go. But one by one we drifted back to the starting point, vexed by the lack of any kind of marker. Except for Karen. She was still poking around, aimlessly it seemed, working her way down, then starting up the next slope. Brett shook his head indulgently. "We may have to go back, except I hate like hell giving up at this point."

"It's the only sensible thing to do," I said. At this point we couldn't even agree on the general direction of Pico Bolivar.

"We could go down on this side and follow the river. Sooner or later we'd hit a village. We'd find our way out," Brett said, either because he'd lost his good sense or hoped we'd lost ours, and he'd have a great adventure.

"You're nuts!" I said. "This isn't the Adirondacks!" Jason waved his hand in dismissal; perhaps he thought it was a joke.

"I think Karen is calling." Brett jumped to his feet. We could see her cutting her arms scissor-like through the air. "We'd better have a look. She probably thinks every loose pile of rubble is a marker."

"Why don't you go," I said, but Jason also picked up his pack.

Stupid waste of time, I thought, forcing myself to my feet, but Karen had indeed located a small cairn, difficult to see from any distance as it was part of the confusion on a moraine. She had spotted the next one as well, thereby saving the expedition.

The climb was slow and strenuous. We stopped to heat a pot of water, and drank tea in morose silence. It started to drizzle, but in spite of heavy fog below us, the visibility remained reasonable. The cairns would be impossible to find if the fog closed in.

We were hoping to make it over the peak, then descend to Pico Espejo where we would take the teleférico to the valley.

"Are we going to make it to the lift in time?" I wondered.

"Oh, sure," Brett said.

Shortly after that encouraging communication, I took a wrong step while crossing a bog and my boots filled with mud. The kids looked at me with half puzzled, half embarrassed expressions while I sobbed over my soupy toes.

"Why don't you just put on dry socks?" Karen asked.

"C'mon, Mom," Brett started sopping up the murky water in my boots with Kleenex. "They'll dry, it's no big deal." When I looked for clean socks I discovered I had lost my fannypack, and cried some more.

The final leg to the summit became precipitous, but we were nearly there. On top would be the bronze bust of Bolivar, the famous South American revolutionary; we would take his picture as proof of our success. For me, it was enough of an incentive to overcome my fear of heights. The last cable car would leave at four; with my habitual worrying, I pictured missing it. I kept thinking of things green and of enough air to breathe.

Now Karen was crying; she was deathly afraid of climbing sheer cliffs and healthy enough to care. Behind me, I heard Brett trying to calm her. He sounded impatient; it wasn't his way to be held back.

"Let's wait for them," Jason suggested when we had almost reached the summit. It had been our tradition all these years to go the last steps together.

The unforeseen reality of being on the wrong summit hit all four of us at the same time. Instead of the statue of Señor Bolivar, there was nothing but ice and wind.

Our sense of calamity was overwhelming. I climbed a spire on my hands and feet, hoping to sight the teleférico, but the world below looked abandoned.

"Get down off there, Mom!" shouted Jason.

Now we had to face the problem at hand—where would we sleep tonight? This was an unlikely place for a camp site; the last flat area I recalled was the bog.

"Brother," I said. "We're not too good at hitting our targets."

"What do you expect without a map?" Brett said indignantly.

Jason deflated any opportunity for witticisms with, "Who cares, anyway."

On the climb down, our hands bled from clinging to the icy rock. A terrified Karen lost her last inhibitions; her wails rang piteously, interspersed with furious "'Jesus Christ Brett-Bretts."

It was dusk when we reached a flat area on a shoulder, where Brett said we would make camp. Jason and I stood incredulous in the pouring rain while Brett started scraping rocks away with his boots.

"You guys, put up your tent before you get chilled," he ordered. Karen was already clipping their tent poles together, her movements efficient, competent.

"Everything'll be soaked before we get the fly up!" I protested.

"Then you'd better hurry."

We pitched the tent and crawled inside with our dripping rain slickers and boots. The inflated pads kept us off the wet floor; we put our space blanket over the sleeping bags for extra warmth.

I wrapped my arms around myself for comfort. With the weather so close, I lost sense of time and place. The rain turned to snow, muffling the clanking of Karen's dishes to a dim tolling of far away bells.

"Hey Mom," Brett's voice drifted by, "Mom? Jay?" I made a mental effort to answer.

"You guys all right?"

"We're fine," Jason answered lazily without lifting his head.

"Do you want tea?"

"Sure." Brett brought over his aluminum pan and swirled

teabags through the warm water. He knelt in the snow and chided, "What kind of mountaineers are you guys anyway? You'll get too weak if you don't eat or drink. Hell, I have a headache, too!"

I chewed gravelly nuts. He opened a can of kippers and harpooned one on the end of his knife.

"Here, try a piece." Eating made me feel useful.

"Good, huh?" said Brett.

Jason didn't eat anything at all.

The night was primeval—immense and empty. I felt myself part of the rock on which we were hurtling aimlessly through space. Now and then I picked fresh snow off the roof to put on my forehead. Warm drops oozed down my neck. It was the pits.

Sometime later I sensed a subtle change in the stillness I had thought complete. I flicked on my flashlight to look at Jason. His mouth hung slack and his lashes stood out dark against his cheek. He was so still that I held my wet hand over his mouth to reassure myself. He had stopped breathing. I slapped him.

"Jason! Wake up!" He took a deep gurgly breath.

"Hm?"

"You weren't breathing!"

"Oh. Sorry." He turned on his side and went back to sleep. My laughing at the courteous "sorry" sounded insane. I had read about breathing problems at altitude. I kept my vigil until daylight came.

Frozen condensation coated the ceiling and made the inside of the tent an ice cave. The sleeping bags were damp. Before I changed into my last clean jersey, I buried my face in it to sniff its cleanness.

While we shook the glazed ice sheets off our tent, I commented to Jason that he'd been decent about the slap in the face. He thought he'd been aware of not breathing; it hadn't seemed necessary somehow.

"Don't tell Karen," he joked. "She'll think I'm stupid." But it was his wavering breath that had helped me to endure the night.

I was glad to get going again—elated with the sun-cupped slopes, the gift of a new day. With the early start, we were optimistic about finding our way. Retracing our steps to where we had seen the last cairn before we had gotten lost, we stood debating the options. Miraculously, the four Indians walked out of the clouds. Their white lips were a dead give-away—they had found my fannypack and used the zinc oxide I kept in it for protection against ultraviolet rays. They were as startled to see us as we were to see them, but we were happier. One of the men immediately grasped what had happened. He produced a notebook and drew a picture of the shelter where we had first met. Tapping the pencil stump on the shelter's roof, he smiled with his white lips, "Get it?" It was a nice sketch. He had observed the details and reproduced them with quick accuracy. We crowded around. The pencil made the scree slope. Four dots on it. The Indian indicated us, laughing loudly. He drew the trail, the ridge over which it passed, the bog, and mountains all around. Then a big question mark—our present location. He crumpled up the sketch, stuffed it into his pocket, then drew the bog again and the turn leading to the teleférico that we had missed.

"Uh-oh!" I said. The third picture, the one that I kept, started at the question mark and led to the station by a shortcut the Indians knew about. He drew a smile there. They would show us.

The sun had come out; already last night's snow was melting. We hiked single file, with me struggling to keep pace with the other seven.

There was one obstacle—the scaling of a cliff with a thousand feet of sky next to your boot. We clambered through a narrow chimney, the Indians familiar with every foothold. They carried Karen's and my pack, which made it easier for us to keep our balance. Neither she nor I dared let out a peep, though I came close to wimping out.

Then, suddenly, cables, a platform, a bathroom, hot chocolate. Pico Espejo! At 15,500 ft elevation this was the station of the highest cable car in the world.

Looking back to where we had come from, we saw a large board with red letters, "Danger! Going beyond this point is strictly forbidden!"

Karen, her tears vindicated, cheered, "Brett! You see?" and focussed her camera. Across the gap loomed the icy summit of Bolivar we hadn't been able to find.

The teleférico brought up fresh tourists who tried to overlook our disheveled appearance. We drank chocolate with our

Indian friends, from whom Karen retrieved my lost fannypack.

Sailing above the haze in brilliant sunlight, I felt euphoric to be borne to the lowlands, the sun-fed green of the living jungle.

"It's so exuberant!" Jason exclaimed.

"It's an oxygen factory," I said prosaically, but I thought I understood now the Inca priest who had said, "Oh Lord Sun, we are probably not good enough to exalt thee."

Preludes and Glass Bullets

When Jason came home from the conservatory for spring break, he stayed in his room a lot. He seemed to find it difficult to fit in now with the family, making excuses to miss supper, keeping conversation sparse. I supposed he was defending his freedom.

Though the vacation was nearly over, there hadn't been an opportune time to talk to him. We no longer shared our morning coffee; he slept until noon, and the rest of the day he practiced his violin, took several showers, and talked on the phone a lot. At night he listened to music shut away in his room. There were no more intense discourses on Schoenberg or late nights of listening together to Mahler's Ninth.

I didn't understand why we couldn't still be friends. I missed the after-school talks we'd had during his high school years, but more than that, I couldn't bear his sullen self-imposed quarantine. I'd also been wondering if he were too old now to go backpacking with his mother; if he'd made different plans, I wanted to look for another companion. But I was hesitant to bring up the subject.

The day before he was to return to school, I rang the dinner bell at ten in the morning. I had coffee ready and blueberry muffins. He came downstairs looking lost. Mornings he always looked especially lost. Forgetting to go to the bathroom, he sat down at the table, waiting for the next prompt, it seemed.

"I hope you don't mind I woke you," I said. "I've hardly seen you. How are you, Jay?"

"Fine. Why should I mind? It's after ten."

"You don't say."

"You're critical of my late sleeping. I can't stick to the same schedule every day. You guys eat at seven, go to bed at twelve, get up at seven, on and on. Boring." He floated a spoon filled with Coffee Mate on his coffee; we watched the dark liquid seep into the powder.

"Your father has responsibilities," I said primly. "You'll have to keep a tight schedule yourself if you're going to maneuver between the conservatory and Tufts."

Jason would simultaneously attend Tufts University and New England Conservatory in September. The previous fall he had withdrawn from Tufts at the eleventh hour for fear he wouldn't have enough time left to practice. Joe, who had counted on an academic education, reluctantly acquiesced. Since it was Jason's first year away from home, I thought it had been a good idea to stick to music. However, when he came home for Christmas, Jason had changed his mind; he needed more intellectual stimulation than the conservatory offered, he told us. He reapplied to Tufts and was once more accepted.

I poured another cup of coffee; Jason seemed to have forgotten his. Disregarding my remark about his fall schedule, he bent back his fingers to keep them supple.

He said, "Why don't you do something fun, Mom, like you used to? Remember how we would go for walks in the middle of the night? And that great Halloween party we had?"

Did I remember? "What are you trying to accomplish with that muffin?" I asked. He had sectioned it into ever smaller pieces and was absentmindedly patting the crumbs into a flat cake.

"I'm going to eat it," he said.

I got into my favorite slouch, put my feet on an empty chair, and dunked my buttered muffin into the sugarbowl.

Jason grinned, "At least you're still doing disgusting things."

I loved being with him when he was conscious.

"Repetition is one of the most basic aspects of human experience," he declared, picking up the thread of our conversation. So. We were going to philosophize about the circles we danced.

"Quite," I said.

"Birth and death, trust and betrayal. Mourning. Joy. The rituals of every day. We move chaotically within a strict pattern."

Ah youth....But here was my opening.

"Like our yearly mountain trips. We go up, we come down. But it's always new."

"Hm. I was thinking in terms of music," he said stuffily. "Take Chopin's E-minor prelude I listened to last night. It's so romantic, so deep...."

"You compare that with someone like Philip Glass," he went on. "He's really too ebullient. His rhythms are layered; they fold into these thick patterns."

"Well, that's very different music. I don't have the patience for Glass."

"Sure it's different. But both composers use an extreme kind of repetition. You could say the E-minor is repetition within change, Glass's piece change within repetition. Listen." He hummed the contrasting passages. "You hear how Glass's rhythms evolve inside exactly repeating notes, right?"

"Now that you point it out. I think that what it boils down to is that there's freedom within structure, and there can be great beauty as well. Thoreau said, 'Always the laws of light are the same, but the modes and degrees of seeing vary.'"

"But you have to be aware, Mom."

"As in Bach's fugues."

"As in life."

He had no knowledge yet of how easy it was to fall into repetition without change, how comfortable to consent to the immutable. Without him around. And if he knew, he wouldn't care. He still had all these possibilities, all this earnestness.

I glanced at him over the rim of my cup. He had that familiar between-worlds look in his eyes.

"Have you thought about the summer at all?" I asked.

"You mean after Norfolk?" He would be at the Norfolk Music Festival for six weeks.

"I assume you're going backpacking. Have you found a friend you want to go with? I'm getting a little too old to keep up with you, you know. Anyway, it'll be more fun with people your own age. I was thinking of asking Helga. She's in terrific shape.

You know how I hate it when people crawl along."
He shrugged, and started to clear the table. "It's up to you."
"What do you mean it's up to me? I thought you...."
"You already told me. I've always gone with you. I was
looking forward to it. I thought we had decided last year to go to
the Rockies."
Whether he said that out of loyalty or not, I knew I would
find out on the trip. The next day I booked seats for Denver.

On the thirteenth of August we drove a rented car from the
airport to the mountain town of Buena Vista in Eastern Colorado.
After spending a few days high in the mountains, but sleeping low
to acclimatize, we set out for the Collegiate Peaks Wilderness.
It was early in the afternoon when we decided on a camp
site in a gorge at 10,000 feet. We were hot from the long uphill
approach. There was no wind and even at that altitude the heat was
stifling.
We dropped our packs and started tramping around the
sloping field in opposite directions to look for a level camping
spot, considering proximity to the river and shelter from high
winds. There were animal droppings everywhere and lots of happy
flies. Our presence signaled more blood-thirsty hordes; the tent
was up in record time, and we dove inside. Soon, the bugs that
snuck in with us dropped dead from the ceiling as the heat was
trapped inside. There was no satisfaction in that; the swelter forced
us to abandon the tent and make for the shaded slope across the
river. Here we waited in uncomfortable postures for the sun to go
down. Usually even a short rest quickly repaired tired muscles, but
not that day.
Rapidly changing mountain weather whisked in thunder
clouds late in the afternoon. We returned to the campsite where
Jason suddenly grasped his head with both hands. His skin was
damp and streaked purplish.
Looking wild-eyed, he mumbled, "I'm going down." I
knew we were having a problem with the altitude, but it was too
late to start hiking down.
"It's the heat," I said, "Take some aspirin."
"It's not the heat. It's the damned altitude. I'm going

down." He looked around as though he had lost something, still clamping his head. "I can't stand it here. I need air," he said again, close to panic.

"Come on, you'll get used to it. We've been much higher than this. Take some aspirin. We'll go down later if we have to, okay? We'll use the headlamps and leave our stuff," I said.

He crawled into his sleeping bag without undressing. I watched lightening zap the blackened peaks until rain began to fall. Jason tossed through the night, groaning in his sleep. I woke him several times to make him drink.

The next morning he was completely well. We were eating porridge while studying the topographical map when a couple of smiling men in snazzy outfits passed by the tent.

"Howdy!" They said they'd gotten up very early and were going to "do" Mount Columbia. Would I take their picture with Columbia in the background?

They struck a classic pose—all white teeth and L.L. Bean in the view finder, then wished us "happy trails." Jason cringed, but I said thanks.

We stayed in camp that day, waiting for my headache to subside. Jason, who didn't share my environmental engineering ambitions, made snide comments while we hauled flat rocks from the river and built an elegant patio. On it we would park our boots and do the cooking. We also made a fireplace for burning trash; there wasn't enough wood for fires. Around two, the sky turned black and thunder rolled in. The grass bent down; giant rain drops punched the thin nylon of the tent before changing to a soporific drizzle. We snoozed the afternoon away.

"Anybody home?" That had to be the Happy Trailers. I stuck my head outside and looked up at the brightly gortexed men.

"We worried about you up there, in the storm," I said, conscious of my rumpled attire. They told me the weather had prevented them from reaching the summit, though they now knew which was the best route. I went out into the drizzle to be instructed.

"Cross the river before it branches, follow the col east...."

"Okay," I said, lost already, "thank you!" Who could

remember? Anyway, we were going to climb Mount Harvard first, then Columbia, then Yale.

"Well, that was nice of them," I told Jason.

"Those fools," he said.

"Don't be mean."

"They were nowhere near Columbia."

"They said they almost made the summit!"

"Of what is the question," he scoffed.

"Then what did I take the picture of?"

"Beats me. It's unnamed on the map."

"You didn't see fit to tell them?"

"Mom, all you have to do is look. You can see that mountain isn't high enough. As long as they're happy, who cares?"

I felt reprimanded on all fronts.

For the next few days we explored the area. Between showers we climbed several cliffs. Then came Harvard, a long day of labor. As in the past, Jason was an easy companion, but the lighthearted joy of living with the trees and the wind wasn't there anymore. Whatever problems he had brought along he kept to himself. He fell asleep as soon as the light faded and left me to think with some nostalgia of the small boy who used to plead, wake me up when you wake up, Mommy, for fear he would miss some mysterious, dark happening. Though his mind had always been elusive, he'd never deliberately shut me out. He doesn't trust me anymore, I thought. Half of our two-week vacation was gone.

On the morning we were to climb Columbia, I got up at daybreak, hoping to get down the mountain before the obligatory afternoon thunderstorm. I shook my sleep-dopey son with an eager, "Sky's clear, get up!" He was unmoved, but by the time I returned from the river with my orange soap dish, wetter from the dew-washed grass than from the river, he had the stove going and sat solemnly in the tent entrance, a formless mass stuck in pounds of down.

"Morning," I said, with cold water vigor.

"Okay." He was always agreeable.

"I just said good morning, Jay, and you said okay."

He came out of his fog reluctantly. "What time is it?"

"Six A.M. Time to do our thing."

"You're exhausting. Are you going to cook something?"

At seven-fifteen we zipped the tent shut. Jason carried the few things we would need: water, the first aid kit, candy, and the camera, and legged away. I had to gather steam first thing in the morning. The distance between us widened quickly.

The new mountain was as exciting as the previous ones had been—an unexplored idea followed by a conquest. Fine weather had us in high good humor, impatient to see what lay beyond.

About an hour below the summit we stopped to discuss the best way up, pointing toward our goal. I wanted to go by the saddle, he, "straight up."

"I don't know," I said, "It looks awfully steep that way. You go ahead."

We separated. Almost at once I ran into trouble; gorges I hadn't spotted from below were hard to cross, loose scree made the surface unstable. I couldn't see Jason and envied the rapid progress I thought he'd be making. The summit seemed to be moving away from me. Abandoned to so much uncompromising rock and wide silence, I felt frail as a dragonfly. In his sure-footed youth, my son didn't know about my trepidation. I continued to grope my way upward until I saw him straddled on a boulder, waiting for me to go the final minutes together.

Jason tapped the summit marker with the toe of his hiking boot, and resting a hand on my shoulder, said with his tentative one-sided grin, "14,073 feet, Mom."

We stood braced by the wind, turning slowly from pole to pole and narrowing our eyes to infinity. There was only the moment—the universe.

Inexorably, our attention was drawn downward again, to the shadowed valleys we came from—the river we'd crossed, tangled briars we'd fought. Away from the wind we huddled low to the mountain, eating chocolate in quiet bliss. It was noon. From our perch we watched cumulonimbus drape shadows over the land. It was time to get off the high ridges before bad weather came. We tied our rain jackets around our waists.

"Which way do you want to go down?" Jason asked.

"Your route's too steep, but mine will take longer."

"I still think we can move faster the way you came up, over

the saddle."

I knew it was settled then. I was getting accustomed to him taking the lead. Very subtly, our roles had shifted over the years. It seemed that with every pound transferred from my pack to his, a pound of decision making had followed. Still, I was often determined to do things my way and more than once had gotten us lost. He would shrug then, with male economy of emotion. By nature, Jason wasn't a leader. He had, however, an uncanny gift to find his way in the mountains, reading contours of stone and committing the information to memory. I found this strange, as he was just about helpless in a city. A year of living in Boston and he still had to ask directions to get back to the conservatory, after jogging.

We didn't get down the mountain much faster than we'd gotten up. Now and then we stopped to watch pikas lug their sun-dried provisions around in their mouths. Every time we came on the small creatures with their furry feet, we laughed at their humorous behavior. The larger, yellow-bellied marmots were too shy to stick around for observation. I knelt to photograph a cushion of purple mountain saxifrage framed by pink heather. I imagined the minuscule bells chiming. It seemed profane then to trip the shutter.

Just as I caught up with Jason, it started to hail.

"Not again," he said.

We still had marks on our arms and legs from yesterday's pelting on the way down from Mount Harvard. Stones the size of marbles had chased us off an exposed ridge.

"Maybe we'll be all one color now," I said, remembering a friend who tried to fill in the white between freckles by lying in the sun.

"They feel like rubber bullets. Ouch!" he held his pack protectively over his head.

"They're only glass bullets."

"Steep as snot here." That was backpackerspeak we'd picked up on the Long Trail, years ago.

"Not as slippery," I said, gingerly hitching down a boulder on my rear.

"You're more disgusting than funny," he laughed.

Walking along the side of a mountain, known as "gouging," is to be avoided if your legs happen to be more or less the same length. But the other choices were crunching through valley brush, or sky diving off a seventy degree bluff. So we gouged through an August afternoon in the Rockies, with a flannel sky overhead and crystal rain bouncing about. I felt connected to it all.

The last stretch of our walk led through scrub forest to the open grassy spot and our tent.

Jason immediately went to sleep. I lay wedged between muddy boots and the stove we'd brought in from the rain, fretting about food, my wet socks, the hail that had changed to the kind of rain you knew would outlast you. I was glad when Jason finally popped up. Reality didn't seem to measure up to his dreams; one look at the mayhem and he slunk back into his sleeping bag.

"Why don't you take a little nap," I said.

"Sorry, I must've dozed off."

"You're great company. So peaceful."

"I'll make tea, okay?" he said apologetically. He spent the next twenty minutes coaxing the stove. Pumping, tilting the fuel line a millimeter up or down, reaming out the jet, and finally dismissing it and its maker as failures. The little stove had accompanied us to the Himalayas and Andes, that's why we stayed loyal to it in spite of its unpredictability. We kept it swaddled in a sock.

The mountains had slipped away and a small pond had formed on the roof. Everything was dripping, hanging heavy.

"Oh well, let's have a Granola bar and some Gatorade," I said. The carbohydrates stoked us up a little. Jason suggested we read until it would get too dark. I held my half of our poetry anthology somewhere near the ceiling.

"I can't see anymore."

"You want me to read to you?"

"Would you mind?"

He started with Dylan Thomas. Not a fine out-loud reader, he read without remembering me. I relaxed to the round vowel sounds: moved, hooved, love, calm, charmed — missing the poem's meaning. Then, reading Wilfred Owen, he began to falter, first after stanzas, then lines, gathering courage for the red words of war.

He paused. The final lines dangled like broken limbs: "The old Lie: Dulce et decorum est - Pro patria mori."

The rain was closing in. I had to strain to hear the next poem, "Arms and the Boy." His voice broke after "For his teeth seem for laughing round an apple. There lurk no claws behind his fingers supple...." He flung the book away. "I can't read this stuff."

There was one sob from him; he covered his eyes with his forearm. I listened to the drip on the roof, finishing the familiar verse in my head, "Nor antlers through the thickness of his curls."

Though I ached to comfort him, his private tears had to be endured. I wanted to tell him that I knew about the claws and the antlers, but here under the open skies there was no rush about things.

Some time later the rain stopped. When I went outside, sweet, foot-deep mist lay in the grass; the mountains towered darkly on either side of the valley. Another seamless day spilled into night. I walked up the trail a bit, stretching, relishing the fragrant soil, my warm sweater.

The stove worked that night. We had magnificent pasta, green pudding, tea. Now and then a half moon set off the charcoal hems of the clouds and brightened the pasture.

After dinner, Jason wandered down the slope to the river. He carried two three-pint plastic bottles, clapping them together in front of his body and behind. I could still hear the ghostly clop-clop after his figure had dissolved into the night. In the darkness I clutched at the memory of the rolling field, the stand of pines across the river. Shadows stretched behind spooky shadows. Tossing the cups and spoons in the spaghetti pan, I set out for the river with my dishes and half cake of Ivory Soap. I heard Jason humming and walked toward the sound.

"Hey!" I called, "Would you like to see me wash the dishes?"

"Are you kidding? It's too creepy down there."

"What nonsense. You think you can scare me?"

"You? No."

I needed the flashlight to clamber down the river bank. My chores quickly done, I sat down on a ledge in the shallow stream. My beam of light rested on a clump of monkey flowers sticking out their hairy yellow tongues, then on the low-growing bells of kinnikinnick. In this perfect garden, my mind wandered to the paved cities where once there had grown flowers, and trees, and grass. Trailing my hand through the water, I lingered a while longer. Then I walked slowly toward a big yellow moon sitting on the field—Jason had hung a flashlight from the ceiling of our old yellow tent, lighting up its dome.

Every evening we burned a candle on the patio. The flame nearly always outlasted our wakefulness. That night it kept sputtering. I brought it inside until it was good and hot, re-planted it, zipped the screen shut, and watched grotesque shapes of grassblades and insects creep on the wall until the candle died once more.

"Just leave it, Mom; the moon's come up anyway." It was true. Light shone through rips in the clouds.

"One more try," I said. I leaned one hand on the hardened wax, half of me outside the tent. From the corner of my eye I thought I saw something move. I peered. Nothing. Then again, I was sure. Slowly a doe emerged from the protection of high grasses. She stood motionless, watching me.

I signaled Jason, "Sh, quiet."

The doe took a few steps forward, stopped, never taking her eyes off us. Two yearlings appeared less cautiously, and finally the buck. He sauntered toward the tent, looking grand in his headdress.

"Uh-oh," Jason whispered. The buck stopped, then took a few more steps. He lowered his head and started to nibble. At that point, the whole family relaxed and enjoyed its evening outing. The deer stayed in the open, the youngsters frolicking long-legged near their mother, untill all of us retired to our lairs.

"That buck was one big sonofagun!" I said. "That was worth the whole trip, wasn't it?"

We celebrated with yet another cup of tea. No doubt the mother deer in the bushes was shaking her head tolerantly. Sleep came easy then, but didn't last. I felt a presence before I heard anything.

"Grrrr." Do deer grunt? I wondered.

"Hruff." That caused Jason to sit up wide awake. "Did you hear that?" He stumbled over me to peek outside. "Mom, it's a bloody bear!"

"You're joking of course."

"It's a black bear. What did you do with the matches?"

"Are you going to burn him?"

"We may have to scare him off." I began to believe him then, kind of. "I don't think he'll bother us, do you?" Jason whispered.

After I had seen for myself, I was in no position to have an opinion. It was light enough to distinguish coarse fur, a nutmeg muzzle. Vapor came off the bear. I could see his claws; he was digging up things. We'd seen bear tracks the last few days, but nowhere near our camp.

"Should I make a racket with the pots? You think? Mom? C'mon! We've got to do something!"

Well, I didn't see why. My mouth felt dry.

Jason shook me and urged, "Get a hold of yourself. It's not a grizzly!"

We had been whispering all that time, but his reassurance that I wasn't going to be killed by a specific species of bear struck me as malapropos. I let out a loud sort of half cry before he covered up my mouth.

"God, you're going to get us in trouble."

"I thought you were going to bang pans." Half the sentence came out garbled before he moved his hand, persuaded I wasn't going to be hysterical. The bear ignored us. He rolled a log over, sticking his nose into some goodies he found.

"Damn," I whispered, "He'll smell our food!" The bear was psychic. He lumbered closer. Instinctively I rolled up into a ball, protecting my head and the front of my body, while Jason added another layer of safety by crouching over me. The bear kept coming. I heard Jason whisper, "Oh shit." There's a blank in my memory between the moment the animal was about to walk over us and when I felt Jason's weight lift off me. Still I couldn't move.

"Mom, are you okay?" My ears heard, my muscles put me upright. Jason was on his knees. The bear had literally stomped over the tent, snapping one fiberglass pole and crushing the water bottle.

"Why shouldn't I be?" I said. We collapsed in the puddle on the floor and laughed ourselves silly, pointing at the sagging tent, the flattened bottle.

"I was so terrified that I didn't hear or feel a thing, did you?" I gasped.

"You think I was taking a nap? God, I could smell him!" I cracked up again when I visualized Jason sniffing.

We had two extra poles. He went outside to fix the tent; I mopped up the floor with tissues. The fabric of the fly was torn; we would repair it the next day.

After climbing a summit, surviving a poetic war and a confrontation with a quarter-ton beast, it was still only eleven-thirty.

I wanted to talk more about the bear; I was wound up. What did he think when he heard the pole splinter? What if the beast had stepped on us? Who had told us there were no bears here?

He was done with it all. "Nothing. Who knows," were his contributions. I had nowhere to go with my nervous energy. I wouldn't let him go to sleep.

"Why is it that you were scared of a bunch of cows in Switzerland, and now don't mind a bear on your pad?"

He had minded; how long was I going to discuss it? Switzerland was years ago. "You want some tea?" he said.

"We have no water."

"I've been thinking."

"Good."

"You want to know about what?"

"Beethoven probably," I said with stale sarcasm.

"I don't want to go to Tufts. I've been trying to figure things out for a long time. Now I know. My life is going to be too short to understand Mozart or Schumann. To learn to play the violin the way I want to play. I'll need a lifetime for Bach. I'm sorry, but I can't go."

"Not again!"

"Are you disappointed?" he leaned on his elbow, facing me, but I couldn't really see him.

"Would that change your mind?"

"No, but...."

"Then you've already made the decision. But you'll have to take on Dad by yourself."

"He won't understand."

"Well, he doesn't have the benefit of a bear stepping over him. You may have to go easy on him." I kissed his cheek. "He loves you," I said.

"Mom?"

"Hm?"

"Nothing."

He fussed around in his sleeping bag, trying to get comfortable.

"Night," I said. "Don't worry," but now he was awake.

"Do you think we could go to Alaska next year?" he asked.

"They have grizzlies there. Are you going to have grizzly-size problems in the future?"

At least for now it was like old times—a surplus of understanding.

"How did those Glass recapitulations go again?" I asked. He began to hum softly.

I fell asleep to piccolo, flute, and organ arpeggios. Maybe there were saxophones. Long calls from the horns. Glass's psychedelic coloring.

-26-

Not The End

When Jason left home, I expected part of me to die a little. It did, as it had when Gaia and Brett moved out. His leaving was the more poignant as he was the last child to go. Yet my occasional secret weeping didn't mean I wanted to keep him. The time of his dependence was finished.

I don't bemoan his absence because, to put it mundanely, I had my full share of him. He gave me enough to last my life, he was the son I had wished for in my most ambitious dreams.

Jason's departure was incremental. It began long before he actually left, when he was busy metamorphosing into manhood. There was a period that lasted into his first college years, that he seemed to be cocooned in some mysterious way—he was simply not accessible. He has emerged a man, looking the same and not the same, but once more recognizable.

My friendship with Jason superceded the parent-child connection. We listened to music, quibbled about books. We cut the Christmas trees in December and decorated the house. We took walks at midnight, chanted, skied, and talked. When the time came, we shared the crises in our lives as naturally as we had sat out the thunderstorms in the hills.

When our hiking continued year after year, some well-meaning people tried to warn me that we should be with people our own age, that we spent too much time together. There were veiled insinuations of Jason becoming that monster of all time, the Mama's boy.

In fact, he was called upon to stand on his own feet and carry his own load at an early age. And how much time with your child is too much? As for the age difference, well, two twelve-year-olds aren't likely to spend a month in the woods, and the chances of two middle-aged women getting a yen to learn ice climbing are slim. The point is that we learned from each other *because* of the age difference.

As with everything, there was a flip side to the idyllic hours spent, but it was not their dissolution. With so many intense experiences shared, the lines between mothering and friendship blurred. I might have been a better mother if I'd been a lesser friend. Having lost my mother at an early age, I never learned from example, but I hope Jason knows that I did what I knew to do.

Joe's passion has been his work; the children and I existed on the curbside of his life. He has been deprived of the sweet sorrow of Jason's childhood's end. Or possibly his loss nags with regret, and he is left with an unfinished and perhaps unfinishable chunk of life. But maybe neither of these is true. As I have said a few hundred pages back, Joe's feelings are off the record.

Jason has made courageous attempts to find his father, overcoming shyness and pride, but if Joe knows what's needed, he doesn't seem to be able to get to that part of himself. He deals with Jason either intellectually or with callow banter, fine as far as it goes, but Jason's young heart is filled with matters of life and death. Watching these dear, decent men trying to show their love for each other is more painful than their long, silent denial.

Sometimes I envy the special glow Jason reserves for his father when things between them do click. I am a given, Joe a gift. Why, I ask then, does it have to be so difficult for them?

I wonder if it is possible to shut out a father who doesn't wish to be shut out. I remember Joe's involvement when Jason was a small boy, and worry that somewhere along the way I drowned him out. Our lopsided life didn't start out this way. Things never do, and you have to watch it all the time.

The summer after Colorado, Jason insisted we go backpacking in the Sierras. As it turned out, we had to make a side trip to Los Angeles so he could visit the young pianist he had fallen in love with. Fortunately, I fell in love with the girl's parents and we all had a wonderful time, but I berated him for bamboozling me into traveling three thousand miles so he could see a girl.

"I'm an unfair target because I love you too much," I said.

"How can a mother love a son too much?" He was dumb-founded at the very concept. "Gee!" he said, dismissing such schlock.

It was apparent that he had become the protagonist and I the sidekick of the final trips we made together, and in the end, the tradition of his childhood summers had to be wrapped up definitively. The next year, it happened that he had to be in Banff, Canada, with his newly formed Pythagoras Trio. Among his luggage were an overloaded backpack, an axe, and a climbing rope. I assumed he'd organized a mountaineering trip with friends, at the end of the Trio's tenure.

Later, when he showed me the route on the map, it turned out he'd gone into the mountains of British Columbia alone. He had crossed a broad glacier to make a high bivouac, and climbed from there. It had been the most beautiful campsite he'd ever seen.

"What about grizzlies, weren't you afraid?" I asked, trying to sound casual.

"I was. And of avalanches. And crevasses."

Seeing my horrified expression, he grinned. "It was okay. I just went to sleep. By the way, we've got to patch the tent; it got torn by the hail. I had to lie in a puddle."

I thought it was the bravest thing he'd ever done, for I know that the long, cold nights in the mountains are among the loneliest times on earth. I was glad I hadn't known about the initiation ahead of time.

"Yeah, we'd better fix that old tent," I said, "It doesn't do to sleep in the rain."